C000197486

WILD GREEN WONDERS

by the same author

THE BUTTERFLY ISLES
BADGERLANDS
COASTLINES
ISLANDERS
WILD CHILD

wild
green
wonders

A LIFE IN NATURE

patrick
barkham

First published by Guardian Faber in 2022
Guardian Faber is an imprint of Faber & Faber Ltd,
Bloomsbury House, 74–77 Great Russell Street
London WC1B 3DA

Guardian is a registered trademark of
Guardian News & Media Ltd
Kings Place, 90 York Way, London N1 9GU

Typeset by Sam Matthews

Printed and bound by CPI Group (UK) Ltd, Croydon, CR0 4YY

All rights reserved
© Guardian News & Media Ltd, 2022

The right of Patrick Barkham to be identified as author of this work
has been asserted in accordance with Section 77 of the Copyright,
Designs and Patents Act 1988

A CIP record for this book
is available from the British Library

ISBN 978-1-7833-5248-7

2 4 6 8 10 9 7 5 3 1

To the first *Guardian* readers I got to know,
my mum and dad

Contents

CONTENTS

Introduction

This collection contains what I hope are the most compelling nature stories from two decades of writing for the *Guardian*. They are mostly what I love best: venturing into the world with eyes wide and mind open and writing honestly about other people and their relationships with other species. These are adventures and discoveries that became stories about wild and not-so-wild places, people and other species.

We are often almost unknowingly drawn to a place that feels like home. In 1998, when the dotcom boom was firing up in warehouses between Westminster and the City of London, I took a shuddery old lift to the converted attic of a tatty commercial building in Clerkenwell for a job interview. Beneath high, whitewashed rafters was an airy space filled with pot plants and beige boxy Apple Macintosh computers that were tapped by self-assured, serious young people in casual clothing. This was the home of the *Guardian*'s new website, soon to be rebranded *Guardian Unlimited*.

I belonged to an extremely lucky generation, graduating during the burgeoning optimism of the first years of the New Labour government, when old newspapers were looking for cheap young graduates to staff their clumsy

1

forays into the 'new media' of the World Wide Web. I'd wrangled a bit of work experience at ITN's website and the *Financial Times* website but as soon as I answered a job ad (paid entry-level opportunities in the media! Ah, those were the days!) for a writer/researcher and stepped into the *Guardian*'s Ray Street office, I knew I wanted to work there. My mum had read the *Manchester Guardian* as a kid; I'd grown up in virtually the only *Guardian*-reading household in our rural village; the *Guardian* was home.

After two years working on the website, I landed the job of the *Guardian*'s sole Australia correspondent and left the Ray Street office. This sounds glamorous, and it was, but in the realm of foreign correspondency it was the most junior role, in a part of the world that narrow-minded London editors deemed relatively unimportant. My job was to supply a bit of light relief: stories about the Olympics, which began just as I arrived, and other quirky, inconsequential reads. My first hit story was about a pre-historic stick insect dubbed 'the walking sausage', which had been discovered on Lord Howe Island.

A few months after I arrived in Australia, I wrote about the northern hairy-nosed wombat, and how this endangered species was threatened with extinction by the destruction of its rainforest habitat. It was the first story I really cared about. I felt so sorry for the wombat, and deep empathy for the sorrows of its human champions. At a trivial level, the wombat was cute. At a portentous level, our relationship with the planet and its species simply seemed like the most important subject. But writing about all this also felt like home.

It was familiar to me because I had grown up in the countryside, the child of parents who cared deeply about the natural environment. My parents did the *Good Life* thing in the 1970s and we were raised on an acre-and-a-half of land with goats, rabbits and plentiful home-grown vegetables. Mum was a geographer, and passionate about natural landscapes. Dad nursed a profound emotional need to be close to wildlife and taught environmental science at the University of East Anglia in Norwich. With the keen ear of a child, I absorbed their discussions about the destruction of hedgerows, the hole in the ozone layer, and the need for people to live more sustainably.

Siding with the planet is to side with the underdog, and this motivated much of my journalism. I didn't write that much about wildlife or environmental issues at first, although after two years in Australia I felt I had covered every possible wryly amusing story about wacky animal happenings, from koalas invading the suburbs of Adelaide to killer jellyfish. The most significant issue I reported on during my time in Australia was the plight of refugees who were intercepted in boats seeking the safety of 'the lucky country' and dispatched to 'offshore processing' – which meant indefinite detention – on the dysfunctional tropical island of Nauru. My big dispatch from Nauru was published on the morning of 11 September 2001 as the twin towers in the United States crumbled. The refugees did not get the attention they deserved.

I don't want to sound grand, because I wasn't: I was a young person slowly learning how to be a competent journalist. Before I returned to London in 2002 I wrote a dispatch from the idyllic South Pacific island nation of Tuvalu, which was – and still is – threatened with inundation as sea levels rise because of human-made global heating. This is the earliest piece to appear in this collection and it remains deeply pertinent twenty years on. Over the next decade I became a general reporter and then a feature writer (writing longer stories), which meant I wrote about all kinds of subjects. I spent two years at *The Times* and was dispatched to report on the Iraq War. Even though I was based in probably the safest place for a war correspondent – a hospital ship – I discovered that I was too much of a coward to do war reporting. I've never had the toughness to be an investigative journalist either. In 2004 a reporter's job was advertised at the *Guardian* and I was able to return to my journalistic home. Here, I reported on the plight of Gypsies and Travellers in this country but I also morphed into one of those embarrassing yoof correspondents, reporting from Glastonbury or writing amusing fluff about being a metrosexual or wearing onesies (my personal favourite).

There is not much I haven't written about over twenty *Guardian* years, from business stories to celebrity interviews to diaries to obituaries – more than 1.6 million printed words and almost another million for the website. A lot of these were deeply inconsequential or not arranged in a particularly alluring order. But whenever I turned to report on an animal or an environmental issue I felt a deep sense of kinship with it. In 2009 I wrote a book about butterflies, *The Butterfly Isles*. Reconnecting with this childhood passion made me more determined to spend more of my time telling the many miraculous stories about other species and our relationships with them. When I half-heartedly tried to leave the *Guardian* in 2013 – they were offering voluntary redundancy and I was tempted to become a full-time book-writer – a particularly kind editor asked me what my dream role might be. My answer was to report on wildlife all the time. He gave me a preposterous job title, Natural History Writer, and, for the last eight years, working part-time at the *Guardian* while also writing books, this is what I've done.

As well as writing an indecent amount about butterflies, I've discovered that the natural world supplies an inexhaustible fund of funny and fascinating revelations, even when many of these stories also bring out a sobering indictment of humankind's myopia, chronic short-termism or greed. I've never been a polemical writer like my brilliant colleague George Monbiot; I've never had a column on the opinion pages where I formulate ferocious arguments about the undoubted stupidity of our species' authoring of a planetary overheating and the sixth great epoch of extinction. Temperamentally, I just can't do it.

When I argue about things I get all ranty and feel ill.

So you won't find me banging on about the state of the world in this collection, although I think these stories together present a clear-eyed view of the challenges we have created for ourselves and other species on our planet. The tritest question David Attenborough gets asked (I'm sure I've asked it of him too) is whether he is hopeful that we can avert a planetary crisis. As the nature writer and *Guardian* country diarist Mark Cocker argues, hope is written into all our encounters with the natural world. Step outside, spend time with other species, including our own, and we are filled with a transcendent joy at being part of a world that is so much larger than ourselves. 'You have only to have the sun on your back, the wind in your face and birdsong in your heart to know their river-bursting powers of liberation,' Cocker writes in *Our Place*.

My writing here is hopeful, and I hope it is open-minded too. Sometimes I know what I think about an issue before I begin to investigate it but mostly I don't, and my mind always changes when I speak to people who have different or better-informed views. I always learn something new when I listen to other voices. Journalism is often a dirty word but good journalism is most of all about listening. I like to pay close attention to divergent views. Critics might say I load the dice when presenting a debate (about the persecution of hen harriers, for instance) but I hope I relay opposing arguments fairly. This may be fanciful but I believe my interest in understanding the multiple sides of an issue derives from a childhood where I tried to keep diverging parents together. Like most parents who argue and eventually separate, my mum and dad had completely different versions of reality. As a teenager, I had to marry their two realities, and make sense of both points of view. Even when writing is superficially impersonal, it always rises from a deeply personal place. Occasionally I write in a more directly personal way: some of the longer stories in this collection are leavened with shorter, more personal, gently opinionated pieces, which come from the little 'nature' Notebook column I enjoyed writing for a few years.

I've been so fortunate to find a home at the *Guardian* for twenty years. I hope my writing reminds us that we all have a home in nature. Being able to enjoy a life alongside other species is what makes us happy and keeps us well. Our planet is a wondrous home, our only home, and its diversity is our wealth. I hope we learn to take better care of it while we can.

PART I

Living with Animals and Plants

The loneliest bat in England: is one greater mouse-eared bat the last of its kind?

We cannot speak of its loneliness, but it must be Britain's most solitary animal. For the last sixteen years, every winter, a male greater mouse-eared bat has taken up residence 300 metres inside a disused and exceedingly damp railway tunnel in West Sussex. The greater mouse-eared bat has been all but extinct in this country for decades. This is the only remaining one we know of. The future of the species in Britain appears to rest with one long-lived and very distinctive individual.

The greater mouse-eared bat is so large that observers who first discovered it in Britain likened one to a young rabbit hanging from a wall. In flight, its wings can stretch to nearly half a metre – an astonishing spectacle in a land where bats are generally closer to the size of the rodent that inspired their old name: flittermouse.

The bat has large, mouse-like ears and its feeding habits are as striking as its size. Rather than zig-zagging through darkening skies collecting flying insects, like most bats, *Myotis myotis* descends earthwards, flapping its wings very slowly as it covers the ground, picking up grasshoppers, crickets, dung beetles and other flightless insects as it goes. Often, it will flop on to the ground, wings out-stretched to fold over its prey.

The solitary individual who spends the winters in West Sussex has never been observed in flight. Where it goes each spring is not known, and what it does is not known, nor which other animals, if any, it encounters. All that is known is that each winter the bat faithfully returns to its dark tunnel, where it hangs, almost motionless, for five months. This place of winter rest is a closely guarded secret, for the bat's select band of self-appointed guardians are adamant: there can be no repeat of the scenes of 1957. That year, a live colony had been found inside an old mine on the Isle of Purbeck in Dorset. Although a reasonably familiar sight in southern Europe, where large colonies roost in caves, this was the first time a greater mouse-eared bat had been found in Britain. *The Times* published photographs, and a media frenzy ensued. Several animals were whisked out of hibernation and transported to TV and photographic studios and filmed for weeks before being returned to their hibernation hole. Disturbing bats mid-hibernation can kill them. Money was also offered for dead specimens and collectors spirited away individuals.

This fascination was fatal: the greater mouse-eared bat was barely seen again in Dorset, apart from reports of 'large, broad-winged bats' in an appropriately Gothic set-ting: flying around Corfe Castle. Although another small colony of greater mouse-eared bats was found in West Sussex in the late 1960s, by 1992 the species was declared extinct in Britain, the first mammal to disappear from our shores since the wolf 250 years ago.

Bats fly beneath our radar. While butterfly sightings have been collected for 400 years and birds have been scientifically monitored for more than seventy years, bats only been systematically counted for less than two decades. Little is known about many of Britain's eighteen bat species, some of which exist in perilously low numbers. Today they are threatened perhaps more than they've ever been by the loss of their insect prey, the conversion of old barns and derelict buildings in which they roost, and the bright lights of new suburbs, wind farms and speeding vehicles that bamboozle or kill them.

The unexpected reappearance of the greater mouse-eared bat in its West Sussex tunnel, in 2002, was a symbol of hope. Against the odds, bats are surviving in our human-dominated land and, perhaps more than any other wild animal, they are constantly surprising us.

Bats are great survivors. The oldest known fossil of a bat, found in a quarry in Wyoming in 2003, is about 52.5 million years old. Bats have been evolving for so long, and with so many specialised attributes, from echolocation to drastically extended forelimbs, that the order of *Chiroptera* – 'winged hands' in Latin – accounts for one in five species of mammal. They are supremely successful animals. As one expert puts it: when you have been evolving for so long, you've perfected the business of being a bat.

That business is becoming trickier in a human-dominated

world. In older times, they were feared and despised. Modern people may be more tolerant, but even beneficent parts of society – from harvesters of renewable energy to vicars – are often hostile to bats. Energy-efficient homes seal up roof spaces where bats once roosted. New roads – and the planned route of HS2 – block traditional foraging routes. LED lighting is particularly disturbing for bats. Wind farms chop them up: according to a study published in 2016, researchers using sniffer dogs to find and retrieve bat carcasses calculated that twenty-nine onshore wind farms killed 194 bats per month – a kill rate that would dispatch 80,000 bats a year across Britain, without accounting for migrating bats taken out by the rapidly expanding rows of offshore turbines.

Earlier this year members of the House of Lords spoke in favour of a bill that seeks to remove bats' legal protection in churches unless there is a 'significant' adverse impact on rare bat populations. The Bishop of Norwich blamed barn conversions for driving bats into churches, with more than half of 12,000 listed churches housing roosts of bats. Worshippers had 'come to the end of their tether', warned the bishop, because of bat droppings despoiling fabrics and fittings. For much of the 1990s and early 2000s the Movement Against Bats in Churches – founded by a vicar's wife – campaigned to eliminate the blight of bats. Is there another animal in Britain that has a dedicated protest movement against it?

Bats that overcome these challenges can live a long time.

Only nineteen mammal species are longer-lived relative to their body size than humans, and all but one of these are bats. (The other is the naked mole rat.) And of these unusually durable mammals, the greater mouse-eared bat is one of the longest-lived of all: it can clock up more than thirty-five years. Scientists recently discovered that its longevity is probably due to the fact that, unlike most mammals, its telomeres – a string-like material at the end of its chromosomes – do not shorten with age. They hope further insights from the unique biology of *Myotis myotis* may one day help humans live longer.

Time passes in a different way for such a long-lived animal, and so it seems with its guardians. I first contacted natural scientist and bat expert Tony Hutson in early 2017, and it was more than a year before he agreed to take me to see the bat. Hutson, a retired entomologist from the Natural History Museum, is wary of any interference in the creature's peaceful existence. Each month of winter Hutson and other local recorders count the bats hibernating in several old railway tunnels, and each month I begged to be allowed to tag along. After the bat was inspected without me in December, January and February, finally Hutson agreed that I could accompany them on an extra trip they would undertake in March, with a big caveat: they didn't normally inspect the bat so late in winter, and could not guarantee it would still be hanging there.

Hutson is the second in a short lineage of champions of the greater mouse-eared bat. The first was a wildlife-loving tea planter from Ceylon called Captain William Watt Addison Phillips. Phillips grew up in Staffordshire during the reign of Queen Victoria, and headed to Colombo to become a tea planter when he was nineteen. Living among the civets, leopards and sloth bears of Ceylon, he catalogued the bat's natural history and published papers including 'On the Habits of the Ceylon Gerbil'.

After retiring, Phillips conducted a survey of the flora and fauna of the Maldives for the Natural History Museum before settling in Bognor Regis in 1959, just after the first greater mouse-eared bat frenzy. Phillips remained active and insatiably curious in retirement, taking an interest in every kind of animal and plant around him. He was also lucky: one day he found a grey long-eared bat – Britain's second-rarest species – sprawled on his dustbin. It was dead. Some years later, Phillips explored some derelict railway tunnels in Sussex with his grandson. In one, they were delighted to discover a small colony of greater mouse-eared bats. Bearing in mind the old shooting aficionado's adage, 'What hits is history, what's missed is mystery,' Phillips shouldered his gun, brought down a couple and donated the specimens to the eager curators of the Natural History Museum, who added them to their collections.

At the time Tony Hutson was working as a scientific researcher in the museum and, by chance, had already met Bill Phillips a few years earlier, during an expedition to the Maldives. Hutson had first become fascinated by bats as a boy, when he saw them above an old priory. He was particularly gripped when he first witnessed the mystery of their motionless hibernation. 'That got me – that they will sit there without moving for three or four months,' he says. Growing up in south London, he joined a natural history youth group that met at the Natural History Museum and, as a young man, applied for a job there. He had a cup of tea with a secretary and asked if he could help its scientists who were studying bats. 'They said: "No, but we can give you a job in entomology."' So Hutson cunningly pursued his passion by studying the ectoparasites – such as fleas – that live on bats.

As one of the museum's bat experts, Hutson spent much of his time coaxing irate homeowners not to destroy colonies of rare bats roosting in their roofs. But there were moments of adventure, too. He undertook an expedition to a cave in Ecuador with Erich von Däniken, the Swiss author of *Chariots of the Gods*, who believed that aliens visited earth and influenced early human culture. The explorers were winched into the cave by helicopter and the astronaut Neil Armstrong came along. 'The theory was that if we did meet any aliens, he would be the best person for them to talk to,' said Hutson. He found no aliens, but did come across a few interesting bat species.

After taking note of Bill Phillips' surprising discovery of a colony of greater mouse-eared bats in Sussex, Hutson first visited the old railway tunnels in 1974, and saw the bats for himself. 'I was working with ectoparasites of bats at the time, so I'd sometimes come down and poke a few around, searching for parasites,' he said. The tunnel was bricked up, with a locked door at one end, to stop visitors from causing a repeat of the scenes that destroyed the Dorset population in the 1950s. (The bats gained access via ventilation grilles.) Each year in the 1980s, Hutson unlocked the door and counted the greater mouse-eared bats inside. Each year, their numbers dwindled. The Wildlife and Countryside Act of 1981 gave bats and their roosts legal protection for the first time, but then, disaster: one winter, all the female greater mouse-eared bats disappeared from the tunnel. It seemed that their maternity roost – the barn or some other unknown place in Britain where the females raised their young during the summer – must have been destroyed, perhaps in a fire, or by developers. By 1992 the greater mouse-eared bat was declared extinct.

But Tony Hutson did not give up. Each winter he continued to check tunnels and disused mines all over the south of England. Nine years later, his vigilance was vindicated. He heard reports of a live bat found, grounded, in Bognor, and raced to the seaside town. By the time he arrived, this old female bat had died. And it presented another puzzle: it was disabled.

'A bat's forearms are usually the same length, but on this bat they were different lengths,' he remembered. 'Whether it spent its life flying around in circles, I'm not sure.' Was there a secret, residual population of mouse-eared bats? It appeared not, for this venerable female showed no sign of ever having bred, and no sign of having communed with any other mouse-eared bats. 'There were no parasites on it that it would have picked up from others of its kind, which is what I was looking for,' said Hutson. But the find put him on high alert.

At the end of 2002 his annual inspection of the old tunnel where the bats had been found by Captain Bill Phillips in the 1960s revealed a single greater mouse-eared bat. It was a young male, born that spring. Hutson and the protectors placed a silver tag on its elbow and wondered how this species would surprise them next.

By March this year I was desperate to see this bat. I met Hutson on a murky day in a lay-by close to the secret tunnel. He had been visiting the bat each month over winter, but offered no crumb of comfort. 'Whether he flew off last night, I don't know,' he said with a twitch of deadpan humour. We set off with some fellow bat enthusiasts: Crispin Scott of the National Trust, and Sue Harris and Martin Phillis, volunteer bat recorders for the Sussex Bat Group and part of a network of bat fans who form the Bat Conservation Trust. This small charity is the national voice for bats in Britain, and Hutson revealed, with characteristic modesty, that he helped set it up.

We walked down the cutting of an old railway line, sharp lumps of chalk and fallen trees tumbling down the banks. The tiniest trace of people having walked along the cutting worried the protectors. 'It's too open,' said Scott. 'We need to fell a couple of trees across here so only people in the know come down.' At the end was a tunnel of red brick, marching into the hillside.

At the centre of its bricked-up entrance was an iron hatch. Phillis pulled out a key, unlocked the top and the bottom, and we squeezed inside. The tunnel was cool but not freezing; dark but not pitch-black. Daylight shone from the grille above our heads and in the far distance, like a mirage, was a crescent of light – another grille, 680 metres away, at the tunnel's end.

I hadn't anticipated the water. There was the sound of constant dripping as water oozed through the brick ceiling and hit the stony floor. The bricks glistened with moisture. 'Bats need it very humid,' said Hutson. 'If it gets too dry, they dehydrate.' There were black stains on curved tunnel walls and ceiling. Only when we later emerged and discovered our faces were streaked with black did I realise that this was archaeological soot, from the steam trains that last entered this tunnel in the 1950s.

The bat protectors wielded head and hand torches and began by painstakingly sweeping their beams up and down the curved walls of the tunnel, inspecting ginger-coloured fungi, straggly like beards, and searching for the bats that clung in crevices where mortar or brickwork had come away. Different species shared this tunnel. Smaller species may temporarily wake from hibernation to pee or feed if it is mild, but the greater mouse-eared goes deeper into the tunnel and remains motionless for longer. Hutson pointed out the different species, with their distinctive features. The Natterer's bat has long, trumpety ears and a Daz-white belly; Daubenton's bat has big feet, which it uses to grab insects off the surface of ponds. These bats are counted three times each winter for Bat Conservation Trust hibernation surveys.

We probably didn't need to, but we talked in low murmurs. I walked past the bats' somnolent bodies with the same care I take while tiptoeing into my children's bedroom when they are sleeping.

The first question Hutson asked when he found the mouse-eared bat in 2002 was: where did it go after its winter hibernation? Answer this question, and he might find other members of its tribe. Hutson contacted colleagues in Portugal who better knew its lifestyle and were familiar with its preferred summer habitats. 'We organised a big survey, well sort of,' he said. 'We met in the pub and looked at prime local habitat. It was a time when they were cutting a lot of hay and these bats often go for freshly cut hay, where they can find more insects.'

During summer, the greater mouse-eared bat roosts high in church and castle turrets in northern Europe, and in caves in the south. Hutson looked in old sand and chalk mines, and in disused lime kilns. He asked industrial archaeologists and consulted other societies for secretive enthusiasts. 'There's always some nut looking for holes in the ground,' he said. 'We combed the region for suitable sites.' The bat group appealed to the media, encouraging people to look for big bats. They collected a hair sample to use DNA to identify its origin, but the lab scientists weren't able to extract DNA at the time.

The broadcaster and naturalist Chris Packham came to film the hunt. But there was no trace of the bat or its kin. The bat did turn up at the Sussex tunnel the next winter, however, and the winter after that. Hutson considered putting a VHS radio tag on the bat, but was worried that the burden of a tag could kill it, and he would be blamed. 'What put me off in the end was if it didn't turn up again that winter, I'd be drummed out of the country,' he said. In 2007, however, the protectors plucked up the courage to carefully take the bat off the tunnel wall during its hibernation and inspect it. Its teeth were a bit worn, but it was in good health – and very alone. During his inspection of its private parts, Hutson found signs that it had never been sexually active.

We were now 300 metres inside the tunnel. A Natterer's was stuffed into a crevice no wider than a centimetre. 'He's awake, isn't he?' said Hutson, swiftly moving his torch away so as not to disturb it. Then he pointed his torch towards a bat that was noticeably larger than the others: solid, and tea-cup sized. 'A very rare bat,' he said, 'but not rare enough for you.' A Bechstein's bat.

What of the mouse-eared bat? 'He has definitely moved,' said Sue Harris, who had noted his position during their previous inspection, in February. We were in the relatively warm middle of the tunnel, where it was 8.2°C, but there was no bat. Harris walked ahead. Suddenly, her methodical movements became frantic. 'I can hardly contain my excitement,' she called out.

High up, where a whole brick had fallen from the wall, hung a large, sandy-coloured bat. A silver ring wrapped around its forearm shone in our torchlight. The greater mouse-eared bat. The Natterer's bats we had seen weighed eight grams. This one weighed more than thirty grams, with a broad pink muzzle, a long, pale underside, and dark-brown wings folded up tight by its side like an umbrella.

It would be hard to bond with a creature you only ever saw perfectly still, in a deep sleep, face averted from the world. Was Hutson fond of it? 'I shall be sorry when it's not there, assuming I outlive it,' he said. 'You never know – it might have another twenty years to go. It might be having an easy time, no stresses. It looks quite tough, sort of robust.' But Harris was worried. 'He's looking damp, especially around the neck area. He didn't look at all damp in February,' she said. Droplets of water glistened silver on his fur. His ring looked tarnished.

The bat's unknowability was frustrating but, after sixteen years, Hutson had become resigned to the unanswered questions about this individual, and the fate of the species in Britain. Where does this bat go? Perhaps to France? Are there really no more? 'After a few years I wondered if we should have done more in terms of finding others,' said Hutson, 'but now I'm convinced it is a loner and whatever we had done wouldn't have made a difference.' Could they reintroduce the species using wild specimens caught in continental Europe? 'The first problem is that they would have to go into quarantine for six months because of rabies. After being in captivity for six months they wouldn't be too good at operating in the wild.'

We reached the end of the tunnel. There was no exit, just a solid wall of breeze blocks. The bat seemed less a pioneer, the first of its kind, than a survivor, the last of its kind – like the tunnel, a dead end.

Not far from where the bat hung motionless, Fiona Mathews was busy moving boxes into her office in the University of Sussex's 1960s campus at Falmer. An enthusiastic, plain-speaking professor of environmental biology and chair of the Mammal Society, Mathews had just arrived from the University of Exeter and was determined to find out more about the greater mouse-eared bat. She had admired them on the continent, and had seen them landing on prey and covering it with outstretched wings. 'We've caught some and you think, "Blimey, that's big." They come out [of the net] teeth first.'

If there really is only one greater mouse-eared bat in Britain, with no possibility of reproduction, then it is as good as extinct. Seven other British bat species exist in such low numbers that no reliable population data exists. But technology such as bat detectors, which reveal bats by the sound of their echolocation, is helping better monitor populations. The Bat Conservation Trust's systematic monitoring of ten species since the start of this century has revealed an unexpected picture: nine of these appear to be increasing in number. If true, it is yet another way in which bats have surprised us.

But counting bats accurately is difficult, said Mathews. They are usually counted where they are known to roost, but scientists have yet to work out a way of counting roosts. 'Unless we know that, it makes it very difficult to understand what is going on with the population,' she said. Current threats to bats seem to spring from misunderstanding of both human and bat nature. Today, every bat and roosting site in the EU is protected by the EU Habitats Directive. But legal protection infuriates many homeowners and developers, and may encourage the furtive destruction of bat colonies.

Environmental legislation usually follows a 'polluter pays' principle, but with bats, the person providing a home for bats is penalised and must meet all the expense of surveying and providing alternative sites. The government is promising that after Brexit, public money for farmers will be based on the services they provide for the ecosystem (clean water, fertile soils etc.). Mathews wondered whether a similar formula could be applied to homeowners who provide bat services.

'You can understand why people find it frustrating when they want to convert their barn and it's got bats in it and it's a complete palaver,' she said. 'Whoever has a bat roost is providing a service to the rest of the community, so there should be a community effort to make sure the bats are protected.'

The second challenge for bats is another visible sign of

society's supposed care for them: the bat bridges that span new roads. These trellises of wires hung between telegraph poles either side of the carriageway are designed to funnel bats up and safely over fast-moving traffic so they are not killed by cars and lorries when they follow their traditional foraging routes across new roads. Unfortunately, they don't work: bats are still killed by moving vehicles. And there is no funding to monitor how bats use these bridges, if at all, or to test whether there may be a design that does work.

'The idea that bats are going to cross a road in one place and not in lots of others is preposterous. They wouldn't have done that before the road was built. Why would they suddenly go to one crossing point? Yes, a bridge may be built on one key flight line [such as following a hedge-row] but the bats probably have twenty key flight lines,' Mathews said. The evidence that bat bridges actually help bats cross new roads is poor, although there is stronger evidence showing bats willing to use tunnels under new roads and broader green bridges over them. Mathews was seeking to raise money to test different bridge designs before a road is built, and was mystified as to why the Highways Agency pumped public money into unproven bridges. 'They just want to tick a box rather than make stuff that works. That's a really bad use of public money.'

Despite the roads, the regulations, the wind turbines and the barn conversions, Mathews feels there are grounds for optimism for Britain's rarest bat. The greater mouse-eared bat may have dipped in and out of extinction in

Britain, but after decades of decline in northern Europe, the species is on the rise again in countries such as Austria. She believes it might be possible to find out more about the lonely bat's mysterious life. 'My first question was: why don't we put a GPS tag on it?' she said.

It's already sixteen. It's now or never. We don't want to intervene and hasten the demise of this animal, but on the other hand, it does seem a rather wasted opportunity not to find out anything else about it. If it had been me, I would've been blitzing the place looking for evidence of greater mouse-eared bats, and I don't think anybody has.

Mathews will start doing just that this summer, putting out special nets such as a harp trap – a large frame with strings between it, which cause a bat to drop unharmed into a collection chamber below:

The same species on the continent is often found in churches and castles and big buildings. We could start looking at these sorts of places. We could also do DNA analysis of historic droppings. Perhaps it does go to France every summer and comes back? Surely it won't be the only one doing that? We could do some more work in the autumn, when these bats exhibit swarming behaviour. If there are others in the area that happen not to hibernate in the tunnel, it's possible they may turn up at that time of year.

Tagging, she admitted, won't be simple. At least the size of the greater mouse-eared makes it easier: you don't want a tag to weigh more than 5 per cent of a bat's body weight, but the smallest GPS tags have now shrunk in size to just 1.5–2 grams, which makes it light enough to fix to the animal. But while tags are revealing hitherto-unknown facts about migratory birds from cuckoos to sandpipers, bat tags cannot be powered by lightweight solar because the wearer flies at night. When bats go underground, the tag needs a special programme to stop it constantly searching for a satellite and draining its battery. Mathews could use a combined GPS and VHS radio tag, but the latter requires a receiver, and if the bat disappears to France it will be out of range. The greater mouse-eared bat's life beyond its lonely tunnel will almost certainly remain unknown for a while longer.

2018

*

Britain's 'loneliest bat' inspired a play, *Vespertilio*, by Barry McStay, which opened in 2019 in a disused railway tunnel beneath Waterloo Station in London. The greater mouse-eared bat returned to his usual winter resting place in 2019 but did not appear at all during the winter of 2020. Tony Hutson feared this long-lived solitary bat had died. Unfortunately we are unlikely to ever discover how, why or where.

2021

Calm down, deer:
in search of the Beast of Bushy

Three hinds shoot me a doe-eyed look of warning. The enormous creature that looms over us is pumped full of testosterone, armed with a sixteen-point set of antlers, and has not had sex for a year. He eyeballs me, throws back his head and emits a groan that Chewbacca would struggle to emulate. Is this the Beast of Bushy?

Every October since Henry VIII introduced them to hunt, the rutting stags of Bushy Park in south-west London have made war with each other to find themselves a female. This year, they have widened the field of combat and thrust their antlers at a swan, a young girl who had to be taken to hospital with head, wrist and chest injuries, and a woman and a man in their fifties, who were both knocked down by stags.

What terror is stalking the wilds of suburban London? Has the heat turned red deers' heads? Are ruminant tourists getting too close? Is there a rogue giant – the Beast of Bushy – after our behinds?

The media will always pursue an alliterative animal tale – last year's seasonal stag story starred the Emperor of Exmoor – which is why I find myself wandering across the park, risking a goring for the *Guardian*.

You hear them before you smell them and you smell them before you see them. The stags – there are 125 red deer in Bushy Park – bellow guttural 'ugh-ugh-ughs' followed by great groans. A pungent scent reminiscent of a randy billy goat drifts over the bracken. And then a gigantic set of antlers rises up.

'They hide and then they appear out of the bracken without warning,' said Diane Arnold, who puts her two dogs, Amber and Millie, on the lead as a stag moves purposefully towards us.

'We got chased the other day,' said her friend, Sarah Shepherd. 'He wanted us off the path. It was hilarious.'

There are two million deer roaming Britain, more than at any time since the Norman conquest, despite an annual cull of up to 350,000 animals. Increasingly deer are living suburban lives, so clashes between man and beast are inevitable in weird, man-made ecosystems such as Bushy Park, where noisy, exotic ring-necked parakeets dash between ancient English oaks and dogs hurtle after grey squirrels.

Eight mums perform elaborate stretches by their baby buggies. Joggers go round and round and round. It's enough to turn a stag quite doolally.

'We're going to ride him!' shouted a young man to his four-year-old daughter, running up to a stag slumbering in the rutting hotspot, which is inconveniently situated between the car park and the children's playground. 'The Beast of Bushy Park, what's that?'

Warned about the rutting season, the man and his family marvel at how the pumped-up stags have waited a year to have sex. 'You get grumpy after a week,' said his wife.

'One of them could kill a kid in two seconds with them bloody horns,' said Robbie Mac, who was obeying the notices banning the feeding of the deer and instead throwing soggy bread to menacing Canada geese – another exotic addition to Bushy Park life.

Is there a Beast? 'I'm so glad you asked that,' said a spokeswoman for the Royal Parks. 'There's no rogue stag. All the stags are charged with testosterone, they are all battling for supremacy, but there is no Beast.'

Rumours about the Beast are multiplying. Some park-goers think the stags have been turned aggressive by the annual cull, which recently ended. Others believe new beasts have been added to the herd from Scotland to mix up the narrow gene pool, and that these are less accustomed to the public. In fact, the last time animals were introduced from Scotland was in 1637, according to the Royal Parks, and the only recent introduction was one pair of red deer five years ago.

The most persuasive theory is, in fact, that the recent fine weather sent record numbers of pesky humans to the park who failed to obey the fifty-metre rule, so got caught between pairs of rutting stags.

'Although they are magnificent creatures, it's important to admire them from a respectful distance – at least fifty metres,' said the Royal Parks spokeswoman.

Park-goers agree. 'People are asking for trouble,' said Sarah Shepherd. 'Stags are wild animals at the end of the day.'

2011

Ancient roots: legal protection for trees

A dark green tree stands on the north side of the medieval stone church in Defynnog in the Brecon Beacons. The tree is broader than it is tall and has divided into two quite separate elements over the centuries. Beneath its low boughs, multiple trunks resemble molten lava. Some limbs twist like sinews, others are ramrod straight. Some patches of wood are as smooth as liquid, other parts are as spiny as a sea urchin. Stag's antlers of dead branches sit alongside spiky fresh foliage that turns ancient stumps into vast shaving brushes.

All forms of tree seem to be present in this fantastical, sculptural yew in a small Welsh village. According to some experts, it may even be more than 5,000 years old. Yet it is, remarkably, far less protected than the church building beside it.

Thanks to stringent English and Welsh heritage rules, about 500,000 listed buildings – including bus stops and skate parks – enjoy high levels of legal protection. Damage to Defynnog Church, a Grade I-listed building of 'exceptional interest', could be penalised with two years in prison and unlimited fines. By contrast, if anyone harmed the yew next to it they could well escape punishment altogether. But campaigners hope all that could change following a petition calling for better legal protection for ancient yews, which has gained 230,000 signatures. The fate of such trees has been discussed in the House of Lords, and barristers are drawing up plans for new legislation to protect them.

Britain is home to far more ancient yews than any other country in Europe. The Ancient Yew Group has identified 978 of the species over 500 years old in England and 407 in Wales. France has seventy-seven, Germany and Spain just four each. For Janis Fry, an artist and yew expert who started the petition, the tree at Defynnog, thought by other authorities to be just 1,500 years old, possesses 'every possibility of creation'. Its red berries show it is female but, unusually, it also has one male branch.

The yew is cherished by its local vicar and parish, but some visitors who worship it have stripped needles from its boughs. Fry tuts as she points to them. 'The pagans have been taking needles off it,' she says, explaining that some believe the yellowish needles possess healing powers. This is one small sign of the yew's cultural and religious heft – many are found in churchyards, with theories abounding as to why this might be. Some have suggested that yews thrive on the soil surrounding corpses, with one seventeenth-century commentator writing that the trees can help keep at bay the odours produced by putrefaction. Others believe the fact that the yew is poisonous would have deterred farmers from grazing their animals in churchyards. Yet another theory suggests that the wood was used to make longbows to support the church's military ambitions.

Whatever the reason, many old yews were planted by Norman church-builders, others by Celtic Christians, and some predate Christianity altogether, showing how the new religion supplanted older sacred sites.

The yew's mystical qualities are derived from its ability to regenerate, producing fresh shoots from apparently dead wood – including beams within buildings. The yew can regenerate humans, too – the anti-cancer drug Taxol is derived from the bark of the Pacific yew – while the ancient trees are home to a wealth of wildlife.

According to Fry, about 500 ancient yews have been destroyed in the last century. Most of these were before the 1980s but there are more recent losses. Fry cites the chopping down of an ancient yew in Penegoes, Wales. Another was cut down on the boundary of Ashford Carbonell churchyard in Shropshire in 2011. And Fry says churchyard trees are often neglected. 'Ivy grows all over them and acts as a sail in the wind and breaks their branches,' she says. Fry has found stowed in ancient yews the remains of an old oil tank, lawn mowers, breeze blocks and bags of cement.

These smaller slights against ancient yews are revealed on a tour of Shropshire with tree campaigner Rob McBride. A magnificent yew in the churchyard at Uppington has a hollow inside containing a garden rake and a lawnmower grass box. Ivy snakes up its limbs, and climbs the ancient yews in nearby Kenley churchyard.

In both, McBride points to stumps where yew branches have been cut, potentially stopping it from regenerating. Although most churchwardens are well-meaning, says McBride, there is no legal requirement for churches to call upon specialist ancient tree surgeons when trimming an old yew 'instead of Fred down the road who has a saw'.

McBride is astonished that there is no legal protection for ancient yews. 'If I took a chisel to the church at Uppington, it would be a criminal offence. So how can people just cut bits off ancient yews?' he says.

Fry is heartened by the success of her petition but believes any moves to translate it into government legislation will be scuppered by Church lobbying. 'If we've got the largest collection of ancient yews in the world, why aren't they protected?' she says. 'It's because the Church won't have it. The Church has always considered such moves an unnecessary challenge to its authority and jurisdiction over its own property.'

The Church of England says it won't support a campaign for extra protection for yews because there is already adequate protection via tree protection orders (TPOs) issued by local authorities. Yews are also protected if they are in a conservation area and the Church of England's own law requires individual churches to seek permission to remove any churchyard trees. The Church of England is wary of adding to the legislative burden its managers already face.

Alex Glanville of the Church in Wales strikes a more

emollient note. 'Clearly, we want them celebrated and it's a really important thing that we happen to own. I'd love them to have special acknowledgement, and maybe special protection is a way of doing that,' he says. 'But if a tree receives a certain designation, is that actually going to improve things?'

Glanville admits that some churches have made 'ill-informed' decisions about trimming churchyard yews in the past. The Church in Wales has introduced a new requirement for churches with ancient yews to seek advice from ancient tree specialists before undertaking any tree surgery, and provides funding for that specialist advice.

'We're not sure ancient yews are desperately under threat,' says Glanville, 'because what's going to threaten them? It's going to be ill-informed work.'

Paul Powlesland, a barrister who founded Lawyers for Nature, says the existing TPO system is 'not brilliant protection' for ancient trees. TPOs only tend to be granted by a local authority if a tree is threatened. A protection order is often too late, and too little. 'The punishments for breaching a TPO are not reflective of the importance of these trees,' argues Powlesland. 'It's an anomaly in our law that we haven't grappled properly with the idea of protecting living things. If an ancient oak was chopped down in 1700 and turned into a building, that oak in the building would now be protected. If it carried on growing, it wouldn't.'

Fry hopes that new legal protection for Britain's

ancient trees, and especially its yews, could be a kind of positive nationalism for a country mired in Brexit. 'The UK could make something of that – we are independent, and we've got the largest collection of ancient yews on earth,' she says.

Powlesland agrees. Protecting ancient trees 'crosses political divides – it can unite environmental lefties and political conservatives', he says.

> It speaks to who we are as a country. What is this land? What does it mean to be British? It's a chance for politicians to make themselves part of history. These yews have existed for thousands of years. Hopefully, if we protect them, they will still exist when this entire civilisation is consigned to the history books. That's a magical thing.

2011

Flying high: London's peregrine falcons

By the four chimneys of Battersea power station, between tower cranes and builders' cabins, is an unobtrusive metal mast. At the top, a watchful figure looks down upon the 3,000 workers bustling around this vast £9 billion construction site.

'Female,' says David Morrison, with a deft glance through his binoculars. 'She's protecting her nest site. There was an intruding female about half an hour ago.'

Suddenly, she's off, arrow-like, steepling down from her mast and over the Thames, in pursuit of an unlucky bird. This year, the first residents and businesses will move into the revamped power station, but the London landmark already has its first family. A pair of peregrine falcons have been nesting here since 2000.

These fearsome wild birds of prey, the fastest member of the animal kingdom, are thriving in the capital. There were three pairs in London at the turn of the century; now there are thirty, probably the second-highest density of peregrines anywhere in the world after New York. The peregrine, once considered a bird of lonely rocky cliffs, almost fell extinct in Britain in the last century. Now it has reinvented itself as an urban creature. Pairs nest in many cities and towns, including Manchester, Derby, Coventry,

Chichester, Ipswich and Norwich. The peregrine is safer in the city than the countryside.

It's spring, and the peregrines of Battersea are laying eggs. We walk closer to the metal mast topped by a wooden nest box. The peregrine peers over the edge, cocking its head to size us up with one enormous eye. This alpha female is the most powerful wild bird in London. Peregrines will bully and sometimes kill much bigger birds, from buzzards to crows. And the female is a third bigger than the male. Over the past three years, this bird has successfully fledged eleven chicks. 'It shows she's a very virile female. She's in her prime,' says Morrison, admiringly.

Morrison is one of the reasons for the peregrine boom in London, alongside volunteers for the London Peregrine Partnership, which also monitors the birds. He was a steel fixer on a construction site in Battersea when he discovered they were nesting in the then derelict power station. He'd always loved birds, and knew that this rare bird enjoys the highest legal protection. He contacted Natural England, the government's wildlife watchdog, and began surveying urban peregrines. Under his watch, pairs of this fiercely territorial bird have taken up residence on high buildings. Once they 'hold' a territory, they sometimes struggle to breed successfully without a purpose-built nest box, so Morrison provided some. Six years ago he retired and became a full-time peregrine consultant and ecologist.

He faced his biggest challenge in 2013. Battersea's peregrines nested just below one of its famous towers but the chimneys needed to be taken down and rebuilt as part of the power station's transformation. The Battersea Power Station Development Company spent more than £100,000 on a relocation plan, building the mast at exactly the same height as the old nest in the quietest corner of the construction site. When the birds finished breeding that year, Morrison closed off their old nest and waited. It was a tense moment. 'It's nature, isn't it? You can't predict what they are going to do.' But the birds took up residence in his new nest box and have successfully bred there ever since. 'There are very few other species that would adapt and wouldn't just go,' says Morrison. 'They will even hunt from the cranes here. They are not going to move.'

They hunt at dawn, before work starts at 8 a.m., and then 'sit up there watching the world go by', says Morrison. Alongside his nest sites, an all-you-can-eat urban buffet is the main reason the birds are thriving. As we gaze at the peregrine, flocks of feral pigeons scurry through the air just below her. If a particularly large flock breaks away, 'it gets too much for the peregrines and they are off in pursuit', says Morrison. 'One of the most spectacular hunts I've ever seen is from the power-station chimneys. They hunt from here every day.'

Peregrines target weaker pigeons but will also devour starlings, black-headed gulls and most migrating birds, which often follow the river. They are also partial to a recent arrival in London: ring-necked parakeets. Every winter Morrison checks his nest boxes and cleans them:

the strangest prey he has found up there is the remains of a hen pheasant.

The naturalist and 'urban birder' David Lindo, who grew up in London, remembers having to travel to the coast as a boy to see peregrines. He first saw urban peregrines as a teenager, when he visited New York.

'Now, virtually every city I visit I expect to see a peregrine,' he says. As peregrine numbers grew in London, he set up the Tower 42 bird study group to monitor the migration of birds of prey. 'From the tower, you can see upwards of six peregrine territories across London.'

Lindo's motto is 'look up'. Seven years ago, he turned up at Tate Modern with a large, empty picture frame, and set up a telescope.

I called my 'picture' peregrinations. I had a queue of people looking through the telescope at peregrines. The kids were going, 'Oh wow, that's amazing,' and the adults were saying, 'Are they just here to cull the pigeons?' They are wild peregrines. The most amazing predator on the planet. They are a symbol of power and speed, but also a symbol of urban birding. You can see some amazing things in the heart of the concrete jungle.

Many city dwellers miss the peregrines above. Most London nests are also a closely guarded secret because they are still at risk from egg collectors and, occasionally, rogue falconers who steal peregrine chicks because wild birds tend to be better hunters than captive-bred individuals. But peregrines can be seen on Tate Modern and Charing Cross Hospital, and a pair nest on the Houses of Parliament, too.

At Battersea Power Station, the workers have embraced the birds. They are a kind of totem for this new development of more than 4,500 homes, restaurants and businesses. When it is finished, the developers plan to put telescopes in its new park so residents and visiting tourists can enjoy watching them. Morrison is quite a celebrity on site.

A middle-aged builder in a hard hat approaches. 'Are you David? I've just seen them, just now,' he says excitedly. 'One peregrine came over and tried to jump on the other' – a mating attempt.

Notices tell builders to look out for fallen falcons and all 3,000 workers have been briefed about the 'falcon recovery plan – what to do if a bird (usually a juvenile taking its first flight) is found on the ground. They may be masters of the sky, but peregrines can become stranded on the ground, where they are preyed upon by foxes. So workers are taught to guard the bird until Morrison or a trained colleague arrives. They take grounded juveniles to a high platform where the parents can feed them until they fly. Battersea's chimneys have almost been rebuilt now, and the developer and Morrison have created a new nest box behind a natural hole in the brickwork. When the building is complete in a few years' time, Morrison will oversee the peregrines' transition back to their old home.

It seems ironic that this supremely wild animal is safer in a busy city than the countryside. In rural Britain, peregrines are still illegally shot or poisoned. Conservationists believe that these birds of prey are illegally killed because they threaten the profitability of lucrative grouse shoots. Lindo also points out that pigeon-fanciers 'absolutely detest' peregrines. 'Any peregrine nesting in an urban area is less likely to be persecuted,' says Lindo. 'Becoming more urban is a blessing, but they still face dangers when they wander. When the youngsters move off into the surrounding countryside, that's where their problems start.'

Peregrine populations in provincial places are limited by the lack of high buildings, apart from cathedral spires. But as London becomes more high-rise, is there any limit to its peregrine population? Just as city-dwelling people adapt to less personal space, so do peregrines. According to Morrison, the average peregrine territory has shrunk from four kilometres in radius at the turn of the century to 2.5 kilometres today. 'I get contacted a lot by people saying, "We've got pigeons, can we have peregrines?"' says Morrison. 'Everyone wants them.'

2017

The riddle of the Orkney vole

A small, short-tailed rodent is an unlikely emissary of ancient civilisation. But the Orkney vole tells us more than we might imagine about our long and intimate relationship with Europe – and small animals. I chanced upon the story of this mysterious mammal while visiting the Neolithic marvels of Orkney, including the Ness of Brodgar, a thrilling archaeological dig which is painstakingly revealing a 4,500-year-old 'cathedral'.

The site buzzes with excitement, as student volunteers from Scotland and North America chisel away at the earth, opening vivid windows into our past: Neolithic people did not live in a world of grey stone, for instance, but painted walls bright red and yellow. And, bizarrely, they surrounded these buildings with 400 cattle shin bones.

Other remains found here include those of the common vole, which still lives on Orkney. This is intriguing because the common vole belongs on continental Europe, and fossil records suggest it has never lived on the British mainland. So where did it come from? And how did it scurry to the islands of Orkney?

Scientists were stunned when DNA analysis answered the first question: these voles originate from Belgium, and have quietly prospered on Orkney for 5,100 years, evolving to be significantly larger than their continental cousins. The answer to the second question is still hotly debated: some archaeologists believe they arrived by chance, carried on vegetation washed north by great post-Ice Age rivers; others think the voles were stowaways in freshly cut hay kept for livestock ferried to Orkney by sophisticated Neolithic farmers.

I didn't see any voles during my visit. Sadly, they are threatened by stoats, which suddenly appeared on Orkney in 2010. Julian Branscombe, co-author of an excellent British Wildlife paper about the voles, fears we are presiding over the 'McDonaldisation' of wildlife as islands end up homogeneously populated with cats, rats and stoats – and fewer uniquely evolved species.

The fact that we have no clue how stoats reached Orkney six years ago suggests we will never solve the mystery of how the common vole ended up there many centuries before. Branscombe's theory is that they were deliberately brought to Orkney as a Neolithic pet, totem or snack. I can't tell you how they taste but they do look very cute.

2016

Save our swifts: the international jet set are disappearing from our skies

It is the most miraculous bird, the ultimate winged messenger, exploring our globe, spending its life on the breeze. Sickle-shaped wings silhouetted against the sky, the swift is the fastest of all birds in level flight and remains entirely airborne for ten months, sometimes more, feeding, sleeping and mating on the wing. These long-lived creatures can clock up four million miles, commuting between English summers and African winters.

Something has changed, though. June is erupting as gloriously as it ever did: roadsides are waving with ox-eye daisies and blackbirds flute during the endless evenings. But summer is a shadow of its former self. The swifts aren't here.

Well, they are. Only not as we knew them. I heard a scream just now, felt that start of wonder, and glanced up. One swift; no, three, darting through the blue. Three birds. It's like returning to the place where you grew up and finding your old home bulldozed. Reality does not compute with the picture you remember. I knew the swift for its screaming parties, marvellous groups of twenty or forty or sixty or uncountable numbers of birds racing together through the sky, flicking their wings, calling in apparent glee.

But this bird is in freefall. A graph produced by the British Trust for Ornithology is terrifying: the British population declined by 51 per cent between 1995 and 2015. And the rate of decline is increasing: down 24 per cent in the five years to 2015.

The decline of globalised animals is always global, and always complicated. So the disappearance of other, equally charismatic long-distance migrants such as nightingales, cuckoos and swallows is bound up in habitat loss or changes in Africa, as well as Britain, and climatic changes en route.

Living in roofs, swifts have also suffered from the conversion of derelict buildings, and our desire for more energy-efficient, impermeable homes. But the biggest cause of changes in animal populations is always food supply. And guess what? Swifts feed on flying insects.

We are belatedly waking up to the global calamity that is the loss of insect life. The German study showing a 76 per cent decline in flying insects since 1989 is no anomaly. In Britain, for instance, three-quarters of butterfly species have declined over forty years, while moth abundance has fallen by more than 40 per cent in the southern half of the country.

Do not accept the vanishing of the swifts. This week is the first Swift Awareness Week. Enthusiasts are taking action: counting swifts, putting up special nest boxes, telling their neighbours to make space for them too.

We should be marching on Westminster about this threat to life. And yet, if we imagine hundreds of thousands of us brandishing banners depicting moths or birds, shouting 'Save our swifts!', it is preposterous, or comical. It shouldn't be.

2018

*

Following this June column, I got chatting to Chris Packham who had already decided to organise a march on Westminster to do exactly this – shout for swifts and other native wildlife. On a wet Saturday in September, more than 10,000 people joined Packham's 'People's March for Wildlife'.

2021

The egg snatchers:
the hidden world of a strange compulsion

When the Operation Easter detectives opened the door of the second bedroom in an ordinary house in Cleethorpes last month, they suspected they would find a shoebox or two of wild birds' eggs. Officers did not imagine they would discover twenty polystyrene fish crates, several biscuit tins and a suitcase, containing a collection of 7,707 eggs. Nestling between layers of cotton wool were the dainty speckled pale-green and blue eggs of blackcaps, corn buntings and yellowhammers, just like Cadbury's Mini Eggs; the larger, blotched chestnut red of the osprey; goshawk eggs the colour of the moon. Each acquisition was meticulously recorded in notebooks; each egg painstakingly labelled in spidery black ink and its insides blown out through a tiny hole drilled in its side. For the collector, these dead things had clearly been a life's work.

Despite being fined, jailed and derided as deviants by birdwatchers, a small band of obsessive collectors known as 'eggers' continue to illegally take the freshly laid clutches of wild birds. Last year, fifty-four egg-collecting incidents were reported to the RSPB. The twelve reports of illegal sales of wild birds' eggs was the highest figure since 1995. The seizure in Cleethorpes came shortly after the unrelated case of Michael Barclay, sixty-eight, a well-to-do landowner, who pleaded guilty to buying prohibited wild birds' eggs and taxidermy and was sent to prison for four months.

Wildlife experts fear the recent arrests reveal only a fraction of the true picture. 'The guy [from Cleethorpes] has never been on our radar before and he's got nearly 8,000 eggs,' says Mark Thomas, one of the RSPB's five investigations officers. 'How come nobody has ever caught this bloke? How come nobody has ever rung up with suspicions about this guy? That's what worries us. How many more are out there?'

Virtually incomprehensible in most other countries, egg collecting is a peculiarly British impulse, a residue of a colonial era when Victorian explorers brought back booty from around the globe and oology, the study of eggs, was a respectable branch of ornithology. Known for his fiery temper, the eminent Victorian collector the Rev. F. C. R. Jourdain would be publicly challenged to identify eggs by his rival, P. F. Bunyard. Oologists earnestly debated bird species at annual dinners held by their charity, which they named the Jourdain Society. And small boys would embark on a lifelong passion for birds by snaffling eggs from hedgerows.

After the Second World War, collecting became more furtive. *Guardian* country diarist Harry Griffin referred to collectors as 'the cloak-and-dagger men of the fells' in a 1952 column. Taking wild eggs was made illegal in 1954, but collecting continued. The extinction in the 1980s of the red-backed shrike, which had the misfortune to lay pretty, speckled eggs, was attributed to collectors. 'It was a little bit cops-and-robbers in the seventies and eighties, but it peaked in the late nineties,' says Thomas. Increasingly professional eggers cracked hi-tech security operations that were attempting to protect imperilled populations of golden eagles, white-tailed eagles and ospreys.

By the late 1990s the RSPB was receiving, on average, one report of nest theft every day. Tayside police set up Operation Easter, a rolling nationwide investigation that is still active today. In 2001 it targeted a hard core of 130 eggers. There was 'the Hoover', so called because he would pitch up at a tern colony and take hundreds of eggs, and 'the Abbott and Costello of egg collecting', Jamie and Lee McLaren, caught in the Orkneys in 1997 with videos of each other robbing nests (in one, a fulmar vomited over their shoes in an attempt to protect its offspring). On another occasion, a warden found his name and 'fuck off' written in lipstick on hen eggs plonked in the raided nest of a peregrine falcon.

Collectors were brazen because they knew they were untouchable. Allowing only for fines related to the convicted's ability to pay, the law was no deterrent. Eggers such as Colin Watson, who died last year falling from a twelve-metre larch he was climbing to examine a nest, clocked up repeated convictions during the 1980s and 1990s. Despite paying fines totalling nearly £6,000 Watson persisted, on one occasion trying to fell a tree in Scotland with a chainsaw to reach an osprey's nest.

Rather than their prey, it was eggers who became threatened with extinction when the law changed in 2001. Collectors could now be jailed. One of the most notorious eggers, who inspired a small following in Coventry, handed over his vast collection to police so he would not be prosecuted. 'That was the turning point,' says Thomas. 'He was almost an idol of the egg collectors. When they saw him give away his collection they thought this new law is really serious.'

Derek Lee, thirty-nine, was the first egger to be jailed for his obsession. Two fines failed to curtail the secret hobby he began when he was eight, captivated by a tawny owl chick his brother's friend snatched from a nest. 'We went to the local park and took common eggs such as blackbirds' and song thrushes',' he says. Most gave up when they got older, but Lee graduated to rarer species. 'For me, it gradually got to be an obsession. When I left school at sixteen I had a bit of spare time and a little money so I travelled elsewhere to pick up a kestrel or sparrowhawk egg. Then the next challenge was a buzzard. Eventually, I came across peregrines and red kites.'

Like many eggers, Lee confided only in a couple of close friends who shared his passion. They would meet in the winter and methodically plan raids in the spring when eggs were freshly laid (nearly hatched eggs cannot easily be blown and preserved). 'It's a bit like a bank robbery.

You've got to do your own work at getting certain eggs. You can't just go into a field and pick them up,' he says.

Travelling from his home in Greater Manchester to Wales or the Lake District, Lee would share information about where birds were nesting – and wardens were waiting. Savouring the adrenaline rush of outwitting the authorities, Lee would pose as an ordinary birdwatcher and chat to wardens, 'getting information from them without them knowing I was taking eggs'.

When they got their hauls home, Lee and his confidants would note the Latin name of each bird and where they found the egg. Then they would squirrel it away. 'You'd look on it again occasionally and reminisce about what you'd been up to, but most of the time it would be tucked away. You couldn't show it off to anybody because you wouldn't know who you were talking to – their dad might be a police officer. It's not something you'd broadcast.'

He still remembers the last egg he ever collected – a woodcock – and the visit at his home at 8 a.m., a few months after the law changed. The police were at his front and back door, brandishing search warrants. They discovered hundreds of eggs. Lee was given a six-month prison sentence. 'It was a bit of a shock. When I came out of prison I decided to give up,' he says.

Others, always men and often working class, followed Lee to jail. Carlton D'Cruze, who kept journals describing how a white-tailed eagle on the Isle of Mull broke one of her own eggs in a desperate attempt to defend her nest from him, received six months in 2002. Anthony Higham, found with video footage showing him stealing red-throated divers' eggs on the Orkneys, was jailed in 2003. Daniel Lingham, a carpenter living in a caravan filled with hundreds of nightingale and nightjar eggs, was put away last year. Custodial sentences are a particularly powerful deterrent, according to Thomas, because fellow prisoners see egg thieves as particularly odd deviants. 'We know that people stealing birds eggs don't get a very good time inside. It's almost seen as paedophilia; it's a crime committed by weirdos in the eyes of the "normal" criminal set,' he says.

Why do eggers still do it? While some, such as Barclay, pay money for collections, the desire to raid nests is rarely financial. 'It's an individual trophy that relates to that person, the location they took it from and the work they did behind the scenes to find the nest,' says Thomas.

It's about a guy in Coventry leaving at night and driving to Scotland, walking fifteen miles through fields of snow, abseiling down the crag, knocking the golden eagle off its nest, stealing the eggs, blowing them, burying them in tins in the ground, driving back to Coventry with nothing and waiting until autumn to return when birds are not breeding so they won't get caught in transit.

Some eggers' mania for collecting extends to drawers of seashells or boxes of toy soldiers. Most of those jailed have speeded their own journey to the cells thanks to the evidence of their own index cards or coded computer files carefully detailing every clutch and theft. An obsessive-compulsive attention to detail can obscure reality. On one police raid, officers were amazed to find an egger reminding them to wipe their feet and not spoil his carpet.

Others seem addicted, gripped by an obsession they can no longer master. When the knock finally comes on some collectors' doors 'there's this dawning realisation of what they've been doing for twenty years or more', says Thomas. 'We've had some break down and cry and say, "I'm so glad you've finally come, this has been controlling me for years. The breeding season comes and I can't stop going out and collecting eggs."'

Lee testifies to its addictive quality. 'There are quite a few who are obsessed with it. Every single spring and summer they can't wait to get out. If you put a child in a chocolate factory their eyes light up with excitement. It's like that. When spring and summer come, the eggers are on edge. They're like big kids.'

While Lee now sticks to bird watching – 'It's not quite the same but you enjoy the birds flying about' – he claims to know several eggers who are still active:

All the collectors are thinking about packing in, but you'll always get a few hard-core collectors who will carry on. You're not going to stamp it out completely. I know of two who are still taking them. One got sent down for it and he came out and he was still taking them. Some people don't learn their lessons.

Eggers are getting smarter at hiding their collections. 'They'll put them somewhere where the RSPB can't find them – in a lock-up garage or in their place of work,' says Lee. When police raided Barclay's grand home, Hanworth Hall, in Norfolk, they discovered a secret door in a wardrobe leading to a concealed room containing empty cabinets ready for egg collections. Most seizures now come from tip-offs, often from disgruntled wives who have played second fiddle to their husbands' obsession for decades or from others in the egging community who betray their friends and rivals.

According to Alan Stewart, wildlife and environment officer for Tayside police, Operation Easter now tracks seventy suspected collectors, down from its peak of 130 five years ago. While some have given up, others, he says, have been driven abroad, taking cheap flights to Madrid, for instance, where they can target Spanish imperial eagles and post the eggs home to a friend's address. The National Wildlife Crime Unit is now liaising with Interpol to tackle egg collectors who go to Europe. 'We can't relax our guard,' says Stewart.

Does it matter? Some might argue that the oologists, who still gather at dinners organised by the Jourdain Society – now without its charitable status – are harmless eccentrics, even if some, reportedly, have convictions for egg collecting. Apologists claim that responsible collectors only take freshly laid clutches and most birds simply lay a second clutch. (Not so, says the RSPB, which points out that big birds of prey only ever lay once a year, while unscrupulous thieves commonly take as many clutches of eggs as a bird will lay in a breeding season.)

But, ironically, egg collections have helped preserve some bird species by assisting vital scientific discoveries. In a pioneering study, the naturalist Derek Ratcliffe pinpointed the cause of a near-catastrophic decline in birds of prey by comparing peregrine eggs from historical collections with eggs he tested in the 1960s. Finding the older eggs were heavier, he proved that pesticides were causing the birds to produce thinner eggshells that often cracked before they could hatch. Some conservationists argue that a form of egg collecting must continue for the good of future environmental science.

An inescapable melancholy hangs over the spoils of the Cleethorpes raid, now being counted in an RSPB warehouse in Bedfordshire. So much energy and care has gone into gathering and recording these eggs, each one a bird that has never flown. 'It would be good to think that this collection is the last major one seized in the UK,' says Thomas. 'It's very encouraging to know that there's not an increase in young people taking birds' eggs. The majority are in their forties. Maybe in a generation's time, the day of the egg collector will be over.'

2006

*

Egg collecting has not quite disappeared. In 2016 a retired solicitor from Devon was fined almost £5,000 for amassing a collection of hundreds of eggs over nearly seventy years. A prison sentence was no deterrent for Daniel Lingham (mentioned above), who was jailed for twelve weeks for egg collecting in 2005. In 2018 he was sentenced to eighteen weeks in prison after being spotted acting suspiciously on a heath near his Norfolk home and found to be in possession of nearly 5,000 eggs including marsh harriers, nightjars and turtle doves. He was sixty-five at the time, again suggesting that egg collecting will vanish with the older generation.

2021

When doves fly:
the race to rescue the turtle dove

Under the torrential rain of a fickle British summer, twenty-five soggy pilgrims gather in front of the Plough, an ancient oak-beamed pub in the West Sussex village of Rusper. Above the drone of planes bringing travellers into Gatwick, the walkers – variously devotees of trekking, folk music or wildlife – raise their voices to sing an old English folk song that is told from the point of view of a globetrotting visitor to these shores:

> 'Fare you well, my dear, I must be gone,
> And leave you for a while.
> If I roam away, I'll come back again
> Though I roam 10,000 miles, my dear,
> Though I roam 10,000 miles.'

The song, 'The Turtle Dove', was discovered by Ralph Vaughan Williams when the Plough's publican sang it to him more than a hundred years ago. It is a forgotten lament for a bird that has inspired writers, musicians and country-dwellers for centuries. This small, delicate wild dove, with grey feathers blushed pink and ginger, is a symbol of renewal in the Old Testament and an emblem of love and constancy for Shakespeare. The romance embodied by the turtle dove has fluttered into countless songs, from 'The Twelve Days of Christmas' to Elvis Presley's 'Baby, If You'll Give Me All Your Love' and Cliff Richard's 'Bachelor Boy'. But this celebrated bird is slipping towards extinction in Britain.

The turtle dove is a global citizen, spending winter in the Sahel region of Africa before flying to Europe to breed. The Victorians observed great flocks of turtle doves assembling to begin their migration south. As recently as the 1960s, there were 125,000 pairs in Britain. Between 1967 and 2016 their numbers plummeted by 98 per cent. Each year, population estimates are revised downwards: there may be fewer than 2,000 pairs left. Most worryingly, there is no agreement about how we can reverse the decline.

The pilgrims, led by the singer Sam Lee, are beginning a two-day walk from the Plough to one of the turtle dove's last strongholds, the Knepp estate in West Sussex. In a quixotic act of faith, they plan to sing the song to the doves. If we all paid more attention to this enigmatic bird, thinks Lee, perhaps we could save it from disappearing.

'We're casting a magical spell,' says Lee. 'Vaughan Williams was passing this pub on his bicycle 113 years ago and he popped in and said: "Anyone know any songs?" The landlord sang him "The Turtle Dove", which he'd never heard before. He took it away to London and he made a global hit.' Vaughan Williams' arrangement of the song has been recorded, in different forms and with different titles, by artists including Joan Baez, Marianne Faithfull and Nic Jones, yet the song's original meaning has been forgotten, explains Lee, especially in its Sussex heartland. 'We're going to rewild this song,' he says. 'The amazing connection is that the song itself is about extinction.' The turtle dove sings of its migration, its disappearance and its devotion to its unnamed love, which could be for a place as well as a person.

The turtle dove is a symbol of the extinction crisis unfolding in Britain. Our intensively farmed, densely populated country can still look pretty, but experts agree that lowland Britain – the turtle dove's home – is one of the most nature-depleted landscapes in the world. More than half of Britain's plant and animal species are in decline and one in ten is severely threatened. More than forty million birds have vanished from this country in fifty years.

The Victorians may have seen flocks of turtle doves, but today they are elusive. The best chance of encountering one is to hear a calling male, which makes the soft 'tur-turr' that gives the dove its name. The sound is gentle, summery and somnolent – one of the most soothing in nature, according to Victorian admirers. When I search for it this summer, I hear it only beside the old walled courtyard at Pensthorpe, a Norfolk nature reserve that has run a trial to breed the doves in captivity. 'It's so sad that the only place to hear them is in our aviary,' says Chrissie Kelley, head of species management at

Pensthorpe Conservation Trust. 'It used to be a common sound.'

Kelley takes me through the turtle dove's troubled recent history. It has been affected badly by recent droughts in Africa, and the by Mediterranean penchant for shooting migrating birds each spring and autumn (traditionally for food, but now more for fun). It has been estimated that three million turtle doves are shot each year. While EU law bans the hunting of birds during periods of breeding and migration, the turtle dove is still shot in many countries during autumn. In addition, BirdLife International estimates that 600,000 are killed illegally each year.

But these trends do not explain entirely the loss of British turtle doves. Although the bird is declining across Europe (down more than a third this century), only in the similarly intensively farmed Netherlands is there a decline to match Britain's. Turtle doves eat mostly grains, living on wild plant and weed seeds. Since the 1950s, Britain has destroyed almost all its wildflower meadows, while chemical pesticides have removed arable weeds. 'Back in the day, when turtle doves were very numerous, they'd feed on farmers' grain spills,' says Kelley. 'Fifty years ago there was a lot more mess – stubble fields and open barns. We've got so clean in our farming practices now, that there's no spillage, no waste.'

Britain has also lost dense hedgerows where the turtle dove likes to nest. 'They need thick, scrubby hedgerows, because as far as turtle doves are concerned they think a couple of twigs is a nest,' says Kelley, pointing out the feeble construction her captive doves have made in a thicket inside the aviary. 'They need food and water fairly close by, sucking up water to make crop milk for their young.'

Pensthorpe is working with a group of mid-Norfolk farmers to preserve hedgerows, restore farm ponds and offer the birds supplementary food. It is a formula being repeated across the turtle dove's last strongholds in the south-east and Yorkshire, as part of Operation Turtle Dove, a partnership by charities including the RSPB and Natural England, the government's advisory body on the environment. But earlier, similar, schemes have not worked. One Norfolk farmer who planted field margins with wild seed mixes succeeded in boosting bird populations, but not turtle doves.

Isabella Tree, the co-owner of the Knepp estate, is critical of recent attempts to provide the doves with additional food. Knepp is one of the few places where turtle doves are increasing: from none at the start of the century, the 1,400-hectare farm now has twenty calling males. In the book *Wilding*, Tree's account of how she and her husband, Charlie Burrell, returned their farm to nature over two decades, she argues that our categorisation of the turtle dove as a 'farmland' bird is misleading. What did it eat before there were farms? What does it eat in sub-Saharan Africa? Tree believes turtle doves that have been observed eating spilled arable grains in Britain are starving and desperate. Any dove breeder will tell you about the dangers of feeding wheat and corn to the birds: cracked grain can tear the throat, while in the gut it absorbs moisture and can cause fungal diseases.

When Operation Turtle Dove launched in 2012, the RSPB wanted to scatter a mix of wheat, oilseed rape, millet and canary seed at sites including Knepp. Tree and Burrell politely refused. Knepp's farm produces no such seeds, yet their turtle doves are thriving. 'Why can't modern conservationists go back to the meticulous records of the Victorians to find out what turtle doves were actually eating?' asks Tree.

While conservationists agree that turtle doves love weed seeds such as common fumitory (which has returned to rewilded Knepp), most weeds do not produce seeds until the middle of summer – the turtle dove arrives in Britain, undernourished, in April and May. In fact, says Tree, there are old accounts of turtle doves eating snails. They may peck at hawthorn shoots, too. Ornithologists have observed continental turtle doves eating berries, fungi and invertebrates.

One theory is that Knepp's turtle doves are thriving because they can easily find seeds on the bare ground created by the rootling of the wild pigs that Tree and Burrell have restored to their farm. 'We know the turtle doves like bare earth, where their little legs aren't having to cope with anything too scraggy or long,' says Tree. 'They want areas where they can see what's coming and fly off quickly.' Turtle doves at Knepp this summer are being caught and fitted with a radio tag that should help scientists identify where they have been feeding and deduce precisely what they need.

Increasingly, however, conservationists fear there are other, even more complicated causes for their demise. Carles Carboneras, an RSPB research scientist who specialises in migratory birds, says that global heating is causing quail, another migratory 'farmland' bird, to move further northwards. But the turtle dove is showing no sign of expanding its range. 'Everybody agrees the main cause for the decline is the transformation of landscape,' says Carboneras. 'The increase in monocultures is very, very bad for the species. In this country, you either have very intense agriculture or very dense woodlands – and neither of these is good for turtle doves.'

But Carboneras points out that this shift to a 'simplified' landscape in Britain occurred fifty years ago. So why have turtle dove populations fallen so dramatically more recently? Carboneras fears that the rapid accumulation of nitrogen from farm fertilisers and traffic pollution in the soil is causing vegetation to grow too quickly for turtle doves. 'If the grass is too high, they can't access the food. In the south-east, we're probably seeing the effect of nutrients, but it's a hunch. We don't have the evidence for that yet.'

It will be difficult to save the turtle dove without understanding the reasons for its decline but, some conservationists warn, endangered species have been 'studied to extinction' in the past. We cannot always afford to wait. At Pensthorpe, Kelley and her team have successfully demonstrated how to breed turtle doves in captivity. Here, turtle dove eggs are fostered by Barbary doves, because these common birds are less sensitive and happy to be kept inside smaller cages. Releasing captive-bred turtle doves into the wild, says Kelley, could be 'an insurance policy for British wild birds before they go extinct'.

The RSPB is opposed to breeding turtle doves in captivity, saying captive-bred birds are unlikely to possess a migratory instinct – they would not depart every autumn and return each spring. As Carboneras says:

> This is like the British solving their own problem – and so what? You still have a declining population internationally. You cannot have millions of captive-bred turtle doves being released across Europe and expect them to behave naturally and link breeding and wintering areas as they have done since they evolved. It might solve the problem for this island, but not for the species.

Other conservation scientists disagree. Carl Jones has used captive breeding to save the pink pigeon and other critically endangered birds from extinction on Mauritius. Now, as chief scientist for Durrell Wildlife Conservation Trust, an international charity, he is looking at whether he can help save British turtle doves with a similarly intensive rescue plan. The RSPB is, he thinks, being 'narrow-minded' and cites other examples of the successful release of captive-bred migratory birds, from the white stork across Europe to the orange-bellied parrot in Tasmania.

'There's no better way of understanding these animals than breeding them in captivity and really getting hands-on with them, rather than just standing back and observing decline or putting fences around things,' says Jones. He argues that a captive-breeding programme, alongside the management of wild populations through supplementary feeding, is the best way of saving endangered species and quickly understanding their needs.

Back at Knepp, the pilgrims arrive, wet and exhausted, at their journey's end. At 4 a.m. they rise from their bell tents and head to great green pillows of sallow and black-thorn scrub in the rewilded landscape. Here they finally hear the 'tur-turring' of the turtle dove and softly sing Vaughan Williams' folk song.

'There's something immensely calming about the turtle dove's song,' says Lee. 'It has this low frequency that suddenly appears and disappears. It's almost the flicker of a film – and such a metaphor for its own situation. The silence around it is as powerful as its presence.' Singing about this bird, he says, makes it 'become more powerful and significant. Suddenly the bird is fuller and you realise every creature has that potential – we've just stopped listening.'

Most of us will never notice if this one small bird with

its soft song disappears from Britain. How would we lose if it does? 'There are so many ways,' says Lee. 'The disappearance of its song is part of a greater silencing of the natural world. Losing the turtle dove is to lose the intelligence of that creature, which understands the landscape around it and plays a part in it.' He pauses. 'It's the burning down of a library. To take these books off the shelves and lose them would be to weaken us as human beings.'

2019

＊

The turtle dove is still Britain's most rapidly declining breeding bird. Each year it fails to reappear in former haunts. Despite intensive conservation efforts, many experts expect it to be extinct in this country by the end of this decade.

2021

Sealed with a bracing dip

Horsey Gap is usually a gloriously empty stretch of sand dunes on the crumbling Norfolk coast. At this time of year, however, it is bustling with rowdy grey seals, arcing their banana bodies protectively around new pups.

This means it is full of people too. A few years ago there were no seals here – now there are more than 750 pups, and over the winter 30,000 people drive down a bumpy track to admire them. Volunteers in high-vis jackets corral the crowds but last weekend there was such traffic chaos that Norfolk police have warned people to stay away.

This is a shame because we are curious about seals and they are curious about us. In summer, when I swim in the waves at nearby Waxham, the seals startle me when they pop their heads out of the water wondering what I'm up to. Common seals may be the smaller and cuter species, but the big grey seals with their soulful eyes and long dog-like faces are my favourite, despite their uncomplimentary scientific name, *Halichoerus grypus*, which means hook-nosed sea pig. Britain is home to almost half the world's population of grey seals: mostly in Scotland, but increasingly found in burgeoning colonies on the Farne Islands and the Lincolnshire and Norfolk coasts. In 2001 just twenty-five pups were born on the National Trust's

Blakeney Point nature reserve – this winter, there were 2,417.

Seal-watching is a cottage industry, with fishing families making a good living from boat trips to see the seals at Blakeney and on the Farnes. There is seal art too. The popular local painter Brian Lewis has produced a funny picture of a boatload of seals gazing at human sunbathers on the sand. Nevertheless, for all the admiration, big populations of large mammals are rarely allowed to live peaceably alongside humans: seals are still shot in Scotland, where they interfere with salmon farms. And in Norfolk some locals dislike the visitors the seals attract, fearful that pilgrims will erode the fragile sand dunes.

Last weekend I avoided the melee by taking my family to a beach a mile from the seals to watch another spectacle: my girlfriend swimming in the sea without a wetsuit. She deserved a few spectators. The seals, busy with their pups, failed to show up.

2015

PART II

Wild Places

This island is not for sale:
Eigg, an object of desire

'It's the difference between black-and-white TV and colour,' said Brian Greene. 'That's what it was like after the revolution.' Greene was giving me a lift in his dilapidated Peugeot along Eigg's only road, waving at every passer-by. It was the kind of explosive Highland summer day when butterflies jinked out of the steaming greenery and every foxglove, fuchsia and yellow flag iris seemed to have simultaneously burst into flower.

Small islands are like celebrities: they loom far larger than their actual size, they are pored over by visitor-fans and they become public possessions, laden with reputations and attributes they may or may not embody. The Hebridean island of Eigg is second to St Kilda as the most famous of the smaller British isles. While St Kilda is renowned for its extinction as a place of human settlement, Eigg is celebrated for its rebirth. After overthrowing its eccentric, authoritarian owner two decades ago, this 31-square-kilometre patch of moor and mountain was reborn as what is sometimes mockingly called the People's Republic of Eigg. This triumph of David versus Goliath has forged an apparently inspirational, sustainable community of a hundred people. On first glance, it appears at once industriously creative and attractively lackadaisical: colourful houses, gardens filled with strawberry patches, hammocks made from old fishing nets and swings from old pink buoys.

Eigg has suffered more than most over the perennial small-island question of ownership. Larger British isles, such as the islands of Shetland and Orkney, or the Isle of Man, have (at least in modern times) avoided the vexation of capricious landlords. Perhaps their remoteness, or the strength of their local culture, militate against individual possession, but it may simply be sheer size. In contrast, the Small Isles – Eigg, Muck, Rùm and Canna – are perfectly formed and of an ideal acreage to be possessed by one person. For two centuries, these beautiful, fecund Hebridean islands have been objects of desire for wealthy men – and it has always been men – who love islands, with disastrous consequences for both sides.

The islophile D. H. Lawrence wrote a satirical short story, 'The Man Who Loved Islands'. It is a cautionary tale: a young idealist called Mr Cathcart buys a small island in order to create his own utopia, downsizes to a tiny one when he realises the native islanders are mocking him, and finally moves to an uninhabited rock. Fredrik Sjöberg, an author I visited on the tiny Swedish island of Runmarö, believes small islands possess 'a peculiar attraction for men with a need for control and security' because 'nothing is so enclosed and concrete as an island'. The literary academic Peter Conrad offers a more Freudian interpretation, suggesting that an island is a 'uterine shelter' surrounded, like the foetus, by fluid, and attracting men in search of a mother or a primal source of safety. Novelists cocoon their creativity – and fragile egos – on islands, too. 'I like islands,' wrote Will Self, 'because they're discrete and legible, just like stories.'

One of Eigg's old Gaelic names is 'the Island of the Powerful Women', which it was respectfully called by male islanders at sea, to avoid bad luck. But its matriarchy was despoiled by a succession of men whose craving for Eigg outdid their means. The English Runciman family were reasonably enlightened – Lord Runciman's wife, Hilda, became one of the first female MPs – but they sold Eigg as a 'perfectly secluded island of the Old World' in 1966. It was bought by an elderly Welsh farmer whose Hereford cattle promptly died of bracken poisoning. Disheartened, he got rid of Eigg for £110,000 in 1971 to Bernard Farnham-Smith, self-styled naval commander, head of an English charity that wanted to run the island as a school for disabled boys. Eigg's own school was so depleted that by 1973 it was down to one pupil. Islanders welcomed the charismatic 'Commander' and his stories of his navy days in China. Farnham-Smith's ingenious ideas were a bit vague, however, and he was soon cutting costs. The island doctor described his regime as 'living under enemy occupation, without the satisfaction of being able to shoot the bugger'. It turned out that the most Farnham-Smith had commanded was a fire brigade, and Eigg was back on the market in 1974.

On 1 April 1975, Keith Schellenberg, a dashing, Yorkshire-born businessman and former Olympic bob-sleigher, acquired Eigg. He was a charming, persuasive adventurer, who, over the next twenty years, fulfilled the narrative of 'The Man Who Loved Islands' perhaps more faithfully than any other real nesomane (John Fowles's term for island-lover). Legend has it that Schellenberg found himself locked in his home at Udny Castle, a grand pile belonging to his second wife, with the deadline for a blind auction for Eigg approaching. Unfazed, he abseiled down the walls to offer Farnham-Smith £274,000; £74,000 more than the state-run Highlands and Islands Develop-ment Board was prepared to pay.

The thirty-nine remaining islanders – an all-time popu-lation low – were initially pleased. They didn't want a takeover by the government, which had shown little inter-est in renovating their pier or reforming the high freight charges on the ferry. At first, Schellenberg promoted a pre-scient modern vision of self-sufficiency through tourism, the miracle industry then hailed by the authorities as the solution to the Highland 'problem'. Farnham-Smith had kept the wooden community hall locked, but in a popular early move Schellenberg gave it back to the islanders so there could be badminton in winter and dances in sum-mer. Dozens of ceilidhs took place during that first golden year. Unlike other Highland lairds, Schellenberg was a vegetarian who objected to shooting, and he encouraged the Scottish Wildlife Trust to create three nature reserves. Buildings were renovated for holiday homes, and flashy boats, including a motor cruiser called *Golden Eye*, brought tourists to the island. Job ads in national newspapers brought an influx of new residents to work for the new owner.

Maggie and Wes Fyffe were running a craft workshop on the east coast of Scotland when Schellenberg turned up and invited them to start a similar project on Eigg. Maggie has keen, twinkly eyes, a Lancastrian accent and an excellent smoker's chuckle. She and Wes loved Eigg and felt an immediate sense of belonging. 'Apart from the fact that it is beautiful, I just liked being part of a small community,' she said as we drank tea in her croft. The couple had two children and, on Eigg, they no longer felt excluded from things. 'Kids go to everything here because if there's something happening everybody goes,' said Maggie. 'It just felt right.'

In keeping with most Hebridean islanders, the Gaelic-speaking Eigg natives were far from insular. 'It's a real misconception that folk have about Hebridean crofter types,' said Maggie. She mentions an old islander who has travelled the globe and fought in Palestine. 'People in general here are very hospitable, it's part of the culture. They were really happy to see young people and kids arriving,' she said. That outward-facing mentality is still a feature of the island.

By the summer of 1979, Eigg was open for business.

The population jumped to sixty and the school, that crucial barometer of small-island health, suddenly had twelve pupils. There was a new tea room and craft centre – moped hire, day cruises, sea angling, lobster fishing and pony trekking were advertised as on offer. Visitors could even help with haymaking or shearing sheep. Unfortunately, when the tourists arrived, these activities were rarely available. Staff turnover was worryingly high. New employees were housed in run-down buildings with polythene for windowpanes. Schellenberg's grand lodge was open house for his society friends in high summer. One likened him to Mr Toad: 'Keith actually wears those round goggles and he's always arriving in places with a lot of noise and clouds of dust.' His prized possession was a 1927 Rolls-Royce. Guests would perch on the running board as he drove them to beach picnics or moonlit games of hockey. 'We spent our days as if we were Somerset Maugham characters, sunbathing or playing croquet on the manicured lawn,' said a friend of his.

In the village shop I met Sarah Boden, one of Eigg's two farmers. She remembers a German playboy landing in the Lodge gardens in a helicopter. Two models dressed in catsuits brandishing toy guns stepped out first. 'Schellenberg was very charismatic, a real showman,' said Boden, who recalled him driving around in an eight-wheeled Argocat, an amphibious all-terrain vehicle. 'He'd drive it to the boat and park it in the most ridiculous place possible at the pier, just so the visitors would watch.'

Schellenberg revived the inter-island games that traditionally took place between residents of the Small Isles, and for his guests devised war games with yellow tennis balls, which were insensitively billed as 'Jacobites v. Hanoverians'. During the 1988 games the island ceilidh band, who had agreed to play for his wealthy guests, decided there would be a small entrance fee to raise money for a new hall. When Schellenberg discovered that his American friends had been charged, he demanded that their money be returned. The band walked off stage and many islanders left the concert in protest, pursued by one of the laird's aristocratic Scottish guests, who shouted: 'Scum of the earth, half-baked socialists!'

Behind the comedy was genuine suffering. In 1980 Schellenberg had divorced his wealthy second wife and, suddenly much poorer, was running Eigg on a shoestring. The farm manager quit, labourers were made redundant and the tractors ran out of diesel. His regime was propped up by generous government tax breaks for new, environmentally damaging plantations of non-native Sitka spruce. The rain came in through the nursery roof – old islanders' homes were by now particularly dilapidated. Life 'was quite grim', remembered Boden, who spent the first six years of her life on the island in the 1980s. 'We lived in five different houses and two caravans. Schellenberg would employ and sack people on a total whim, so there was no security.' Inadvertently, though, he created an island community that would ultimately depose him.

Many of the outsiders Schellenberg hired and fired, such as Maggie and Wes Fyffe, liked Eigg so much that they stayed, and scratched out a self-sufficient life on crofts in Cleadale, the fertile valley that had been the island's traditional centre. Older inhabitants were welcoming, if perplexed to see newcomers adopt the life they urged their children to escape. Old and new bonded over house ceilidhs while Schellenberg fretted about Eigg's 'hippy' population. He characterised them as misfits fleeing the mainstream, 'wandering itinerants who found the island a nice refuge but were not mentally strong enough to cope with the life and earn a living'.

The laird was struggling to earn one, too. Planned golf courses and tennis courts never materialised, and tourism petered to a halt. 'I've kept its style slightly run down – the Hebrides feel,' he claimed in later years. Eventually, Schellenberg's ex-wife, who still jointly owned Eigg, took him to court, accusing him of mismanaging their declining asset. Across the Highlands, by the 1990s, there were growing calls for land reform. Tom Forsyth, an unsung hero of Scottish land reform who had helped regenerate crofting on an isolated peninsula north of Ullapool, imagined that Eigg could become a new Iona – like that much-visited Scottish isle, a place of spiritual pilgrimage, creativity and prosperity. Together with Alastair McIntosh, a Lewis academic, Robert Harris, a Borders farmer, and Liz Lyon, an artist, Forsyth would found the Isle of Eigg Heritage Trust. In 1991 they launched a public appeal:

to raise millions of pounds so they could buy the island.

The following May Schellenberg was forced by his ex-wife to put Eigg up for sale. In July 1992 it was bought by the highest bidder: Schellenberg. He planned to take his Rolls-Royce on a 'triumphant tour' of the island, reported the *Scotsman*, 'once it was rendered roadworthy'. The car's days were numbered, however: early in January 1994 the sheds on Eigg's pier burned down, with Schellenberg's Roller inside. The police arrived to investigate but the culprits were never identified. 'It was once the laird's factor [his estate manager] who went about burning people out. Now it seems OK to burn out the laird himself,' fumed Schellenberg, blaming 'hippies and dropouts' for subverting island traditions with 'acid-rock parties'. Eigg's indigenous population responded with an open letter refuting his 'ludicrous allegations'.

Schellenberg was determined not to let the islanders take over, and in 1995, needing money after a split from his third wife, he abruptly sold Eigg to a fire-worshipping German artist and self-styled 'professor' who went by the name of Maruma – Gotthilf Christian Eckhard Oesterle had read his new name in a pool of water in Geneva. Schellenberg returned to Eigg one last time to requisition an 1805 map of the island from the craft shop. Islanders heard he was on his way and parked a disused community bus against the shop's door to block it. Then they took the day off to see what would happen next. A local police officer told the furious ex-landlord that if no one claimed ownership of the bus within thirty days he could remove it. Schellenberg stormed off, by boat. 'You never understood me,' was his anguished parting shot to the islanders. 'I always wanted to be one of you.' Brian Greene, who came here from England as a young man responding to a job advert, almost felt sorry for him. 'He was like an alien. The Scots can be pretty hard on their thousand-year-old oppressor sometimes,' he said. 'Everyone has good points, but he refused to show his.'

Maruma arrived with grand plans. He declared it was impossible to own Eigg and vowed to improve opportunities for the community, build a swimming pool and replace the dirty diesel generators that provided electricity with an integrated system of wind and solar power. The press discovered that, unfortunately, Maruma was not quite what he seemed: he was unknown in the art world, he wasn't a proper professor, and he had used Eigg as security for a £300,000 loan at a punitive 20 per cent interest rate. He promised to remove the island's rusty old cars, but a pile of wrecks soon accumulated by the pier: locals dubbed it 'The Maruma Centre'. In July 1996 the island was put up for sale again, at an inflated price of £2 million.

The Trust redoubled its fundraising efforts. The story of the islanders who wanted to buy their own island was portrayed as a jolly romp in the style of Compton Mackenzie's *Whisky Galore*, in which Hebridean islanders rebel against British bureaucrats. Eigg folk didn't particularly relish this stereotype, but it captured imaginations and raised money.

Maggie Fyffe, who became the Trust's administrator, sorted through the mail from well-wishers: donations began flowing in at the rate of £1,000 per post bag – soon it was £30,000 per bag. Concerts took place in Edinburgh, Glasgow, Tyrone – and even Detroit – to raise funds. A mystery benefactor, a woman from northern England whose identity Fyffe still won't reveal, gave £900,000. According to Alastair McIntosh, most donations came from England. Outsiders were shocked by the feudalism that the islanders endured – the owners even decided which of them, if any, could eat Eigg's seaweed – and worried about the possible fate of its pristine environment. The wildlife trusts, including the Scottish Wildlife Trust, were particularly effective at mobilising their members to help Eigg.

Meanwhile, the island's Trust feared that Maruma's German estate agent would sell Eigg to another international client. The agent described the Scottish islands on his books as 'the Van Goghs' of 120 personally inspected paradises: 'There is a sense of romance in buying islands. It is the ultimate purchase you can make, a complete miniature world of which you can be king.' Maruma's creditor, a German clothing exporter, finally put the islanders out of their misery. After Maruma defaulted on his £300,000 loan, the creditor used the Scottish courts to force Eigg's sale. His solicitors accepted the islanders' offer of £1.5 million on 4 April 1997. Finally, the people of Eigg owned their island.

Community-owned Eigg is twenty years old now. Like a celebrity, it must handle fame, fans, negative publicity and hangers-on. A constant stream of film-makers, journalists, anthropologists and scientists pitch up to study the place, so I sense a certain weariness when I pull my notebook from my pocket. Sarah Boden moved back to Eigg in 2010, after years as a music journalist in London. She's amazed by how many members of her former tribe arrive on storytelling business each summer and expect her to delightedly drop everything. 'A lot of them come with a script that they expect you to conform to – "As a community we are forging forwards and revolutionising X, Y and Z" – but usually the reality is a lot more complicated than that. They don't really listen to what you say and go away none the wiser.' Or, as her partner Johnny Lynch – the musician Pictish Trail – put it: 'I find it quite embarrassing because there's folk here who say, "I saw you on the TV, you fanny."'

At the time of the buyout, Simon Fraser, then chairman of the Trust, called it 'a triumph for all that is good in humanity and certainly one in the eye for everything that is mean-spirited and self-seeking'. The islanders celebrated independence day on 12 June 1997 with ninety bottles of malt donated by Skye's Talisker distillery, which had been founded by two brothers from Eigg. The hangover, an eruption of mean-spiritedness, came six years later. A Scottish-German journalist, a critic of land reform, visited Eigg and penned an unflattering portrayal of the new island rulers for *Die Zeit* in Germany, which British tabloids were only too happy to echo. Islanders were quoted speaking of a 'clash of cultures' – between Hebridean residents and incomers – and Keith Schellenberg chipped in, claiming Eigg had been despoiled 'by people who had lived in Tibet and had "Make Love, Not War" painted on the sides of their vans'.

Fables seep into our consciousness, and the newspapers' cautionary tales about Eigg appear to have lodged in the minds of many who briefly visit. I met two tourists on Barra who passed on gossip they had heard about Eigg politics, claiming it was a cliquey, 'clannish' place. I encountered an ex-resident of Rùm who declared that Eigg was 'a bit too full of scandals and growers and dropouts', and suggested residents needed to grow up. Robert Louis Stevenson, who adventured through the isles of the South Pacific in the 1880s, described the drifters in the Marquesas as 'people "on the beach"' – beached like driftwood – and more than once before I reached Eigg, I heard that familiar accusation: it's full of people who flee to a small island because they can't hack it in the mainstream.

There was another charge too: its residents were grant junkies, sustaining their laid-back lifestyles with mainland subsidies. I chatted to the owner-captain of the little boat *Shearwater* on my way to Eigg and he criticised his larger rival, the government-subsidised CalMac ferry. I assumed he'd attack Eigg's subsidised existence too, but he unexpectedly defended the island: everyone talks about

Eigg's grant money, he argued, but no one on the mainland describes the National Grid or roads or hospitals as state handouts, whereas Eigg built its own electricity grid and doesn't have hospitals or proper roads. Subsidies are hoovered up by whoever owns land in Britain. Eigg's former owner, Keith Schellenberg, benefited from tax breaks on his forestry. It does seem unfair, then, to criticise the islanders for applying for the subsidies enjoyed by wealthier landowners. As islanders point out, taxpayers' funds provided just £17,517 towards Eigg's community buyout.

Plenty of outsiders look more positively upon Eigg. On my way home from the island, I stopped for supper in Glasgow with Alastair McIntosh, the author and activist who invigorated Eigg's independence movement. I found him volunteering at GalGael, a charity based in an old workshop in the redbrick terraced streets around Rangers' Ibrox stadium. Young people were carving wood and learning how to build boats.

McIntosh's beard is turning white and he controls a hearing aid with his mobile phone, but he still possesses an aura of both vitality and peace, and is as inspiring as the best kind of preacher. To my surprise, this man of Lewis was born in Doncaster to an English mother and a Scottish father. When McIntosh was four years old, his father took the family to Lewis, which remains his son's heartland, and worked there as a GP. The island is the foundation for McIntosh's belief in the importance of communities rooted in a local culture that can transcend the spiritual paucity of global capitalism and its veneration of consumption.

He cherishes Eigg, which represents a rare win for activists. 'When we set up the first Eigg Trust, the original vision was about renewable energy, cultural renewal and renewal of the spirit. Not only has all of it been fulfilled, but it's been considerably surpassed.' He's not claiming the credit – it's the islanders who've exceeded the Trust's hopes. He recently returned to Eigg. 'The ones who were heavy on the drink were still heavy on the drink, but the thing that impressed me was the number of young people who were back, balancing babies with a rich matrix of economic activities by which they held their lives together and built their homes, unfettered by an absentee landlord.'

The old divide between indigenous people and new-comers has disappeared on Eigg with a younger generation who are a melange of both. The supposed Hebridean–hippy divide was never so stark or so simple, and many islanders working quietly at the heart of the community are from indigenous families. Eigg's success has come from a genuine fusion of Hebridean culture and mainland counterculture. Incomers who have fitted in with island life, and not just come to buy the view, have taken on the best Hebridean traditions of spirituality, co-operation, hospitality and music, and Eigg has attracted people wanting to participate in a less materialistic community. But to create a community less focused on money, people need a platform to share it, argues McIntosh, and that platform is 'the land'.

The fact that the community owns the island of Eigg makes it different from alternative-minded communities in, say, Totnes or Hebden Bridge, or almost any place in England where daily life, and most possibilities, are mediated through the land-ownership of private individuals. The community-owned Eigg is 'not a selfish endeavour. It's not about just wanting to be landowners, it's about the community having life and individuals having life within that community,' said McIntosh. 'In Scotland, we spit the word out – "property". You can't own the land, the land owns you. What I found in England is there's such a lack of physical space, and it's usually upper-class-controlled. England has never recovered from the Norman Conquest. That deeply embedded class system is so divisive.'

In contrast, community ownership enables Eigg to run its own housing association and provide cheap rents – currently about half the market level of 'affordable housing' in this region of Scotland. Low-rent societies where residents are liberated from the grind of earning a lot to pay for a house are likely to be more radical, creative places: people have the freedom, and time, to pursue less money-oriented goals.

McIntosh echoes an earlier writer of the Highlands, Hugh MacDiarmid, by raising the question of what a small island might bring to a bigger one. His great hope twenty years ago was that Eigg would be 'a pattern and an example unto one another', to quote George Fox, the founder of the Quakers. The centre needs the periphery as a source of inspiration and renewal, just as the periphery relies on the centre. Eigg may be able to give the larger island at its side some practical lessons in affordable housing, renewable energy and land reform. A small-island manifesto for the 'mainland' might begin with the realisation that we need to treat other people more carefully. Be open to outsiders and to the world. Live as generalists, not as sclerosed super-specialists. Spend more time outside. Reduce our consumption. Make our own energy or, at worst, buy it by the sack, and then we will use less. Consider animals and plants as well as people. Live more intimately with our place, for it is a complex living organism, too.

I spent several days walking across Eigg's moors to meet different islanders who run its democratically elected 'government', the Isle of Eigg Heritage Trust. Apart from replacing feudalism with scrupulous democracy, the Trust's first priority after buying the island was to ensure that the islanders, who mostly lease their properties, had one basic right they never enjoyed under individual owners: security of tenure. They renovated dilapidated homes and built a shop and tea room, with toilets and showers for visitors.

The early years of the Trust were not riven with conflict, but the historian Camille Dressler revealed some tensions in her 2007 book *Eigg: The Story of an Island*. The directors of the Trust realised, to their 'bafflement and frustration', that 'the suspicion towards power-holders, which was once directed at the landowner, now found itself directed at the Trust'.

The Schellenberg–Maruma era was, at best, a negligent one, and the islanders were used to sorting things out themselves. Many had enjoyed this feeling of liberty from bureaucratic conventions, and were not sure they liked the box-ticking demanded by democracy. As one islander told Dressler: 'The more efficient we try to make this organisation, the more we end up like the mainland.' But Dressler now says any unease has disappeared. Maggie Fyffe believes that almost every decision is reached by consensus. A high proportion of residents volunteer for the Trust or for various committees that manage everything from the island's rubbish to its culture, but there are some refuseniks. Farmer Sarah Boden is currently serving as a Trust director. 'We still struggle with an us-v-them mentality,' she said. 'Sometimes decisions get made and people moan about "the Trust this" or "the Trust that". You have to remind them that they are the Trust.'

Eigg has thrived, said Alastair McIntosh, because the community has developed a way to manage disputes. 'That's of such importance. In my view, the main inhibitor of community land-ownership is that people are afraid of themselves, they are afraid of what might be set loose if they don't have a controlling figure above them.'

Many portraits of island dystopias are suffused with this fear. On his tour of Scotland, Samuel Johnson wrote of the dangers of brooding brought on by small islands: 'The evils of dereliction rush upon the thoughts; man is made unwillingly acquainted with his own weakness.' Mr

Cathcart is confronted by precisely this in 'The Man Who Loved Islands'. Perhaps D. H. Lawrence was scared of small islands, too. William Golding brooded much upon this danger, not only in *Lord of the Flies*, in which the schoolboy inhabitants of a small island rapidly turn feral, but in *Pincher Martin*, in which a wrecked sailor's small island is revealed to be a hallucination of his own ruined mind, or perhaps even purgatory. In reality, the residents of Eigg have faced their inner demons and won.

I sat in Maggie Fyffe's croft, where water-and-wind-powered fairy lights twinkled over the mantelpiece and the air smelt of roll-ups and woodsmoke. Is Eigg a utopia? 'Utopia is a bit strong.' She cackled wildly at my question and then paused. 'I think it is. I love it here.'

2017

All aboard for the UK's newest tourist attraction: the M25

Long in tedium, short in dramatic action and inescapably circular, the M25 is not so much the Road to Hell, as Chris Rea once sang, but life itself. On a bright spring morning yesterday, however, Britain's least-loved motorway was almost beneficent when viewed from the seats of the first sell-out coach tour of the 188-kilometre London orbital.

The Middlesex County Asylum, Heathrow Terminal 5, South Mimms services, Badger's Mount; all took on a pleasing sheen when subjected to the scrutiny of Nigel Pullen, the guide for the Brighton & Hove Bus and Coach Company's surprise-hit day trip.

With his strawberry-blond thatch and light-reactive glasses, Pullen looked the tour-guide part and did not disappoint with his deadpan delivery of a stream of trivia that flowed as freely as the traffic.

We joined the motorway at Godstone and climbed Reigate Hill to the dizzying heights of 220 metres, the most elevated spot on the orbital. 'Oxygen masks will be dropping from overhead shortly,' quipped Pullen. Later we passed a farm where meerkats live twenty metres from the carriageway. 'They would be out to sell insurance if we were stuck in a queue,' he observed.

After lunch at South Mimms, one of three service areas on the motorway, Pullen was surprised to still have a full coach. Some punters were just surprised to be there.

'I'm speechless and I don't think that's ever happened,' said Julie Hayes, forty-five, taken on the £15 tour as a surprise by her boyfriend, James Smith. 'What have I learned?' mused Hayes. 'Never to go out with a man from south London.'

We learned about the man logging every set of concrete steps on motorway edges around the country and the meaning of those enigmatic blue signs with M25 and a random number on them, which give the distance in kilometres from the Dartford tunnel for the emergency services.

Like life, the M25 seduces you with its banality before subjecting you to occasional dystopian extremes. Severe weather on the nation's biggest car park in 2010 caused the Red Cross to provide blankets and tea for motorists stranded in their cars for seventeen hours.

Death is also always just around the corner, from the adverts for prostate cancer awareness above the urinals in the services to the coach's own warnings about the risk of deep-vein thrombosis (hence two 'comfort breaks').

Just as we entered Buckinghamshire – one of six counties passed through – Pullen gave an intake of breath. 'This is what we've been waiting for – an incident, folks,' he declared as dot-matrix signs ordered us to slow to 50 mph. It was nothing – just a lorry on the hard shoulder.

There were several coach tours of the M25 in the 1980s and perhaps it is no coincidence that the 2012 version has proved so popular. The M25 was opened by Margaret Thatcher in 1986 and will endure as a monument to her era.

As we completed our road to nowhere, applause broke out. 'Please tell other people,' implored Pullen. 'Now I've got this far in my research I want to do it every week. Is that all right, Graham?' The driver shuddered. 'Find another driver,' he growled.

2012

Driving to my car-free idyll

I realised it would be an unusual Easter holiday when we were met at the jetty of St Martin's, in the Isles of Scilly, by a 1965 Massey Ferguson tractor. Its tiny trailer transported me, my children and our luggage to our chalet. Here was a rural idyll of the kind that vanished from mainland Britain in the last century: sparrows chirruping from every bush, roadside stalls with open money boxes selling free-range eggs, and everyone saying hello.

But what really transformed our experience of roaming this beautiful Atlantic island (population: around 100) with my four-year-old twins and my two-year-old was being able to cast aside our fear of traffic. When the twins went careering down the hill, out of sight, I didn't need to worry about safety or whether their lungs were being clogged with diesel particulates.

There was freedom for them too – no parents barking instructions and no hand-holding, except for pleasure.

I had no idea small children could walk so far. We skipped five kilometres one day and three kilometres the next, albeit incentivised by fish and chips or ice creams. At night, the children fell asleep like well-exercised puppies.

Every parent and grandparent I met said the same thing: 'This is how things ought to be.'

And then – oh, the irony! – we drove home.

On the long trek from Penzance, a freak hailstorm turned the M5 into an ice rink and we missed a nasty accident by a few seconds. I saw a motorcyclist slide off his bike and a car spin into the central reservation. People sat, stunned, airbags inflated, in crunched cars. Driving at 70 mph in a noisy, delicate metal box suddenly looked crazy.

We have embraced this madness (even car-eschewing environmentalists depend on motorised transport for food and other pleasures) because these amazing machines give us unprecedented freedom. For this, we have traded the liberty of our children.

The miles of public space I enjoyed as a youngster are out of bounds to my children because of the volume of traffic. We must, somehow, rebalance the power on smaller roads to favour pedestrian over motorist. But I drive: I accept I'm part of the problem.

2016

On safari in the Essex rainforest

Around a roundabout in the Thames estuary, beyond a Morrisons supermarket and just off an old concrete road, stand great hummocks of bramble, scrubby hawthorn and silver birch. An old car seat is dumped in tangled grass amid the ruins of an abandoned oil refinery.

These desolate flatlands, behind where the old Thames does flow, do not look like a biodiversity hotspot. But Canvey Wick is a 'brownfield rainforest': one of Britain's most precious nature reserves, it is an atmospheric, accidental landscape that teems with some of the country's rarest insects.

Nearly 2,000 invertebrate species have been recorded here and more are being discovered every year. There's the shrill carder bee, one of Britain's rarest bumblebees, and the declining brown-banded carder bee. Three insects previously thought to be extinct in Britain have been rediscovered here. There are fearsome predators (the bee wolf, a brutal-looking wasp), exploding bombardier beetles and ingenious parasites such as *Hedychrum niemalei*, a wasp that lays its eggs in the burrow of the rare five-banded weevil wasp, so that its larvae can steal the wasp grubs' food.

It is a cool, grey autumn day and I'm hoping to see some of the rare treasures of Britain's first and only bug reserve with the help of entomologist Rosie Earwaker. She works for nature conservation charities Buglife and the RSPB, which manage this unique place. (It is owned by another charity, the Land Trust, which bought the site in 2012.)

'It's a bit of a mecca for entomologists,' says Earwaker as we walk through strong metal gates, designed to deter the motorcyclists who break in and tear around this wilderness. Inside, there's a profusion of what almost resemble rooms: rough meadows of long grass, glades sheltered by sallow clumps, reed-filled ditches and huge, dark circles of asphalt.

Canvey Wick was once flat, green grazing marshes, rather like West Canvey marsh, a conventional RSPB reserve up the road. Then humans wrecked the place – and in doing so turned it into something much more marvellous. It was used as a dumping ground for sediment extracted from the Thames, so the meadows were covered with gravel, sand, chalk and fragments of old shells. In the 1970s the ground was prepared for an oil refinery – thirteen circular pads of asphalt are the foundations for huge, cylindrical tanks. But the oil price crash of 1973 meant the refinery was abandoned before it opened.

This history has created a wide variety of soil types and habitats in a small space. It is more like a savannah than a rainforest: hot and sunny, not swamped by dark trees. Ecologists call this 'open mosaic habitat'. I put my hand close to the crumbling asphalt – even on a cool day, the surface is warm. Reptiles – such as slowworms and common lizards – thrive in such conditions, as do rare insects. Newly arriving species from the continent enjoy the estuary's low rainfall, too.

The first insect to land on me is a mosquito. Not a good start. Next, we stroll through the meadows and carefully lift a small square of black roofing felt that has been (deliberately) left on the ground. 'Bombardier beetles hide under things like this,' explains Earwaker. These striking beetles, which have metallic, blue-green wing cases, detonate an explosion inside their abdomen if disturbed, spraying hot liquid at attackers, whether insect or human.

We don't find any bombardiers, but Earwaker detects a flying insect and, with a decisive swish of the net she's carrying, catches one of Britain's 5,000-plus species of parasitic wasp. 'I wouldn't be surprised if this is a new species,' she says. It is black and spindly, with four bright-orange front legs and two black rear legs. Often rare and beautiful, parasitic wasps do no harm to humans, but skilfully parasites other insects.

Autumnal Canvey Wick is surprisingly floral. There's a great deal of narrow-leaved bird's foot trefoil underfoot, plus clumps of sea aster, a mauve, daisy-like plant that is the sole food of the sea aster mining bee. This rare bee builds a waterproof lining around its underground cell, so it can survive an unexpectedly high tide.

The site has a random mix of exotic plants, non-natives that have arrived here as ship stowaways or through other unfathomable accidents. Fennel and pale-yellow evening primrose stand tall beneath a broken lamp post. There's even a succulent (a house plant) sprouting on an old bridge.

Particularly useful for rare bees are the lurid-pink flowers of everlasting pea. We scour a patch and spot a dainty bumblebee. It has a dusting of primrose-yellow colour and a distinctive square of black on its thorax: it is the shrill carder bee. This extremely rare bee doesn't forage far from the nest, so it needs nearby flowers and, crucially, late-flowering plants. Unusually for a bumblebee, it can still be seen in mid-October, when its queens require nectar to survive. Earwaker beckons me to listen to their buzzing. 'They really do have a high-pitched buzz, which you can get a feel for, which explains their name,' she says.

A green woodpecker cackles in the trees and a ship – larger than I expected – slips up the Thames, just the other side of the sea wall. A sand hill is covered with miniature volcanoes, made by the hairy-legged mining bee, also called the pantaloon bee. Hairs on the females' hind legs help collect pollen and really do make them look like they are wearing baggy trousers.

Many insects are disappearing by autumn, hunkering down for the winter, but we still see the last meadow browns of the year, a silver y moth and a brown-banded carder bee. There is even more to find at Canvey Wick in June, a time of orchids, and July, when marbled white and wall-brown butterflies jink over the reserve. Summer days are also when the bee wolf strikes, a wasp that pounces like a raptor on honeybees.

Canvey Wick is at its most atmospheric in autumn and winter, though. This hybrid edgeland, which blends the gorgeous bubbling call of the curlew with the beeping of a reversing lorry, is replete with surprises. It is a hopeful place, too, showing how nature bounces back – and how we sometimes possess the vision to protect it.

2017

Seeking St Kilda:
longing for a distant land

Like most visitors, I had formed a picture in my head of St Kilda before I finally set foot last week on the most remote of the British isles, which was reluctantly abandoned by its last thirty-six permanent residents in 1930. The reality of this small archipelago of towering sea cliffs and seabird cities more than 160 kilometres west of the Scottish mainland was far grander, and more complicated, than I expected.

St Kilda celebrates its thirtieth anniversary as a World Heritage site this summer, and is the only place in Britain to be awarded such status for both cultural importance and natural riches.

Cruise passengers stop off in summer and rangers and radar-station employees reside for short periods but it remains an obstacle to our hyper-mobile modern world. It's three hours on a fast boat but, typically, bad weather caused my trip to be cancelled and I had to kick my heels on Skye for four days. For one fellow visitor, our successful crossing was her eighth attempt. Other pilgrims I met included Russ from St Kilda, Melbourne, in full St Kilda Football Club regalia, and Stephen, a Scottish builder whose number plate reads: SKI1 LDA. The visitors' book is full of comments from people who have hankered after the place for fifty years.

Anywhere you can see the curvature of the earth drives you to think, and I wonder if we imbue peripheral places like St Kilda with such significance because they challenge our mainland, mainstream lives – and how hectic, sustainable or important they are. For all its isolation, I was struck by St Kilda's connectedness. It is well protected by the National Trust for Scotland but its seabird citizens today are no more immune from external forces than its former human population: its puffins and fulmars are in decline because of the loss of fish in the Atlantic.

On a blissful sunny day, I climbed its hills and admired a great chain of Outer Hebridean islands, hazily visible almost over the horizon. That old cliché about no man being an island might apply to islands too.

2017

A wagon to nourish the soul: Roger Deakin's wild farm

My frog's eye view takes in a carpet of duck weed, turquoise damselflies and a retreating newt. The water is dark and cool, and the temperature turns head-chilling when I dive to touch the soft clay and decomposing leaves at the bottom. My first question for my hosts at the ancient Suffolk farmhouse that was author and environmentalist Roger Deakin's home for nearly four decades was: can we swim in the moat? The answer is yes, and on a blistering summer day I discover my own version of the magical experience that opens *Waterlog*, Deakin's account of swimming through Britain – a book that frog-kicked wild swimming and nature writing into the mainstream.

In the thirteen years since Deakin's death, devotees have found their way to Walnut Tree Farm, the sixteenth-century timber-framed house rescued from dereliction by Deakin in 1970. The low building, its spring-fed moat (not as grand as it sounds: as Deakin notes, yeoman farmers in Suffolk followed a Tudor fashion for ornamental moats) and fields totalling twelve acres nourished his soul and his writing. Place and person grew together.

When fans come, they're often allowed to wander around the farm by its current owners, Jasmin Moss and

Titus Rowlandson, who are childhood friends of Deakin's son Rufus. For much of their twelve-year residency, the couple have lived with the reverberations of their famous predecessor – 'Rog', as Titus calls him.

'Over our first few years at Walnut Tree Farm, we found that most of the jobs that needed doing around the place entailed an unspoken dialogue with Roger,' says Titus in *Life at Walnut Tree Farm*, a new pictorial biography of the place he has written with Rufus Deakin.

The couple have just put two of the farm's old cabins on Airbnb. I suspect they agonised over this move, because they clearly want to honour Deakin's legacy. But I think it makes sense, given the yearning of Deakin pilgrims, and others who might find joy or inspiration staying in a cabin where he lived and worked.

Like every admirer of Deakin, I've formed a vivid picture of Walnut Tree Farm and the real version does not disappoint. Down a rough track near the village of Mellis, the farmhouse is hidden by vast, overgrown hedges. Deakin practised rewilding decades before it was fashionable. Its walls are covered in climbing plants and shaded by the walnut tree Deakin named it after. Meadows are neck-high in grasses and bounce with meadow brown and peacock butterflies.

From a distance at least, Deakin lived every writer's fantasy. Nursing a self-declared weakness for sheds, he would periodically abandon his house to sleep and write in a shepherd's hut he rescued in 1980 (where original thinkers begin, David Cameron and the rest of us follow) and a railway wagon. 'There's more truth about a camp than a house,' he wrote. It better represents a human life, he thought: we desire permanency but in reality are just passing through.

My wife and I stay in his railway wagon, which provides an unexpectedly elevated view and is beautifully decorated by Jasmin, an artist. There's a wood-burner, a sofa, a double bed and Jasmin's paintings on the wall. An open-air kitchen beneath a sunshade is made from an old workbench, with a gas camping hob plus an open fire on which we barbecue supper.

The shepherd's hut is not let out, but visitors can also stay in a wood-cladded caravan (with en suite). It is like a miniature house, with a tiny double bedroom, a kitchen and a big living space with wood-burner, artworks and books (including Deakin's, naturally). The cabins are in separate corners of the farm, so there's plenty of privacy.

As well as swimming in the moat, we explore the wild fields, finding traces of Deakin. He was a hoarder, and abandoned various beloved Citroën DS Safaris to decompose in hedges – there are also sheds full of salvaged sash windows and church organs. The woods he planted are mature now, as are an ash bower he made and ur-apple trees (ancestors of the domestic apple) he brought back from Kazakhstan. His books almost exist in physical form – here the farm still maps his mind and embodies his values.

A woodpecker cackles, a moorhen parps, and a profound peace settles upon us. We watch bats on a dusk walk, and admire the stars. Twice an hour, the London–Norwich train scythes through the silence beyond Deakin's wood; it adds to the drama of the place.

We sleep deeply, door open to the meadow. As always, Deakin describes the experience best. 'To sleep half a field from the house, tucked into a hedge, with an open door facing south into the meadow and plenty of cool night air, must surely add very much to the chances of sleep,' he wrote in his last book, *Wildwood*. 'The closing of the door on all the daytime stuff in the house, and so little in the shed to encumber the thoughts: just a few rugs, a stove, a bed, a table and chair.'

2019

*

Roger Deakin's old farm was so suffused in wild magic and his spirit that I was inspired to ask if anyone was writing his biography. Fortunately no one was, and I am currently working on the story of his life.

2021

You, me and the deep blue sea: the guardians of small islands

After supper, while Eddie Stubbings was washing up, huge flocks of puffins would come whirling past his kitchen window. Later, when the sun had finally dipped into the ocean, the Skomer night filled with the bizarre caterwauling of 350,000 pairs of Manx shearwaters, which fly under the cover of darkness to burrows dotted across the small island.

'Living on the island was absolutely amazing,' says forty-year-old Stubbings. Alongside his partner, Bee Bueche, forty-one, he has completed six years working on Skomer, 290 hectares of seabird-populated rocks off the Pembrokeshire coast.

Whenever a job advertisement for warden of a small island appears, hundreds of islophiles apply, seeking to flee the tyranny of modern life. It wasn't always this way: historically, many of the 6,200-odd small islands that make up the British archipelago have been prisons, literally or figuratively, with their isolated residents eventually choosing to leave for a mainland that offers more comfort, companionship and opportunities.

Now there is a reverse migration, as people escape the centre for the periphery, chasing the liberation of less choice, and intimacy with nature. As conservation charities have found a new use for small islands – as sanctuaries for rare seabirds – formerly 'empty' ones have been repopulated by wildlife wardens.

Stubbings and Bueche left at the end of last year, but they have not had enough of small islands: they are now doing conservation work on Islay, in Scotland, after a spell helping seabird researchers on the Balearic island of Sa Dragonera. They met on Malta, where they were volunteering to protect persecuted raptors.

The appeal of a small island, Bueche says, is not just being closer to nature – it is being self-sufficient. 'Everything that breaks you have to fix yourself,' she says. 'It's challenging and exciting – you have to look after yourself, use your brain, initiative and imagination. When things break, I love solving these puzzles. Even not being cosy is great – you wake up and feel the cold and chop wood and put the wood-burner on. It makes me feel really alive.'

Like most people overseeing the wildlife of small islands, Stubbings and Bueche were drawn to this work through their love of birds. Skomer was 'absolutely incredible' for them, Stubbings says: thousands of guillemots, razorbills, puffins and, most of all, the noisy, nocturnal shearwaters. Many people struggle to sleep in this cacophony – Stubbings and Bueche found it soothing.

It was a visit to Skomer that inspired the photographer Alex Ingram to document the lives of small-island wardens. As part of his project, The Gatekeepers, he has visited five islands around the UK and plans to capture life on twelve in total. His evocative images tantalise us with illimitable horizons and an alternative way of life.

People who escape to islands where humans are a tiny minority might be assumed to enjoy solitude, if not misanthropy. Plenty of people apply for jobs on Skomer seeking to be alone, Stubbings says, but they would be disappointed. 'You have to tell them that's really not what you're going to find. It is a "hustly bustly" workplace,' he says. 'You never get five minutes to yourself. People come and knock on your door asking questions at 8 p.m., 9 p.m., 10 p.m.'

Their working day as Skomer wardens began with a call to the boatman to see if the weather would permit boats to run. Skomer receives 250 day-trippers during the peak bird-breeding months of May and June and accommodates sixteen overnight guests. As well as birds and seals to count, there are beds to make, staff and volunteers to organise, and VIPs from international ecologists to film-makers to support. 'People probably want to hear we're wild and remote and cut off from the world,' Stubbings says. 'The brutal truth is, these days, you're not. Everyone has got Internet and mobile phones in their pockets and there are plenty of people on the island.'

Stubbings and Bueche's former neighbours on nearby Skokholm, Richard Brown, thirty-eight, and Giselle Eagle, thirty-four, are also a couple – unsurprisingly, island-warden partnerships are a popular way to cope with the rigours of the job. They have it slightly quieter: a mere 90,000 pairs of Manx shearwaters to monitor and only two boats a week, bringing twenty paying guests to the island.

Skokholm is where small-island wardening began. The naturalist and writer Ronald Lockley took a lease on the island in 1927 and established Britain's first bird observatory there, studying its puffins and writing prolifically, and romantically, about his island life.

Brown and Eagle live in a lighthouse, surrounded by puffins, but appear more practical than dreamy. 'We're a bit like tour reps,' Brown says, as if striving to make his job seem particularly unappealing. 'When people first think about island residents, they think of an isolated existence. But I imagine we meet more people during the year than most people on the mainland.'

They receive a fresh food delivery by boat once a month and have inspiring news for mainlanders worried that Britain's imported salad supplies will dry up after Brexit. 'There's no reason not to eat well on an island. We have a lot of root vegetables,' Brown says. 'We've got loads of tinned and dried stuff if our delivery doesn't happen,' Eagle laughs.

It sounds austere, but Brown says it is much more luxurious than when he began. 'When I started out on the island, it was still gas lights and no hot water unless you boiled it. These days, we've got solar power and solar hot water and a 4G signal. It has got much easier. I've so much respect for Lockley and others who did it back in the day.'

The wardens' sense of service to a place is rather like that of a vicar. Both roles have a pressing feeling of being at the mercy of forces much grander than oneself – in a warden's case, the tides, landscape and weather. On Skokholm, Brown and Eagle are also contributing to long-term wildlife recording. 'There has been daily monitoring of birds on Skokholm for ninety years and we've done six of those,' Brown says. 'We definitely do feel we are carrying on something very special. It's a vocation. It's a way of life.'

The weather is the force that most shapes the life of Dean Woodfin Jones, the warden of Lundy, across the Bristol Channel from Brown and Eagle on Skokholm. 'Everything we do is dictated by the weather – mother nature is truly in charge here,' he says.

Lundy – 445 hectares of granite, sitting high above the waves – feels like a huge ship and is likened to one by Woodfin Jones, who sees Lundy's twenty-nine residents as a kind of crew. They are employed by the Landmark Trust, the charity that protects the island. When I visited a few years back, I asked one islander how she got on with her fellow residents. 'Carefully,' she replied. Small island communities can be claustrophobic. As Stubbings puts it: 'If you can't cope with the insularity, you're going to explode, because you're on a small island with a small group of people. You still feel it. You just have to cope with it.'

Small talk is crucial on small islands. Social bonds must be renewed each day and misunderstandings nipped in the bud before they blossom into feuds. But Woodfin Jones is ebullient about Lundy's tiny society, mostly populated by couples in their late forties seeking a change of life after their children have left home. 'You get some brilliant characters here. We've got a really good group at the moment. Everyone gets on really well. We're quite social and like having a drink in the sunshine or going snorkelling together. There's always tiffs between people, but they tend to work themselves out most of the time.'

Unlike on Skokholm, Skomer and Lundy, the permanent population of Enlli, or Bardsey, off the tip of the Llŷn peninsula, north-west Wales, is not all employed by a mainland charity. There is a tenant farmer and his family; the wardens of an independent bird observatory; and a ferryman, Colin Evans, who doesn't live on the island, but is the son of the last island-born resident.

For the past three years, Sian Stacey was island manager of Bardsey after quitting her job in Cardiff. She had holidayed there since she was six and during a volunteering break as an adult met her partner, Mark Carter, an assistant warden. 'It was a second home for me, so it was an absolute honour to then call it home,' Stacey says.

She would walk across the island and suddenly hear the rushing of a peregrine's wings. 'It was the equivalent of a car zooming past, but there are no cars on Bardsey. That would give you goosebumps,' she says.

The currents between the island and the mainland make it famously inaccessible: did she feel cut off? 'That's a very mainlander thing to say,' she says. 'You go three or four weeks without a boat, but I didn't feel cut off, because I was prepared for that. When the post was delivered in the winter, it was like Christmas.'

As well as wildlife, Bardsey was once home to early Celtic Christian monks. Like Lindisfarne in England and Iona in Scotland, it has been a destination for many subsequent generations of religious seekers. The past, wrote Adam Nicolson in *Sea Room*, his story of the Shiants, a tiny trio of Hebridean islands, is unusually present on small islands. Stacey agrees. 'Bardsey is not just a conservation area: it's also farmed; island waters are still fished by fishermen who live on the island; withies [willows] grown on the island are still used to make baskets. You feel like you're in living history.'

The role of small islands as sanctuaries for endangered wildlife seems wholly positive, but this view was challenged by Evans, Bardsey's boatman, when I visited a few years ago. Tourism, he felt, was degrading. Conservation groups too often sought to control small islands with mainland rules and constrain their evolution. 'If you don't have development, what have you got – a museum? I'm keen on sustainable development and I'm keen on work,' he told me. 'The island's fish and meat is the only thing we've got left, and both have been devalued. So, we're stuck with tourism and this industry of conservation, which depends on rules and subsidies from elsewhere, which makes the island dependent. How can we kickstart the island into how it once was, economically independent and proud?'

Since we spoke, Evans – who lives on the mainland with his young family – has bought Bardsey's lighthouse and wants to open an island brewery and even a helipad.

Stacey agrees with Evans that Bardsey must have an identity beyond tourism. 'There used to be over a hundred people living there and it was a better place to live than the mainland. I'm of the opinion that it's still a better place to live,' she says. Although she is back living on mainland Wales, she is still a trustee of Bardsey Island Trust and supports plans for an island orchard to cultivate Bardsey's famous variety of apple, and to lease one of the island's ten holiday lets to a long-term resident. 'We need people with that drive to make it work economically. This can go hand in hand with conservation. I don't think they should be in conflict,' Stacey says.

Her long-term goal is to return to Bardsey, but she is living on the mainland now because she wanted to put her energy into a new project and is considering having a family. 'I'm nearly thirty, so if I want kids I wouldn't have wanted to have them there, because my job was so physical,' she says. While there are couples raising young children on islands so small they don't have a school, it is notable that most island couples have grown-up children or none at all.

Every small islander seems permanently touched by

their life as a minority species, surrounded by salt water, space and, occasionally, peace.

Stubbings and Bueche departed Skomer because Stubbings had long dreamed of working in the Arctic. 'It's not for everyone,' Bueche says of small-island life. 'If you wanted a family, you'd really struggle, but we decided this life is for us and we're not going to have a family.' She finds her appreciation of the mainland deepened by her small-island exile. 'A hot shower! Central heating! A comfy bed! If you fancy a cucumber, you can go to the shop and get it. When you live on the mainland, you don't get any elation from going and buying a cucumber. After being on an island, you start to really value these things again.'

2019

A place to mend the soul: the subtle magic of a Norfolk Broad

In the autumn stillness, I didn't immediately notice the large brown bird flying low over a golden-brown expanse of reeds at Hickling Broad, Norfolk. It was a bittern, a famously elusive creature that became extinct in Britain as a breeding bird 150 years ago. The bittern is thriving again, after beginning its comeback in 1911 at Hickling, the largest of the lakes created by medieval peat-diggers, which now form our wildest lowland landscape. Today, Hickling Broad is a wetland of international importance, home to endangered species such as the marsh harrier, the swallowtail butterfly and the holly-leaved naiad (an aquatic plant so rare that botanists make pilgrimages to admire it).

Hickling is probably one of the ten most important nature reserves in the land, so it was a shock last month when half was put up for sale. People feared a developer would ruin it with a new 'ecotourism' marina but luckily an offer by its current tenants, Norfolk Wildlife Trust, has been accepted. This charity has launched an appeal to raise £1 million to complete its purchase.

It is no coincidence that, alongside the bittern, the common crane also first returned to Britain near Hickling.

This large bird began breeding again on adjacent marshes tended by a local farmer and self-confessed 'craniac', John Buxton; this year a record forty-eight pairs bred across the country.

These revivals show that reserves such as Hickling are not simply fragments where we witness the death throes of endangered species: they are creative places of recovery, where the natural dynamism of wild things enjoys free and glorious expression.

Last week, as I watched the bittern and marvelled at how this great expanse of marsh and reeds was uninterrupted by any human sound, I spied a plaque bearing a quote from a local conservationist, Ted Ellis. The Broads, he wrote, are 'a breathing space for the care of souls'.

Spots such as Hickling are places of recovery for us too. We need these wellsprings of solace and inspiration more than ever.

2016

PART III

Animal Rights and Wrongs

'Kill them, kill them, kill them':
saving the red squirrel

One snowy dawn in March, I went hunting for squirrels in the Lake District. In the silent and empty woods beneath the Aira Force waterfall, the only thing moving was a solitary red squirrel, balanced on a nut-filled feeder hanging from a tree. If you grew up, as I did, with the grey squirrel, seeing a red squirrel is a shock. We're used to the grey – a sleek, North American import, swaggering across parks, raiding bird tables, all fat haunches and bulbous black eyes. In contrast, the red squirrel, although native to Britain, looks exotic: so dainty and alertly pretty, with fine tufts of hair above its ears as extravagant as the eyebrows of Denis Healey. Here, in the snow, this forest sprite quivered with improbable, balletic grace and then – *clang* – slipped on the icy lid of the feeder and fell to the ground. It landed on its feet.

Julie Bailey, a former gymnast with a cascade of red hair, had picked me up from the nearby town of Penrith and driven her black 4x4 along slushy roads to admire this natural acrobat. At Aira Force, she stepped out of the car and, leaning on a stick, walked carefully across the snow. She and her husband, Phil, used to enjoy watching red squirrels at their feeders in the garden – these animals were still a common sight across northern Cumbria a decade or so ago. Bailey worked in pharmaceuticals and coached boys in gymnastics, including her son. But in 2005 she broke her back. She couldn't walk for four years. Seventeen spinal operations later, she only walks thanks to a spinal cord stimulator, powered by a battery in her stomach. When it malfunctions, she collapses. She doesn't make a fuss, but she is in pain twenty-four hours a day and is intolerant to painkillers. 'Because I was stuck at home,' she said, 'I started taking more notice of my squirrels. They really gave me a purpose.'

During the Christmas holidays of 2009, she was startled to see a stranger in her garden: a grey squirrel. Over the next three weeks, her reds became sick, their faces swelling with terrible sores before they dropped dead. 'It was absolutely devastating,' said Bailey.

Bailey joined a band of concerned Cumbrians – accountants, police officers, cleaners, carers, construction workers, retirees – who spend their spare time working to stop red squirrels in their county slipping towards extinction.

Red-squirrel conservation is not like most other efforts to save wildlife. It consists of exterminating one rival species: the grey squirrel. A few weeks after the death of her red squirrels, Bailey began to fight back on the side of the reds. She set up strategically placed feeders so that she could pull up quietly in her car, wind down her window and shoot the greys with an air rifle. Her husband got a gun and joined in. The first time I spoke to Bailey by telephone, I asked her how many squirrels she and Phil had eliminated since they began. She paused. I could hear the clicking of a mouse through a spreadsheet. 'Four hundred and sixty-nine,' she replied.

When I visited her home a month later, I found a shrine to the red squirrel. The time was told by a red-squirrel clock, the wood-burner was adorned with cast-iron squirrels, Bailey's study walls and carpet were squirrel red – there were ornamental squirrels made by a local sculptor, a red-squirrel jigsaw, goblet, boot brush, paperweight and piggybank. We drank tea from red-squirrel mugs, and sat by a grey-coloured freezer. When I asked what was inside, Bailey opened the door and pulled out neatly butchered hunks of grey squirrel. 'All our greys go in that freezer and we eat them. Not everyone's cup of tea, but that's what we do. Very healthy meat. Phil loves his squirrel curry, because he just loves curry. I love it in a stew, so it falls off the bone like pulled pork.' Bailey was collecting the pelts to make a grey waistcoat.

Britain, Ireland and Italy are the only countries in the world inhabited by both red and grey squirrels. In Britain the greys, which were introduced in the late nineteenth century from North America, appear to be exterminating the reds. Britain's 140,000 red squirrels have been pushed to the margins – islands, such as the Isle of Wight; Northern Scotland, Cumbria and Northumberland – as 2.5 million greys have taken over.

An epoch of human globalisation is mixing up species like never before. It has also created a new academic field, invasion biology, which examines how some non-native animals and plants wreak havoc in new settings, spreading disease or outcompeting native flora and fauna. Some consider the grey squirrel one of these 'alien' invaders imperilling the red. But is its slaughter a futile expression of nativist xenophobia? And is it ever ethical to target one species for destruction in order to conserve another?

Many mainstream conservation charities have, quietly, decided that a cull is an acceptable solution. There will soon be thousands of volunteers working to kill grey squirrels in England, Wales and Northern Ireland. (Scotland has its own, rather successful anti-grey campaign.) This army is being assembled by Red Squirrels United, a new campaign supported by more than thirty conservation groups and £3 million from the Heritage Lottery Fund and the EU Life programme, the European Union's funding body for environmental projects.

Red Squirrels United is the largest programme to eliminate an invasive species in Europe. It is also the most controversial. More than 95,000 people have signed an anti-cull petition. Their comments reveal an abhorrence for this kind of conservation: 'This plan is barbaric.' 'My son and I love watching the grey squirrels play where we live.' 'Humans do not OWN animals' lives.' 'These creatures are here to stay and part of our countryside now. You cannot turn the clock back.' As these remarks show, the conflict between two very different species of squirrels is also a dispute between their very different kinds of human champions. How this battle plays out – reds v. greys, conservationists v. animal-rights activists, northerners v. southerners – could eventually shape the fate of other non-native species around the globe.

The red squirrel, *Sciurus vulgaris*, is a common animal across much of Eurasia. *Sciurus carolinensis*, the grey squirrel, is one of more than 2,800 non-native species in Britain. Like the signal crayfish, a North American creature that has been outcompeting the native white-clawed crayfish since it was introduced in 1975, or the Asian hornet, a hefty wasp that turned up in Gloucestershire last summer and devours honeybees, the grey squirrel is classified as an IAS: an invasive alien species. The International Union for Conservation of Nature puts it in the top hundred most harmful invasive species in the world. It strips and eats bark, damaging and sometimes killing young trees, which can prevent the production of high-quality timber. Grey squirrels are also accused of preying on birds' nests (although scientific evidence of greys causing declines in bird species is, so far, scant). Most emotively, they appear to be consigning the red squirrel to oblivion.

In 1876 Victorian landowners shipped the first grey squirrels from North America and released them into English parkland as amusing ornaments alongside peacocks, muntjac deer and other exotic status symbols from distant lands. When squirrels spread, at first people welcomed this 'sociable, easily tamed animal', as the 1912 *Manchester Guardian*'s country diary put it. In 1916 another country diary approvingly noted: 'It appears to be more ready to make friends than our British squirrel, but possibly it has not the same hereditary recollection of stone-throwing boys.'

As the stone-throwing boys suggest, the native red has not always been adored. In the early nineteenth century, 20,000 red squirrels were sold to London meat markets each year. Later, reds were widely culled by foresters because they too stripped bark in new conifer plantations. In 1903, the year the red squirrel was immortalised by Beatrix Potter as plucky Squirrel Nutkin – a defiant representative of the working class, according to one critic – the Highland Squirrel Club was formed to protect timber plantations from damage. Club members slaughtered 85,000 reds over the next three decades. Where reds were driven to extinction, landowners and conservationists shipped in new individuals from Scandinavia.

In the 1920s people noticed that greys were increasing at the expense of reds. In 1932 it was made illegal to release a grey squirrel in Britain. It still is: if you inadvertently trap a grey squirrel in your garden shed, you're breaking the law when you free it. The first of many campaigns to eradicate the grey was launched in the 1930s, and the Ministry of Agriculture issued free shotgun cartridges to squirrel shooters for many years. In the 1970s greys were poisoned by the Forestry Commission with warfarin, commonly used to kill rats.

For the last eight years, Prince Charles, as patron of the Red Squirrel Survival Trust, has promoted campaigns to exterminate the greys. He grew up enjoying the reds on his mother's Sandringham estate in Norfolk and still feeds them at Balmoral in Scotland. 'My great ambition is to have one in the house,' he once said. 'Sitting on the breakfast table and on my shoulder.'

Despite royal intervention, all attempts to eradicate the grey on a national level have failed because, for many decades, the precise reason for the reds' decline remained a mystery. Ecologists agreed that the larger greys were outcompeting reds. Greys were more willing to forage on the ground, better able to digest acorns, and would consume unripe hazelnuts, whereas reds had to wait until they were ripe – so greys were beating reds to sources of food. This theory was not wrong, but it did not explain the often dramatic disappearance of reds after the arrival of greys.

For years, people had noticed that reds were succumbing to an aggressive viral disease that caused swollen ulcers to break out on their faces. These lesions prevented the squirrel from feeding and killed it within a week. Greys were untroubled by this virus. Scientists finally uncovered the full story in the early 1990s, when new blood-testing technology revealed the role of greys as a carrier of squirrelpox. The test found that 60–70 per cent of greys carried the infection but did not succumb to it. No British grey has ever been found dead from the virus, but every red squirrel that has ever contracted it has died. It is a pattern repeated around the world when non-native animals introduce new diseases to 'naive' populations.

Greys are well adapted to squirrelpox, say scientists, because the squirrel and the virus evolved together for centuries in North America. One study has found squirrelpox antibodies in America's greys – a sign that they have had the infection but have fought it off. In Britain, the disease decisively shifts the balance of power from defenceless red to resistant grey: scientific modelling predicts that where the virus is present, greys replace reds up to twenty-five times faster than where it is not present. Professor Julian Chantrey, a veterinary pathologist at the University of Liverpool, has studied an isolated red-squirrel population at Formby on Merseyside, which has been hit by squirrelpox brought in by arriving greys. He believes that the reds' extinction is inevitable if greys are not kept away. 'We've seen it happen across southern Britain. Where the habitat hasn't been kept grey-free, invading greys will spread the virus to any recovering red population and it will crash again. The population gets to a lower and lower level, and then they are wiped out.'

Two decades ago it was predicted that reds would be extinct in Cumbria by now, but they are not. Red squirrels may be defenceless against squirrelpox, but their cuteness has given them a staunch ally: humans. 'I don't think there would be any squirrels left around Cumbria if it wasn't for

Julie Bailey,' said Andrew Hodgkinson, a softly-spoken, earnest conservationist who has worked in the county as a red-squirrel ranger, monitoring reds and killing greys, for two years.

Bailey began volunteering for Penrith & District Red Squirrel Group after her accident. Because her back pain caused her to be awake for much of the night, she worked all hours and soon became administrator, treasurer and trustee. She also supported some of the several dozen local squirrel groups across northern England. If the accident hadn't happened, said Bailey, she wouldn't be 'making the difference I think I'm making for red squirrels, so some good has come out of it'.

Red-squirrel conservation attracts lots of grassroots groups (such as Bailey's) that support a confusing array of national campaigns, as I learned at the Red Squirrels United Knowledge Fair, which was held in an upmarket Belfast hotel in March. Red Squirrels United is a three-year project supported by groups including Prince Charles's Red Squirrel Survival Trust, the European Squirrel Initiative and the UK Squirrel Accord. The latter is a mix of government agencies and charities that is developing an oral contraceptive for grey squirrels.

Beside a banner declaring 'I'm nuts about reds!', a series of scientists and conservationists gave PowerPoint presentations to describe their plans to halt the march of the greys, featuring military-style maps of marching grey dots, and punctuated with battle metaphors (defending red

'strongholds'). The audience was comprised of passionate volunteers, gentle, fleece-wearing charity workers and
tweedy representatives of big landowners, who hate the
grey squirrel because of the damage it does to their valuable plantations. 'It's absolutely wonderful to come here
and talk about controlling greys,' announced Andrew Ken-
dal of the European Squirrel Initiative, which is funded
by landowners and lobbies the EU. 'Fifteen years ago, it
was virtually taboo.' I learned about growing propaganda
efforts on behalf of the red squirrel – Ulster Wildlife Trust is
developing a new children's book called *The Greedy Grey*
– and discovered innovative dispatch devices, such as a new
trap that automatically kills the grey squirrel caught inside.

Conventional traps catch the grey squirrel alive and
rely on someone then shooting or hitting it over the head.
Opponents describe this as 'bludgeoning' them to death,
but the Wildlife Trusts prefers to call it 'cranial dispatch'.
The approved, legal method is one firm 'tap' on the head
with a stick. Nationally, conservation charities such as the
Wildlife Trusts and the National Trust are coy about their
role in controlling greys. They lose members when they
speak in support of killing the non-native squirrel. But in
areas where there are still reds, such charities often facil-
itate culling. Once red-squirrel conservationists have the
support of landowners, the key, according to Julie Bailey,
is 'boots on the ground': both volunteers and professionals willing to devote their days to killing greys.

Private landowners are often reluctant to allow

conservation volunteers on to their land, especially if they are wielding traps or shotguns. They prefer professionals, so Bailey's Penrith & District Red Squirrel Group must raise £100,000 each year for three full-time and two part-time squirrel rangers. 'We're struggling, if we're honest,' she said. 'We don't get a penny from the government – we're voluntarily led and self-funded.' But Bailey's group covers a quarter of Cumbria, and she has gathered some impressive data. In 2014 her group recorded 2,702 sightings of reds and killed 2,224 greys. In 2016 there were 3,306 red sightings and 1,806 grey kills. Fewer grey kills indicate that the cullers are winning.

New technology is helping. Last year, 69 per cent of the greys killed in Penrith were shot – the rest were trapped. Shooting greys has been revolutionised by thermal-imaging cameras. These expensive devices, which reveal the warm bodies of live animals in dense woodland, make it much quicker for shooters to locate greys. In January this year, 74 of 143 grey kills by the Penrith rangers were assisted by these cameras. Personally, Bailey prefers shooting to trapping. 'I don't do cranial dispatch, it's just too close for me,' she said. Not that shooting is easy.

It's bloody awful. Because I shoot grey squirrels, people think I'm a heartless, murdering cow. It hurts to kill something, but if I want to keep my red squirrels, I want to do it.

When I look at a grey, I see a rodent. When I look

at a red, I don't, even though they are the same thing. It's the cuteness factor. The tuft on the ears and the native/non-native gets me every time - they should be here and the greys shouldn't. I've got no problem with greys in North America. I certainly wouldn't support culling them in their country. But here we can't have both living side by side. We've got to make a choice and undo what the Victorians did.

During my two days with Bailey in the red-squirrel territory of Cumbria, I asked every person I encountered about squirrels and could not find a single supporter of the greys. Down south, where the only wild squirrel any-one under fifty remembers is the grey, there is much more hostility to the idea of killing them.

There haven't been red squirrels around the Tonbridge, Kent headquarters of Animal Aid since the 1960s. Here I met John Bryant, a courtly, white-haired man who is a pioneer of humane pest control. He's a consultant for the charity, which has been drumming up opposition to the grey cull, and fears this hostility to a non-native animal is a product of xenophobic times.

Bryant's experience as a humane pest controller has taught him the futility of killing species to 'control' their numbers. Kill one urban fox and another one quickly takes over the territory. Rat poison is a food, which attracts more rats. Rather than trapping grey squirrels, Bryant removes them by putting a cat-scented cloth in their drey.

The mother will then take the babies somewhere else.

The new drive to cull greys is backward, said Bryant. 'It's just, "Kill them." The same old thing. It won't work.' He identifies many hypocrisies in killing greys. The red is not globally endangered – it's common across Northern Europe and Siberia – and argues that the native/invasive distinction is nonsensical when so many reds were reintroduced from Scandinavia. For Bryant, the worst aspect is volunteers being taught to kill the greys by hitting them. 'Clearly, that's a horrific way to die,' he said. Most animals we hunt are also spared during their breeding season, but greys, like rats, can be killed all year round, and so lactating females will die, leaving babies to starve to death.

Bryant is unmoved by the scientific consensus that the red squirrel will become extinct in Britain if we don't control the greys. 'I don't think that is the case, but so what? It's a squirrel,' Bryant replied.

Does it matter what colour it is? They are the same thing. The damage they do – which is very little compared with the damage we do – is to strip bark and take eggs. That's what squirrels do, whatever colour they are. It's just this 'invasive species' label, where what I call biodiversity geeks say, 'It's all got to be native.' I don't go along with it.

Bryant cites two environmentalists who argue against the prevailing view that we should kill the grey to save the red. Stephen Harris, professor of environmental sciences at Bristol University, now retired, wrote ten years ago that we should accept that the grey squirrel is here to stay, and that the best place for the reds was small islands. More recently, the environmental journalist Fred Pearce has argued that ecosystems are always changing and invasive species should be celebrated. The vast majority of Britain's flora and fauna arrived in the last 10,000 years. Nothing is 'native' – everything is visiting. For Pearce, the alleged damage caused by most 'invasive' species, such as Japanese knotweed, is overstated by grant-seeking bureaucrats and sensationalising media. The government claims knotweed costs the British economy £170 million a year, but Pearce calculates it as far less. The Environment Agency calls it 'indisputably the UK's most aggressive, destructive and invasive plant', but only spends £2 million each year on knotweed eradication. Pearce also notes that, in 2009, the racist BNP branded the North American signal crayfish 'the Mike Tyson of crayfish . . . a diseased, psychotic, evil, illegal immigrant colonist [that] totally devastates the indigenous environment'.

I asked Bryant why he thinks wildlife lovers and scientists are killing grey squirrels. 'It's this immigration thing. It looks as if the whole of Europe is turning into a barricaded society. "We don't mind people as long as they are our people. We don't like these foreign squirrels coming in and taking over." It's intolerance, and it's illogical.'

Opponents of culling grey squirrels believe there must

be a way to save the red without killing greys. There are three technological solutions, but it is unlikely any of them will work quickly or thoroughly enough to deter volunteers from their efforts at grey-squirrel eradication. One is a vaccine to save reds from squirrelpox. Dr Colin McInnes, a scientist at the Moredun Research Institute in Scotland, developed a prototype vaccine. 'It gave us hope that we were on the right lines, but unfortunately we have no funding at the moment,' McInnes told me. Vaccine research is not cheap. If granted further funding, scientists must develop a method of delivery, such as an oral bait, and trial and licence the vaccine. McInnes doubts that a vaccine would ever be cheap enough to save reds across the land. 'We always envisioned that the vaccine would probably be used to protect specific vulnerable [red] populations that we could trap and inoculate,' he said.

Another option is a contraceptive for greys, which the government is funding. But a workable formula is at least a decade away. A contraceptive could never eradicate grey populations and nor could it be used in territory shared by reds and greys for fear of accidentally sterilising the reds.

There is more excitement about a third fix – a 'biological' control. The pine marten is a predatory member of the weasel family, which is also a native species. Research by Emma Sheehy in Ireland has linked a surprising grey-squirrel population crash to the pine marten's resurgence. Ecologists think the pine marten may create a 'landscape of fear' for the greys. They also believe that because the reds (which have evolved alongside the marten for centuries) weigh less than greys, they will be more easily able to escape by running to the ends of tree branches, where they cannot be reached. Dr Sheehy is studying the impact of martens on red and grey squirrels in Scotland, but says there is no guarantee that the impact she observed in Ireland will be replicated there, as the pine marten has more alternative prey to the grey squirrel, such as field voles.

Some animal activists also argue that we should leave the greys alone because, over time, red squirrels will develop immunity to squirrelpox, citing the example of myxomatosis, which was deliberately introduced in the 1950s to reduce Britain's rabbit population. This disease killed more than 99 per cent of rabbits, but over the past fifty years the population has bounced back. If a virus wipes out its host, it eradicates itself, so, over time, a virus must become less virulent to survive. The host – the rabbit – also develops immunity; survivors pass it to their offspring.

But squirrelpox, as Professor Julian Chantrey explained to me, is different. The virus already has a perfect host – the grey – and so there is no evolutionary imperative for it to become less deadly to reds. 'The reds will acquire some immunity, but it's going to take a long time, with successive epidemics driving the evolution of red resistance,' he said.

I wanted to see for myself whether 'cranial dispatch' – killing a grey squirrel by hitting it on the head – was cruel. So I drove to North Wales to spend a day with Craig

Shuttleworth, an ecologist responsible for the cullers' greatest achievement: an eighteen-year effort to clear the island of Anglesey of grey squirrels, which was completed in 2015. Since then, its red population has rebounded from near-extinction to 700.

We met at 7 a.m. and headed out in Shuttleworth's battered blue Land Rover with a mismatched red driver's door. In the back was a large translucent plastic sack filled with yellow maize and black sunflower seeds, and a sixty-centimetre-long, square-edged stick. Shuttleworth is a tall, independent thinker who had resisted the professorships of a conventional academic career. 'Scientists are a bit like an under-tens football team,' he said. 'They are all around the ball. The clever kid is waiting on the wing for that ball to pop out.' He is now working to clear greys from a small corner of north-west Wales.

He and two other contractors were funded by Red Squirrels United, but Shuttleworth was a little insulted by the fact that the project claims that killing grey squirrels is 'a last resort' on the Wildlife Trusts' website. To Shuttleworth, it's the only option: 'It's not a last resort. We have no choice, so it's kill them, kill them, kill them.'

Shuttleworth takes the lives of around 1,000 greys every year, and prefers cranial dispatch to shooting. 'Scientists in the southern hemisphere have said, "You're pissing in the wind. You're trapping, which is hugely labour-intensive – why aren't you using poison?" But we're not dealing with a rat eradication on a remote island, we're dealing with a place where sixty million people live with their pets.'

Fast-moving but Zen, like a postman on his rounds, Shuttleworth checked his traps by jumping over slate walls and weaving through overgrown cemeteries, rubbish-strewn parkland and beautiful, mossy oak woodlands. Each trap was a small wire cage containing maize and sunflower seeds. When a squirrel stepped on to a metal plate inside, the door closed. Each had a plastic sheet roof to prevent the animal catching a chill while held inside.

By midday, we'd checked several dozen traps. Each one was empty. Shuttleworth remained calm. He was phlegmatic about his human opponents as well. 'As a scientist, the message I give has to be honest, and therefore it's complicated. The [Animal rights groups'] message is simple. They say: "You're lying, it's bloodlust, it's cruel, you smash them on the heads – you're like the Nazis." There is all this nonsense.'

Animal Aid fears that psychopaths will volunteer to kill squirrels, and believes that amateur red-squirrel conservationists should be vetted, like people who work with children. Shuttleworth finds such fears overblown. Volunteers work in pairs, he told me:

We know where they are and what they are doing. Can we be sure someone doesn't take a knitting needle and push it through the squirrel in the sack a hundred times? I can't be sure, but it's very unlikely. Why would they bother becoming a volunteer with a local group when you can go to a DIY store, buy a trap and legally trap as many grey squirrels as you want?

Opponents worry that killing greys is not just inhumane but tinged with xenophobia. The late Philip Pauly, an American historian of biology, believed there was an alignment between legislation to curb invasive species in the US and the imposition of controls on human immigrants. California introduced a plant quarantine law in 1881; a year later came the Chinese Exclusion Act, which barred Chinese immigrant labourers to the US. Over the last two decades, a rising concern for the future of native species in the developed world has coincided with growing nationalist feeling and hostility towards migrants.

Invasion biologists have pointed out that xenophobia towards migrants within the single species of *Homo sapiens* is not comparable to taking action against invasive species that threaten entire species with extinction. But these academics are increasingly careful with their language. Instead of bandying about terms such as 'alien invaders', biologists now prefer phrases such as the 'McDonaldisation' of ecosystems to describe the damage caused by some non-native species. In effect, writes Peter Coates, a professor of environmental history at Bristol University, they are championing a kind of 'tasty' local diversity, rather like those campaigning for regionally specific cheeses or varieties of apple against the bland produce of globalised agribusiness. Shuttleworth used a similar analogy. If we don't control invasive non-native species, he said, 'we will end up with a homogenised world where it's all seagulls, magpies, crows, bracken, rhododendron and grey squirrels. A bit like high streets – they are all the same.'

Animal rights campaigners' attempts to paint invasive species in a more positive light co-opts the widely accepted view among ecologists today that there is no 'balance' of nature, and ecosystems are never stable. But Shuttleworth argues it is wrong to infer that we should learn to love destructive invasive species. In fact, he said, they prevent dynamism in human-dominated landscapes. For instance, as climate change threatens the survival of some native flora, British foresters will need to bring in new tree species that are better suited to our future climate. But we can't bring more drought-resistant European hardwoods into Britain because we don't know if they can survive the bark-stripping of grey squirrels.

Finally, after crashing through a scruffy copse near Bangor, Shuttleworth and I found a grey squirrel in a trap. It dashed from end to end as we approached. Shuttleworth drew out his stick, kneeled down and took perhaps ten seconds to shift the squirrel from cage to clear plastic bag. Another three seconds, and he had rolled up the plastic, pinning the animal on its side against the earth. Its shiny black eye briefly examined us through the bag. Whack-whack-whack. He pulled the squirrel from the bag. There was a spasm in its long rear legs, but the squirrel was dead. He touched its eye. 'No eye reflex,' he said.

Why did he hit it more than once? 'We don't want squirrels coming back to life. We don't want uncertainty,' he said. He was confident every squirrel he killed was dead after the first blow. His hardest kill was at the beginning of his first eradication project. A young squirrel showed no fear when caught in the trap, turning its back on him to hide the food it was eating. Were Shuttleworth's dreams haunted by all those dead grey squirrels? 'Quite the contrary. They become more and more anonymous, and that's hard for me to accept,' he said. 'One of the things I'm acutely aware of is becoming desensitised. How has that changed my relationship with other animals? It hasn't. I don't have any urge to kill anything else.'

Culling grey squirrels in perpetuity to save the reds is a hard sell, as Shuttleworth and Julie Bailey both admit. 'I suppose this is a bit like nuclear waste,' said Shuttleworth. 'We've got to manage how long "for ever" is.'

On Anglesey he had demonstrated that culling can work and red squirrels will then recover in a grey-free 'strong-holds', but he fears that his current project to remove greys from north-west Wales won't succeed by the end of its three-year funding. Still, he said, it could be successful in the longer term, and Red Squirrels United's EU funders are interested in whether this eradication project can be transferred to other problematic non-native mammals. For animal lovers horrified by culls, Shuttleworth mounted a more philosophical justification. On Anglesey, he argued, a comprehensive cull ultimately saved more lives than it took – the 6,000 greys culled will be surpassed by the number of reds born in years to come.

Five weeks after visiting Julie Bailey, I phoned for an update. She'd had a 'slight fall' and had been in and out of hospital, but had still managed to shoot five greys. One of her rangers was a bit down because there had been another outbreak of squirrelpox and a dying red had to be shot. Did she ever lose energy for this apparently eternal struggle? 'Never, ever, ever,' she said. 'We don't lose any faith in it. We know that if we didn't do what we're doing, we wouldn't have any red squirrels. It's as simple as that.'

2017

*

Since I wrote this story, further fascinating research has revealed how the pine marten reduces 'naive' grey-squirrel populations, thereby assisting the reds. But pine martens won't live in urban areas. Scientists expect the safe, city-living greys to repeatedly recolonise rural areas where the species has been ousted by the martens. In such situations, evolutionary pressure is likely to rapidly select grey squirrels who wise up to the martens; in comparable cases overseas, 'naive' species have quickly adapted to evade novel predators. So the pine marten is unlikely to be a panacea.

British trials of oral contraceptives distributed via hazelnut spread in feeders that can only be accessed by grey squirrels (reducing the risk of affecting other species, or reds) suggest that 90 per cent of a local population of greys can be treated in this way. There is also hope that in the more distant future, grey squirrels could be humanely controlled through 'gene drives', altered genes that can be implanted in males and create infertility in the genome of their female offspring. The gene drive is inherited by males and so female infertility spreads through the population. But this control raises fears that such destructive gene drives could be accidentally spread back to native populations of greys in North America.

Contraceptives and gene drives still raise ethical objections, especially when grey squirrels remain popular among many people in regions where there is no memory of wild red squirrels.

2021

'When their tails go up, leg it': on the trail of the beasts of Dartmoor

The wild boar stood over the stricken body of Bosun the dachshund and gazed at Rosemary Hamilton-Meikle with baleful yellow eyes. Screaming with rage, the eighty-year-old from Plymouth twirled the dog lead around her head like a lasso and clipped its hairy snout, before rescuing her dog from the gorse thicket.

Prehistoric in appearance, with the strength, speed and something of the temperament of Wayne Rooney, wild boar were hunted to extinction around the time Cistercian monks founded Buckland Abbey in Devon in 1278.

Now they are back – and breeding. A group of at least seven adults with around fifteen piglets – pale and stripy like mint humbugs – are terrifying dogs walkers on the western fringe of Dartmoor. There have been dozens of sightings since Mrs Hamilton-Meikle's dachshund was 'tossed' on the snout of a boar on New Year's Day.

Wild boar are heftier than a rugby forward, run faster than a sprinter, can hurdle five-bar gates and swim across rivers. One farmer claims he was chased up a tree by one of the Buckland Monachorum boar, who were let loose by a rogue farmer or animal-rights activists in October last year. The *Guardian* wanted me to track them down.

'When their tail goes up and the hair on their back stands on end like a porcupine, that's when you leg it,' said Jo Cameron, a local farmer who sees the boar almost every day. On Thursday night she watched seven with fifteen piglets feed on a decomposing sheep.

First stop, Mrs Hamilton-Meikle. Bosun was badly winded but is fully recovered. Mrs Hamilton-Meikle, however, hasn't been back to the moor. 'He would've eaten Bosun,' she said. She points out on the map the exact gorse thicket where the dachshund stumbled across the boar.

The smooth swath of Dartmoor near the village of Buckland Monachorum is popular with dog walkers. Dartmoor ponies and sheep wander across the open country. But now it looks more like a ploughed field. The boar have been rootling for worms and shoots, turning up turf like a tractor. The boar are in clover. Oak woodlands by the River Tavy are full of fallen acorns. Then there are the bulbs, crops, worms, insects, grasses, nesting birds, dead sheep and dachshunds from Plymouth. Is there nothing wild boar don't scoff?

Wild boar were hunted to extinction 800 years ago, according to Martin Goulding, a former government scientist and author of *Wild Boar in Britain*. They were reintroduced by James I, but these too ended their days on hunting lances.

When they began to be farmed there were soon escapees, assisted by disasters like the storms of 1987, careless owners and animal-rights activists. Dr Goulding estimates there are at least 'hundreds' in thriving colonies in Kent, East Sussex, Herefordshire, Gloucestershire and Devon.

Normally nocturnal and elusive, the boar of Buckland Monachorum seem to have taken to modern times. Mrs Cameron had just finished her cigarette on the moor when a boar hove into view. It sniffed her discarded butt – wild boar have a sense of smell as keen as a dog – and troughed it up. The dustbin truck has proved attractive. 'I saw a young one frolicking around, enjoying the smells from the bin lorry,' said Luke Scott-Pritchard, manager of Long Ash garden centre on the edge of the moor.

They have shown little fear of people. 'One followed my wife into the garden,' said one resident. 'We just shooed it out again.'

According to Mrs Cameron, they seem attracted by the sound of her quad bike – a sure sign they were domesticated boar used to being fed in a field by a farmer. So we bump out on to the moor.

Some of the 'commoners' – graziers who put their sheep and horses out on Dartmoor – have been feeding the boar in the hope that they can eventually round them up and recapture them. Other locals have been creeping out at night with lamps and rifles – a minimum of .270 calibre is needed to bring down a boar – and poaching them.

'They will kill lambs in the spring. They are scavengers, aren't they?' said Alan Glanville, a retired farmer. Another farmer who did not want to be named said he wanted to shoot them all.

Mrs Cameron is not so sure. She points out fresh trotter prints in the mud. 'They will definitely have a go at dead sheep, but I don't know how true it would be that they would pull down live stuff. They are not aggressive.'

Matriarchal like elephants, wild sows are more likely to attack dogs when they have piglets to protect, according to Dr Goulding. But he believes they are of no risk to people – unless dogs are involved – and would only take dead or dying livestock. Every dog walker on this patch of Dartmoor seems to have seen the boar and lived to tell the tale. But the wild beasts don't show themselves for the *Guardian*.

The government has conducted a lengthy consultation on what to do about burgeoning populations of boar but has yet to deliver any conclusions.

Mrs Cameron believes they could be managed sustainably. Dr Goulding hopes they could be too, with numbers controlled by a restricted hunting season so the boar are not cruelly killed when they have piglets, and warning signs for dog walkers.

'They are not the killing machines people make them out to be,' he said. 'Any wild animal needs to be treated with respect. I fear domestic dogs more than I fear wild boar.'

2011

How native are your daffs?
Exotic species aren't all vandals

Sunrise, Golden Harvest, Cheerfulness, Magnificence, Soleil d'Or – the names of cultivated daffodil varieties are as evocative as the spring flowers themselves. But how do you feel about hefty suburban daffs in wild places? Britain has a native daffodil (my dad used to spend weeks in the woods studying this slender flower), but many nature lovers dislike the incursion of brash cultivated varieties into our countryside.

Naturalist Mark Avery has written about his hatred of 'feral' daffodils anywhere wilder than gardens or suburban verges. They're like graffiti in the countryside, he says, triggering a debate about belonging and beauty – particularly pertinent in what is Invasive Species Week. This may sound obscure, but invasive species – from rhododendron to Japanese knotweed in Britain – raise big ethical questions, and are one of the prime contributors to extinction, after habitat loss.

But the language is problematic. 'Invasive' suggests the species is to blame, when it is usually moved by globe-trotting humans. Protecting 'native species' sounds like nativism, or even racism, which is why many people instinctively side with animal-rights campaigners against proposals to control (i.e. kill) non-native species.

We need another word for species moved by humans on to islands or continents where they cause harm. And 'weed' won't do either. Killing destructive exotic species is not analogous to anti-migrant prejudice (although, intriguingly, history suggests that native species' protections increase in times of anxieties about human migration), because we are a single species.

Globalisation is creating homogenised ecosystems. Unique local plants and animals are being erased by species that accompany us on our planetary march. We risk substituting the extraordinary range of life on earth for a denuded landscape of feral cats, rats and goats: admirable, intelligent creatures with a right to life but also possessing destructive tendencies. Like us, really.

Who lives and who dies? We tend to be more protective of invasive grey squirrels than Asian hornets or *Hymenoscyphus fraxineus* – but does the fungus that causes ash dieback have a right to life too?

A pragmatist would scientifically measure the damage caused and act to stop extinctions. So splashes of domesticated daffodils beyond suburbia get a reprieve because they're not decimating other species. And there's another benefit: if they're not dug up, they may stop the needless scalping of roadside verges that destroys so many wilder flowers.

2017

Who's afraid of the big bad wolf?

The story of a kill is told in the snow. On the Finnish island of Porosaari, we find the first paw print. 'That's a male,' says Asko Kettunen, retired border guard, hunter and tracker. How can he be sure? 'It's big.'

Five ravens rise from dark pines, croaking in the icy silence they will scavenge anything caught by the wolves. We wade through knee-deep snow. There's a spot of vivid blood and a tuft of moose hair, cleanly cut, which Kettunen deduces has been ripped from a living animal. This, he says, is the moment the wolves made contact. First they try to puncture the intestines – if they succeed, the moose may run on, but the damage is done.

We find moose tracks, each hoof print far apart: the animal was running. Kettunen points to wolf prints on either side, to where a second and third wolf joined the chase. There are blood spots and more hair and a pine sapling snapped in two. 'The moose collided with a tree, so it was not that well,' Kettunen says, with Finnish understatement.

There are spots of blood by every moose print now. Finally, up the hill, is the kill zone. A young moose has been reduced to two front legs and a skin detached precisely from the body, intestines that spill like butcher's sausages and a mound of freshly chewed grass where its stomach once was. Kettunen thinks that five wolves feasted here the previous night. We find faeces and a curved bed of snow where a contented wolf took a postprandial doze.

This wolf pack may be momentarily content but many country folk in Finland are not. 'Before, wolves were afraid of people,' says Kettunen. 'Now people are afraid of wolves.' There are too many wolves, say rural Finns, and livestock and hunting dogs are being killed. Some parents are scared wolves will attack their children. For the last three years the Finnish government has assuaged these fears with a wolf cull. Last winter, forty-three wolves were killed in the 'management hunt' but total fatalities numbered seventy-eight, including 'problem' wolves shot by police and road casualties – almost a third of the country's estimated population of 290. Hunters insist that more must be shot.

This winter Helsinki authorised another cull, permitting the death of fifty-three wolves, to include those shot by police and traffic fatalities. The cull is controversial: the wolf is a protected, endangered species. Critics say Finland is in breach of EU law. A candlelit vigil for slaughtered wolves took place in Helsinki last month, and a wolf-hunt saboteur group has sprung up on social media. Hunters say they've been disrupted by fireworks, vandalised trail cameras and a hunting shelter burned to the ground. One angry hunter offered a bounty of €50 (£42) to Russian hunters for each wolf they kill, promising to tip them off when they spot a wolf crossing from the Russian border.

In this apparently calm and phlegmatic country, the wolf polarises opinion.

All across Europe, the wolf is on the rise. Driven to extinction by the middle of the twentieth century, it trotted back into France in the 1990s and into Germany in 1998. Wolves are roaming through Denmark, the Netherlands and, late last year, reached the Belgium–Luxembourg border for the first time in 118 years. Europe (excluding Russia, Ukraine and Belarus) now hosts more than 12,000 wolves, twice as many as the United States (excluding Alaska) – despite being half the size and more than twice as densely populated. Recent reports of wolves on the edge of Paris have been treated sceptically by scientists, but they are nevertheless thriving in suburban Germany and other densely populated areas.

Inevitably, there has been a human backlash. Last year, Norway announced plans to kill 70 per cent of its wolf population of just sixty-eight, to protect sheep flocks, before outrage prompted the authorities to backtrack and propose a cull of just fifteen wolves. Two years before that, Tuscan farmers dumped wolf carcasses in town centres in protest at their burgeoning population. French farmers have also demanded that its authorities shoot more wolves. For them, the wolf poses a threat to their way of life – for others, it stirs deep fears still, given cultural expression in everything from fairy tales to music videos. The animal may be a symbol of freedom and nature's ability to bounce back, but it also embodies two very contemporary

ANIMAL RIGHTS AND WRONGS

tensions: the gulf between countryside and city, and the chasm between ordinary people and an uncaring political elite.

Pia Ikonen's family life is recognisably twenty-first century: inside her modest bungalow, her eldest child, Lukas, nine, is transfixed by a tablet. Lotta, eight, and Lucia, six, watch *Kung Fu Panda 3* on the telly, while Linda, four, reads a picture book showing a wolf pulling a sledge carrying two happy kittens. But during her ten years living two and a half kilometres from the Russian border, Ikonen has seen wolves become ever bolder. Four years ago her dog, Ninni, was snatched in broad daylight from her garden and killed by a pack. This winter she has found two sets of wolf tracks in her snowbound yard.

Dusk is falling. Would she let her children play on the trampoline outside? 'If we have wolves circling, they can't be outside in the daytime alone, and in the darkness, not at all,' Ikonen says. 'It is very much a problem if you can't let your children run around or walk your dog freely.'

The local community pays for an expensive 'wolf taxi' to transport her children, and thirty-one others in the region, from their front doors to school, so they don't have to wait at remote bus stops. Is Ikonen tempted to move to a safer town? She laughs. 'It should be the wolves who don't stay,' she says. This is a territorial dispute.

Wolves were driven to virtual extinction in Finland after a spate of attacks on children at the end of the nineteenth century. The story of a pair of rogue wolves that killed thirty-five children over eighteen months in the early 1880s is still widely repeated. Are such fears of wolves rational, I ask Ilpo Kojola, research professor at the Finnish government's National Resources Institute (its acronym is Luke and its newsletter is *Leia* – Finnish scientists have a sense of humour). 'The risk of a wolf attack is really, really tiny nowadays,' he says, explaining that the historic attacks happened in an era when children led cattle into the forests, and when there were no moose for the wolves to eat.

Wolves can kill people – a jogger was killed in Alaska in 2010 – but a scientific study in which humans approached wolves 125 times in Scandinavia found no occasions of aggressive behaviour: on 123 occasions the wolves ran away; on the other two, an alpha female exhibited harmless 'defensive' behaviour near her pups.

Instead, the hostility towards wolves in rural Finland is mostly because they take hunting dogs. Finland has 300,000 amateur hunters, more than 5 per cent of its population. Helsinki airport is decorated with stuffed hares and wolverine, and much of its rich animal life – beavers, lynx, bears – can be shot under a strict licence system. Moose hunting is particularly popular, a pursuit that has evolved over decades, with GPS collar-wearing dogs chasing moose up to fifteen kilometres beyond the hunter, who follows it on a screen. 'They bark when they stop the moose,' explains Kai Tikkunen of the Finnish Hunters' Association, and then 'it's like an ice-cream truck calling the wolves.'

So the wolf is a rival, killing moose that hunters would like to catch? 'The big problem is not that they eat the moose; the big problem is that they kill the dogs. It's sometimes very scary when I go to the forest: I don't know if my dog is going to come out alive.' Hunters are compensated for dogs killed by wolves, but it can take eighteen months and does not bring back a pedigree animal they may have spent years training.

The snowbound track sparkles under my headlights as I drive eighteen kilometres beyond the nearest shop to meet Ari Maattanen, who lives alone with Minni, his Finnish Spitz. This dainty, bird-hunting dog is on a long leash in his snowy yard, as some dogs are still kept in Finland. 'I like the countryside very much,' Maattanen says. 'It's just nature and it's free. There's no noise and I can see the stars.' He also enjoys all but one of his dangerous fellow species. 'I like the bears, the lynx, the adder,' he says. 'If ten bears are around this house, that's fine. But one wolf? I do not like it, not at all.'

Maattanen's beloved previous dog, Kessu, was killed on 22 January last year. His description of the loss sounds like the abduction of a child. He saw two wolves thirty metres from his window in December 2015. 'They don't jog for pleasure,' he says. 'They were looking for food. And after that, the wolves knew I had a dog.' The 'wolf circle', whereby a pack of five or more wolves scour their 1,000-square-kilometre territory for food, takes two and a half weeks in Maattanen's neighbourhood. 'They took one circle and the dog was not outside. But on the second circle it was there. It was 12.30 p.m. and I remember Kessu was staring into the forest. He started walking in that direction' – he points to a place where his garden blends into the forest – 'and vanished from sight.'

Later that afternoon a neighbour called to warn him that two wolves had crossed the road nearby. 'I went out with a gun but it was too late.' He found scuffle marks, then wolf tracks. 'They had been waiting 100 metres away for my dog. They had invited the dog to play and then . . .' He pauses. 'My dog ran into the wolf's mouth.' There had been no barking. There was no blood. The wolf was so strong it took Kessu without a sound. How does he know the wolf was big? 'Because on Sunday the hunters shot it,' he says. Local hunters had quickly obtained a permit to kill this 'problem' wolf.

Maattanen throws a fluffy object on to the kitchen table. 'That's what's left of my beautiful dog,' he says. It's Kessu's tail. A few days later, hunters found something else in the snow. Maattanen shows me a photo on his phone: Kessu's head, so neatly severed it looks like a surgical operation.

Ari Turunen, a paramedic who lives with his wife and two young children in a wooded village, is the leader of the local hunting group in Ilomantsi. Underneath his snowsuit, a white and grey camouflage for winter hunting, he wears a black T-shirt that says, in English, '99% bear hunter'.

According to Turunen, the local wolf population has

ANIMAL RIGHTS AND WRONGS

grown from two packs to seven or eight. 'Five years ago it was rare for normal people to see wolves. It would be written about in a newspaper. Now they see them daily,' he says. 'We should never let the wolf population grow this quickly, because it disrupts the balance of nature.'

One reason for the wolf's resurgence is rural depopulation. Outside its cities, Finland does not look prosperous: the mechanisation of forestry has stripped jobs from the countryside and picturesque cottages lie derelict in snowy forests. For those who remain, hunting is a social glue. 'We don't have any ice-skating halls here,' Turunen says. 'All my friends and friends' wives hunt. It's part of everyday life. I spend a lot of time in nature, fishing, and picking mushrooms and berries with the kids. I'm a nature conservationist.'

Five days ago, Turunen and his fellow hunters went after two wolves. One of them had been attracted to lard put out for songbirds. It also encountered a jogger near a village. 'It was a very bold one,' Turunen says. He has taken his three-year-old son hunting since he was a baby, but he doesn't take him wolf hunting: there's too much waiting around in the cold. On last week's hunt, they began at 4 a.m. and killed both wolves by midday. The bodies were then dispatched to government scientists for DNA tests – these help to map the wolf population, and confirm the animals are wolves and not wolf-dog hybrids.

Hunting a wolf is tightly regulated: only a few permits will be issued for each region, and hunters stand more chance of obtaining one if they identify a 'problem' wolf. Wolves can't be chased on snowmobiles, and no more than fifty people can hunt at a time. Usually, a few hunters on skis will move through the forest with dogs, attempting to flush resting wolves towards a circle of waiting guns.

Across the nearby border the Russian authorities reward hunters for killing some of their 50,000 wolves, which are considered vermin. Turunen says it is illogical to have two such different approaches, when wolves move freely between the countries. 'It's stupid that, on the other side, it's considered a pest and you get money for killing it, and on this side you go to prison.' His own view is that the wolf should be a 'valuable and respected game animal, a hunting prize'.

Does the Finnish government understand the concerns of rural people? 'No,' Turunen says. 'This discussion is dominated by people who have never seen a wolf or lived in a wolf area. The matter should be decided in the areas where it takes place, and not in Helsinki. If I managed street cleaning in Helsinki they would be equally screwed,' he laughs. 'And the problem is, some things are not decided in Helsinki but in Brussels, where they understand it even less.'

On the train from rural Finland to Helsinki, I chat to a young suburban Finn. He says he can understand both sides of the wolf debate but when I ask him how many wolves there are in Finland, he guesses at 5,000. I tell him there are barely 200 and he changes his mind. 'This animal should be protected,' he declares.

Most Finns, says Sami Säynevirta, manager of Luonto-Liitto, a Finnish wildlife charity, have no idea the country has so few wolves. 'Finnish people are really surprised when we tell them it's an endangered species. They don't realise we have so much poaching.' Säynevirta argues that Finland needs help from the EU, punitive or otherwise, to stop the wolf cull. 'This is not good for Finland's reputation for ecotourism,' he says. 'Wolves could be more valuable for Finland alive than hunted.'

The Finnish government has calculated that if it maintains a minimum of twenty-five wolf packs, it won't be breaking EU law. The first year of its wolf hunt, 2015, was considered a success but the second, last winter, was not, because eight alpha females were killed – too many.

Filmmaker Stefan Gofferje has lodged a criminal complaint against Finnish officials for violating EU law. Gofferje, a German who lives in Finland, tells me he has loved wolves since he was a boy. His pet dog is 55 per cent wolf: he 'lives in my apartment, sleeps in my bed, goes for a thirty-kilometre walk every day and is a local star here in my village. It's practically impossible to train a wolf. When I ask him to do something, I ask him – I'm not telling him.'

Gofferje's legal complaint is currently undergoing what he calls 'client ping pong', shuffled between government departments and jurisdictions. He plans further challenges, contrasting the Finns' apparent willingness to shoot any wolves found near houses with Germany, where 'problem' wolves spotted close to human habitation are first tracked with GPS to understand their movements, then deterred – and destroyed only if displaying direct and threatening behaviour towards humans. Germany has invested millions in public education programmes focused on its new wolf population and only education will help people and wolves coexist, Gofferje argues. 'It's not enough for the government just to make rules or prosecute poachers. They must educate people,' he says. 'If your child is afraid of something, do you remove the cause of the fear, or do you educate the child to combat the fear itself?'

'We have people standing on both sides of us kicking our ankles. If both our ankles are sore, then we've done something right,' says Sami Niemi, the likeable official in Finland's Ministry of Agriculture who oversees its wolf policy (and doesn't hunt himself). 'This is not an issue where you can find a solution that suits all: we have to find the middle way. That leaves everyone unhappy: there are either too many licences or too many wolves, so we can't win.'

The stated purpose of Finland's cull is to reduce poaching. When the wolf was completely protected, Niemi explains, 'illegal hunting was a big problem for us. If the population grew to 140 or 150, the next year it went back down. It's not just hunters, it's local people in general. They put pressure on the hunters to deal with the issue [illegally], so we had to do something.'

But conservationists say this argument is equivalent to introducing government burglaries to reduce stealing. The only winner is the government. 'With the ministry doing this legal hunt, they get fewer phone calls and emails from angry hunters,' says Mari Nyyssölä-Kiisla, chair of Luonto-Liitto's wolf action group. 'They think this is a good thing: "We've got more peace. The people are happy."'

In a recent study, ecologists Guillaume Chapron and Adrian Treves analysed wolf population growth rates in Michigan and Wisconsin and found that government-sanctioned culls in those US states caused a change in wolf population, which they suggested was most likely the result of illegal killing. 'Wolf culling may have sent a negative message about the value of wolves or acceptability of poaching,' they concluded.

In that sense, culling is a political act, Chapron explains on the phone from the Swedish University of Agricultural Sciences. 'The wolf conflict is not strictly about wolves,' he says:

It's a conflict between people about who controls the land. The wolf is associated with wilderness only in our minds – it is a species that can live everywhere. I'm not saying that wolves do not create damage. But the wolf is like a predatory roe deer, and we don't associate roe deer with wilderness. Hunters often consider that wild animals are their property to harvest, while environmentalists are more fired up by the wolf than the roe deer.

'The wolf asks very disturbing questions,' Chapron continues:

In France, when wolves kill livestock in their national parks, farmers say, 'We can't survive with wolves, they are destroying our livestock.' But environmentalists ask in return: 'Why do we even have sheep in our national parks?' The farmers will say that it is a tradition. But is subsidised overgrazing a tradition? The debate becomes very heated, because the wolf is questioning economic practices, land use and the allocation of power in the countryside.

Even in consensus-loving countries such as Finland, wolf-haters and wolf-lovers do battle online, trading threats, insults and wild conspiracies about illegal poaching or zoos deliberately releasing wolves. On the border with Russia, fearful locals share pictures of what they claim is a burgeoning population of Russian wolf-dogs. (The research professor Ilpo Kojola tells me that genetic testing of 450 Finnish wolves over twenty years has revealed only three cases of wolf-dog hybrids.) A suspicion of experts, scientists, entrenched power and political elites is a common thread in many of these discussions.

Among local people who fear wolves, there is a particular

dislike of the EU. Chapron is not making a political point but tells me his research has led him to conclude that EU protection has been key to the wolf's resurgence, as well as that of other large predators including the brown bear and lynx. 'If there wasn't this strict legislation, there would be very few or no large carnivores in Europe.'

Back in snowbound Finland I ask local hunter Asko Kettunen, who is also a wildlife photographer, if ecotourism (spotting live wolves) could replace hunting. 'No,' he replies firmly. 'Feeding or photographing the wolves gets them comfortable with people and more problems will come.'

Does he hate the wolf?

No. I don't like that they kill my dogs, but I don't hate the animal, not at all. It's so intelligent, it's so difficult to catch and it adapts to its surroundings so quickly, faster than other species. The wolf belongs in Finnish nature, just not in yards and gardens. Many people say that hunters hate wolves, but we tolerate them and hope they don't do any damage. It's not hatred – it's realism.

2017

*

There continues to be controversy over the Finnish government's use of licences to kill significant numbers of the country's wolves.

2021

The hen harrier whodunnit: who has been murdering one of England's rarest birds?

Last spring, when walkers on the Lancashire moors came upon two hen harrier nests, they alerted local conservationists. Not because these powerful birds of prey represented a danger to wildlife, but because the harriers themselves are under threat.

When they got the call, staff and members of the RSPB, helped by local volunteers, set up a 24-hour watch to protect the nests. Over the summer, under the gaze of their guardians, the harriers raised nine chicks, four of which were named by local schoolchildren: Sky, Hope, Highlander and Burt. By late summer, as they prepared to leave the nests, the fledglings were fitted with satellite tags so their movements could be monitored.

The Forest of Bowland, a striking landscape of boggy, open upland carpeted with heather and bracken, is home to some of the last breeding pairs of hen harriers in England. A male hen harrier's silhouette gliding low over the moorland is an eerie sight greatly prized by bird-lovers, but the bird is best known for its aerobatic displays of climbing, twisting and rolling, known as sky dancing. Like other birds of prey, the harrier has been protected by law since 1954, but while buzzards and peregrine falcons have recovered their numbers, in England, hen harriers are now close to extinction.

At dusk on 10 September last year, a few weeks after the juvenile birds had successfully left their nest, the 9.5-gram tag on Sky's leg abruptly stopped transmitting. Three days later, Hope's signal was lost. Both birds had disappeared. The scientists and local bird-lovers who had worked so hard to protect them were convinced someone had deliberately shot these birds out of the sky. And they had strong suspicions about who was responsible.

The harrier is a stealth predator. A disc of feathers around its face gives it the piercing gaze and acute hearing of an owl. It can snatch a creature as small as a beetle or as bulky as a duck, but its favourite food on high moors is a plump little bird greatly prized by game shooters: the red grouse.

For four months after the 'glorious Twelfth' of August each year, wealthy sportsmen pay up to £3,000 a day to stand with a gun on private moorland while beaters – usually farm workers or local lads – flap and shoo grouse towards the shooters' sights. Gamekeepers are employed on the upland estates to ensure plentiful supplies of wild grouse. Their job involves eradicating animals that might want to eat these small game birds: foxes, stoats, weasels and, in the days when it was legal to do so, birds of prey. When Hope and Sky disappeared, many suspected they had been killed by gamekeepers protecting grouse for the shooting season.

Since 2000, twenty gamekeepers have been found guilty of 'raptor persecution' or poisoning offences on grouse moorland, including one who killed a hen harrier in Scotland. In 2013 the RSPB logged 238 reports of birds of prey being poisoned, shot or beaten to death. But convictions are vanishingly rare, especially in England. Even when a naturalist working for the government witnessed two hen harriers being shot out of the sky seven years ago, the Crown Prosecution Service brought no charges. The birds had been killed close to the royal estate of Sandringham in Norfolk and the only people known to have been shooting in the area that day were Prince Harry, his friend William van Cutsem, and a Sandringham gamekeeper. The bodies were never found.

Inside the Hark to Bounty pub in the Lancashire village of Slaidburn, I found taciturn young gamekeepers, cheeks flushed red from a day outdoors, quietly discussing their shoot by the open fire. It could almost have been Bowland in 1915, when sportsmen clocked up Britain's record grouse bag: 2,929 birds in one day. Although the RSPB is at pains to stress it is not opposed to grouse shooting, and its staff devote days to visiting gamekeeping colleges and attending rural game fairs to encourage greater co-operation between conservationists and law-abiding gamekeepers, the organisation has made enemies.

While many local people in Bowland celebrated its status as a stronghold for the hen harrier, the RSPB has struggled to win over significant parts of the community.

Some locals said they felt insulted when the charity installed 24-hour watches on Bowland's two hen harrier nests: the implication was that locals could not be trusted. 'They come with an attitude – as if the bird is the most important thing in the world,' complained one local in the pub. 'If you're living in the countryside, a job is the most important thing in the world.'

'Are they gamekeepers that killed these birds? It's supposition,' said Phil Gunning, a retired police inspector who runs a grouse syndicate, a small group of friends holding an exclusive right to shoot on 2,600 hectares of Bowland each season. We were speaking on the landline in the Hark to Bounty pub, as there is no mobile phone reception on the moors. 'There's an awful lot of birds of prey out there and an awful lot of people don't particularly care for them. You'd have to be pretty naive to say a gamekeeper has never killed a bird of prey but to generalise and say, "It's gamekeepers," is simply not fair.'

Gunning rejected the idea that his Bowland shoot was an anachronistic country pursuit for the upper classes. 'We're not toffs. We're not the landed gentry. It's just ten chaps from various walks of life who enjoy each other's company – farmers, retired dentists, a chef, an engineer.' A day on the high moors in pursuit of grouse, he explained, was the game shooter's equivalent of a cricket fan playing at Lords, or a tennis-lover getting to Wimbledon. 'The killing process, it's completely the opposite of bloodlust,' he said. 'It's not a fairground duck shoot where you go pop-pop-pop, it's a supreme test of skill. These things are fully aerobatic, they can be going 60 mph. If you want to shoot, you want to shoot on a grouse moor.'

The distinctively British sport of driving a small wild bird towards waiting guns became popular in the nineteenth century, establishing a rural tradition that has remained unchanged ever since. By 1900 the hen harrier had all but disappeared as a breeding bird in England and Wales. When grouse shooting declined after the Second World War (overgrazing by sheep and the conversion of moorland to conifer plantations had destroyed much of the grouse's heathery habitat), harrier numbers revived. Today, grouse shooting is booming. As a business it's worth £67.7 million a year in England and Wales, and the hen harrier has gone into dramatic decline once again. Ecologists calculate England's heather-clad uplands can naturally support at least 300 pairs of hen harriers, but in 2013, no hen harriers bred successfully in England at all.

Conservationists say there is no ecological reason for this wipeout – no habitat loss, no food shortages, no killer disease – only a conflict of interest between a lucrative business and one of our most impressive predators.

When Sky and Hope's tags stopped transmitting in early September last year, the RSPB's Investigations Team dispatched one of its detectives, Howard Jones, to discover what happened. The Forest of Bowland is a triangle of bleak Lancashire moorland, which most visitors swiftly pass in search of the more scenic Lake District. I met Jones early one frosty morning in Slaidburn village car park, six weeks into his investigation. Unusually for an RSPB employee, Jones did not carry binoculars. Between supporters of the shoot and protectors of birds of prey, feelings were running high, he explained. 'People get abuse just for watching birds on a grouse moor.' He wore all black, and although he usually rides a mountain bike to minimise the likelihood of being seen, today he was driving a nondescript white Transit van with blacked-out windows.

The moors, covered with bracken turning a rusty brown, stretched as far as the eye could see. We parked the van and walked over the moor close to where Sky and Hope vanished. There was no trace of human life, only the croak of a raven and a trickling stream. 'Our job is not to be seen,' said Jones. 'The best chance we have to detect these crimes is by avoiding people at all costs.'

Sky and Hope's disappearance had been reported to Lancashire police but until their bodies were recovered, it was impossible to conclude that they had been deliberately shot. After the harriers' tags stopped transmitting, Jones and another RSPB investigations officer spent a week quietly scouring the moorland where the two birds disappeared, using hand-held scanners. The weather was excellent, so the tags should have been recoverable if the birds had died of natural causes, but no signal was found. Jones concluded that whoever killed them had disposed of the tags and bodies.

Two years ago Jones had caught a keeper beating two buzzards to death. In February 2013 members of the public found two live buzzards caught in a large trap designed to – legally – catch crows. They called the RSPB, and the next day Jones mounted a hidden camera over the trap. Four minutes after he left, a gamekeeper arrived, and let himself into the cage-like trap. What happened next was recorded on tape. The video is disturbing: you can hear the thud of stick on skull as the keeper beats the buzzards to death.

'He had an incredibly blasé attitude to controlling birds of prey,' said Jones. 'These sorts of crimes are committed on private land, hidden away – every time we detect one of these incidents it's a minor miracle.' Jones called the police and his evidence helped convict the gamekeeper, who was given a seventy-day suspended sentence.

In the hunt for Sky and Hope, covert surveillance was no help. The RSPB investigators went public straight away in the hope that someone would come forward with evidence. The local community was caught up in the harriers' fate – children at the primary school who had named Sky were distraught. Blanaid Denman, who had led a hen harrier project for the RSPB in the area, said she felt 'crushed'. Even Phil Gunning was outraged. He had been anxious to foster good relations between the grouse shoot, bird-lovers and the local community. 'I can say this on behalf of everybody in the area. They were all absolutely, totally and utterly disappointed,' he told me over the phone. 'If they have been killed by somebody then it's brought a whole load of nonsense on top of everybody's head that we don't need.'

Much of the time, Jones's investigations relied on tip-offs. 'You get to know the players – the bad estates, the bad people,' he said. Despite RSPB appeals on the web and in local press, with an offer of a £1,000 reward, no one in the area has yet identified the perpetrators. 'Unless we get a good Samaritan who might have known what has happened to these birds and comes forward, we're really struggling.'

Conservation groups have put substantial resources into preserving the hen harrier population. As a scientist working for Natural England, the government's conservation watchdog, Stephen Murphy has spent the last eight years fitting hen harriers with £2,700-satellite transmitters to better understand the lifestyle of these birds, and the reasons for their demise. On an overcast day at the end of October I clambered into Murphy's battered Mitsubishi pickup for a tour of the Forest of Bowland where Hope and Sky had vanished.

Murphy, an ebullient, fast-talking Scouser, has studied the hen harrier's habits. The hen harrier must consume a fifth of its body weight in food each day to stay alive, he told me. 'That's either chasing a load of voles around all day or whacking a grouse every two days.'

Wiry and with short-cropped hair flecked with grey, Murphy had worked on building sites most of his adult life, never realising his birdwatching hobby could be a career. He was nearly forty when his mother encouraged him to pursue his passion – birds – and study for an ecology degree. 'I've loved birds since I was a child. My mum says I used to run around the garden flapping my wings thinking I could take off,' he said. After his degree he undertook research for Natural England on turtle doves, another endangered species, but when that survey was finished, he was unemployed and walking his dog when the organisation called to ask if he fancied studying hen harriers for another research programme. 'I punched the air,' he remembered, as he drove me slowly to the moorland edge. 'To work with them is a dream. Some days I get up in these hills at first light and I'm above the clouds – I feel like I've died and gone to heaven.'

When Murphy discovered that Sky and Hope had disappeared, he was saddened, but not surprised. Of forty-seven hen harriers he has tagged since 2007, only four are alive today. His cheery manner subsided. 'I seem to be impervious but I'm not. My wife knows. She comes in and says, "Something's happened to one of your birds, hasn't it?"'

Murphy's satellite-tagging programme, which he was writing up for a PhD on the ecology of the hen harrier, has shed new light on the bird's varied and nomadic life. Birds tagged in Bowland have been tracked making lightning trips 480 kilometres north to Scotland and beyond. One commuted so frequently between Scotland and Spain he was nicknamed McPedro. The small polygamous male and larger female behave so differently that early ornithologists considered them separate species – Murphy found that a male might fly 3,000 kilometres while his sister moved five kilometres in her entire life. 'We're dealing with a species that can shift time zones in a couple of hours or be a couch potato,' said Murphy. 'That's a hell of a range of behaviours to conserve.'

The tags could not, however, explain why so many birds were dying. Around 70 per cent of hen harriers die of natural causes in their first year and of Murphy's forty-seven tracked birds, thirty-seven disappeared without a trace. There could be innocent reasons for this: transmitters were reliable but might fail, and it was possible a sudden loss of signal could be caused by a fox dragging a bird underground. If a body was taken into a den, or even if it lay in a ditch, the tag would be undetectable. 'With regards to evidence – and Natural England is an evidence-based organisation – we didn't have a lot to go on,' said Murphy. There was no way of telling how many birds had been trapped or shot. 'For us to disentangle the persecution incidents from the rest is nigh on impossible without a body.'

If a harrier died naturally, its body would eventually be found. Teams of up to nine people, with tracker dogs, had searched, sometimes for weeks, for each of the thirty-seven birds that went missing. The harrier-lovers' conviction that grouse estates were behind their disappearance had been hardened by a case in 2011, when Murphy had fitted a tag to a juvenile hen harrier, Bowland Betty. Betty became a celebrity among birdwatchers who delighted in her rapid journeys between Wales and northern Scotland, searching for a mate.

During the wet summer of 2012, Betty's signal abruptly ceased on the Yorkshire Dales. Murphy showed me what resembled a small aerial for an old-fashioned portable TV: it was a hand-held scanner mainly used by the US army to locate downed drones. It picked up a 'grounded' signal that the satellite tag emitted if the bird stopped moving. He had taken it on to remote moorland to hunt for Bowland Betty in the area where he had received the last reliable fix from her transmitter. At 11 a.m. on 5 July, he found her. All that remained was a skinny carcass of bedraggled wet feathers on a patch of bilberries, the tag's antenna sticking into the air. She had been shot. Whoever fired at her hadn't been able to track her down with dogs and dispose of the tag because the shot had not immediately been fatal: Betty had flapped on for several kilometres before collapsing on the ground.

To gain a more complete understanding of how grouse shooting benefits the economy of upland Britain, I crossed the Pennines to meet Amanda Anderson, the director of the Moorland Association, at the home of one of her members, farmer Stephen Mawle. Over homemade cake in his grey stone farmhouse at the head of Coverdale in the Yorkshire Dales, Mawle explained how his expanding grouse shoot not only created jobs but funded a much wider conservation effort. According to the Moorland Association, just 10 per cent of moor owners' £52.5 million annual spend on land management comes from government subsidies – the rest is private money, brought in by grouse.

Mawle employed three keepers whose work included controlling predators (foxes, stoats, crows) by legal means to ensure a healthy wild grouse population. He admitted that the presence of hen harriers was a threat to the profitability of the grouse shoots. 'It's one thing to let the lion prowl around your stock pen, it's another to open the gate and let him in,' he said. 'You've got a huge financial incentive for hen harriers not to nest on your land.'

'A landowner is not going to encourage them to settle,' added Anderson. She suggested that hen harriers could be easily scared off. 'They are very flighty birds.'

On twenty days each season, nine 'guns' would arrive at Mawle's farm. These included a syndicate of German, Italian, Belgian and French clients who called themselves 'the Euroshots', paid £30,000 between them for a day's shooting and enjoyed its unique atmosphere. 'They can't get this get anywhere else,' said Mawle. 'They love that feeling of wildness.'

These clients expected to shoot seventy-five brace (150 birds) in a day between them. Conservationists criticise the intensification of grouse shooting and argue that hen harriers are only killed because grouse shooters want to bag so many birds. It's 'not mass slaughter', Anderson pointed out. 'We don't have any clients saying, "We're not coming unless we shoot 200 brace,"' said Mawle. Then why not shoot fewer? 'You're not going to get people paying for eighty brace and only shooting twenty. They want value for money,' he said. If the farm only offered 'walked-up' grouse shooting – where bags are much smaller because no birds are driven towards guns – Mawle said he would not be able to charge more than £5,000. Much of the shoot's revenue went into the Dales economy: Mawle bought his food at the local shop, serviced his farm vehicles locally and employed local people: the thirty beaters required to drive the birds towards the guns were paid £50 a day.

Mawle offered to show me his grouse moor, and so we clambered into a noisy Kawasaki all-terrain vehicle driven by Neil Taylor, Mawle's Scottish gamekeeper. We then scaled boggy slopes on tank-style metal treads. 'There's Shortie,' said Taylor, spotting a short-eared owl. We strolled across springy heather and moss as wet as a sponge, and a strange cackling call of 'go-back, go-back' rose on the wind: small coveys of red grouse whirred away from us.

Three-quarters of the world's heather moorland is found in Britain – the heather flowers purple in August, the bracken shines bronze in the autumn and the moors are dusted white with snow in midwinter. This wild land-scape is preserved, Mawle argues, thanks to funds gener-ated by grouse shoots. Managing his land for grouse, he added, provided conservation benefits that groups such as the RSPB would approve of. By legally trapping and killing stoats and foxes to ensure plentiful supplies of grouse, he helped conserve endangered birds: woodcock, snipe, golden plover, lapwing, ring ouzel, and 'buckets and buckets of curlew'. Some birds of prey also thrived on grouse moors because of these plentiful food supplies: merlin were four times more numerous on grouse moors than in other locations (although this may be because, unlike hen harriers, they are too small to kill grouse). Mawle had restored heather moorland, 'rewetting' his land by blocking ditches to restore blanket bog, which is rich in rare sphagnum mosses, and also allowed his river to break out of its artificial banks and meander down the valley, reducing flood risk by slowing the progress of water into lowland Yorkshire. 'If the shooting wasn't there, could we afford to do it?' asked Mawle.

If driven grouse shooting were banned, Mawle argued, the cost of keeping the moorlands in their attractive, wildlife-friendly state would have to be met by the tax-payer. He believed that anti-grouse-shoot campaigners were driven by a hypocritical distaste for those who take pleasure in killing wild birds. Perhaps grouse could be 'harvested with nets as a food source, which would achieve the objective of not allowing people to enjoy themselves shooting', he said drily. 'It's completely illogical.'

Since May last year, in a bid to protect hen harriers, more than 20,000 people have signed a government e-petition calling for a ban on driven grouse shooting. The petition was started by Mark Avery, an intense, fiercely intelligent former director of conservation for the RSPB, who last year also launched Hen Harrier Day in protest at the grouse industry's perceived persecution of the harrier. I spoke to Avery the day after he had travelled to Margate to admire Jeremy Deller's painting of an enormous hen harrier grabbing a Range Rover in its talons, which Avery saw as a compelling statement about class-based power still defining what lived and died in the British countryside.

'I'm not a shooting person but I can imagine how shooting would be fun – it's difficult to do and grouse shooting takes you to fantastic places,' said Avery. 'But once you've shot ten birds in a day, why do you have to go on to shoot a hundred? It seems like carnage rather than sport.' His call to ban driven grouse shooting was not supported by the RSPB but Avery remained convinced that, like fox hunting, the sport was 'past its sell-by date' and would one day be banned. What about the argument that declining birds such as curlew thrive on land managed for grouse? Avery had visited a grouse moor earlier in the year:

There were golden plover and curlew and lapwing displaying and it was pretty impressive but if there had been a pile of 400 stoats by the road and however many foxes and weasels and a pile of illegally killed hedgehogs, badgers, peregrines, goshawks and short-eared owls then the lapwing and curlew don't look quite so impressive. That is the trade-off.

Against these growing public protests, Amanda Anderson spent much of last year making the three-hour train journey from her home near Bowland to London for meetings with the Department for Environment Food and Rural Affairs and other members of its 'hen harrier recovery group', which included the RSPB. She took on the newly created job of representing moorland owners a year ago, convinced she could find a bridge between apparently conflicting interests. All sides agreed that diversionary feeding (scattering dead chicks on the moorlands – room service for harriers) was a good way to reduce nesting hen harriers' predation of grouse.

A second way to reduce the impact of harriers on grouse – a method of forced migration known as brood management – proved more contentious. Unlike most birds of prey, which are territorial and fight each other over nesting and hunting grounds, the hen harrier nests close to other harriers. 'They pile in there together like footballers pile into a bath at the end of a match,' said Anderson. In 2013 there were just two harrier nests on Langholm Moor in Dumfries and Galloway, Scotland (an experimental site where harriers are protected), but in 2014 ten nests produced forty-seven fledged hen harrier chicks on the same 119-square-kilometre site. So many grouse-guzzling hen harriers thriving in the area meant the grouse population was reduced too far to sustain a commercial shoot.

Moorland owners, Anderson explained to me, wanted to be allowed to move hen harrier nests. Brood management would guarantee that if more than one hen harrier nested in any ten-square-kilometre area of grouse moor, government scientists would remove additional nests, raise the chicks in captivity and release the young birds into lowland areas. 'There would not be a feather on a hen harrier chick's head harmed,' said Anderson. This, she argued, was the key to stopping their persecution. Why would anyone harm hen harriers if they posed no risk to the grouse shooting industry? 'It just needs the RSPB to give it a try.'

In the recovery group's final meeting of 2014, however, it became very clear that the RSPB was not willing to give it a try. It refused to countenance moving nests until there was an end to the illegal killing of hen harriers and their population had recovered. It would be 'ludicrous', said Blanaid Denman, to remove the nests of a bird that barely exists, just to placate grouse shoots. RSPB negotiators expressed their fears about the long-term implications: if nests of one of the rarest breeding birds in England were removed and the chicks reared in captivity, which rare species would landowners want to control next?

In the weeks after the latest stalemate, these fears seemed to be borne out by a gamekeeper seeking permission to protect the pheasants he breeds by 'controlling' buzzards. That case will be decided in the high court later this year. A rather eccentric populist-aristocratic campaign called You Forgot the Birds has also been launched against the RSPB led by the former cricketer Ian Botham, claiming that the charity neglects small songbirds in its veneration of birds of prey. 'More and more people are realising that the hen harriers' biggest enemy is the RSPB – not rogue gamekeepers,' Botham told the *Mail on Sunday* in November after the charity restated its opposition to moving nests. Hen harrier campaigners including Mark Avery were convinced that these were not the authentic concerns of bird-lovers but the increasingly rattled shooting industry: Botham runs a grouse shoot in North Yorkshire – the *Mail on Sunday*'s editor-in-chief, Paul Dacre, also owns a grouse moor in Scotland.

The two sides were so polarised it was no surprise when moorland owners and the RSPB failed to reach an agreement at their meeting in November.

When I contacted RSPB investigator Howard Jones in late December for news on the loss of Sky and Hope, he was driving north to investigate another case of raptor persecution. 'Unfortunately we've had no further information,' he said. 'It's very frustrating.' At least, he added, Sky and Hope's siblings, Highlander and Burt, who had also been tagged, were still on the wing, exploring the uplands of Dumfries and Galloway, the Yorkshire Dales, the Lake District and the South Pennines. 'We hope they'll make it through the winter and breed next summer,' said Jones.

Back in Bowland, Stephen Murphy was close to finishing his PhD. His satellite tags had provided vivid new information of the remarkable distances travelled by these unpredictable predators during their brief lives. When I called, he was still buzzing after another day on the chilly moors, seeking out his birds. But when I asked if things had improved or worsened in the decade since his studies began, his natural exuberance once again deserted him.

'If anything, it's changed for the worse,' he said:

> The keeper sees the harrier now as not just the thing that can eat their grouse but can upset their day-to-day life. With the harrier comes what they call 'the pig circus' – us lot, the RSPB, the birders, the wildlife-crime copper. By focusing on the harrier we forgot about the generic landscape – what happens here and what's made the harrier come here in the first place. We wanted to make it a harrier reserve by stealth. Even when we had fourteen pairs here, the RSPB still wanted more, instead of dispelling the myth that the harrier could take gamekeepers' livelihoods away.

Grouse moorland is 'the best and the worst place for the hen harrier,' added Murphy. 'These birds span the whole range of human emotions. They inspire love and hate. There's not many birds that do that.'

2015

*

In 2020 the hen harrier recorded its best breeding success in England – sixty chicks fledged from nineteen nests – since Natural England began working on the bird's recovery in 2002. This success was hailed by supporters of 'brood management', whereby chicks are removed from some nests on grouse moors, reared in captivity and released elsewhere, as vindication of their scheme. The first 'trial' brood management intervention occurred in 2019 and brood management is licensed until 2021. The Natural England scheme has been disavowed by most conservation charities, including the RSPB. Hen harriers continue to be widely persecuted: in September 2020 a satellite-tagged bird called Harold disappeared from a grouse moor on the Yorkshire Dales.

2021

Don't knock whale selfies

When a sperm whale was washed up on the Norfolk coast, the great polymath Thomas Browne raced from his home to inspect the animal. Braving an 'abominable scent', Browne took samples and roasted some flesh in an attempt to discover the secret of the 'oyl' or *spermaceti* after which the whale is named.

The seventeenth-century scientist wasn't the only disrespectful whale poker. A 1602 engraving by Dutch artist Jan Saenredam depicts crowds around another stranded whale: people clamber on it; one holds up a toddler to see it better. Our curiosity when these deep-sea mammals are washed into our shallows is timeless. But our condemnation is a very modern phenomenon.

There has been anger over the fact that a few people took smiling selfies by three sperm whales found dead on Skegness beach this weekend. Particular rage has been directed against a dad and his toddler son, grinning together, in front of a mighty jaw. The authorities erect cordons and warn that dead whales are a health risk but these dead creatures still apparently made Skegness as busy as a bank holiday. In Hunstanton, where a fourth whale distressingly died on Friday night, hundreds of people clambered over rocks to view it. A fifth washed up yesterday in Wainfleet.

I think it's heartening that we are still so curious about a dead whale – it would be more tragic if one was stranded and no one took a look. What if that smiling toddler's cetacean encounter bequeaths a lifelong love?

Obviously we shouldn't spray 'CND' on a whale tail (as has happened in Skegness) or ride the carcass (as people did on a minke whale washed ashore in Barry in 2009). It is right that only scientists are allowed to cut away the jaw or flesh to discover why these animals died. But can't we admire these whales without inhibition? The reason we are expected to behave in the presence of a dead whale with the same decorum as when attending a funeral is because the whale is such a powerful symbol of the harm we are inflicting on our wild world.

As Hugh Aldersey-Williams writes in *The Adventures of Sir Thomas Browne in the 21st Century*, whale strandings were considered an ominous symbol of squandered riches 400 years ago. 'We read a different loss,' he writes, 'the loss that we are inflicting upon nature, and the loss that this in turn threatens to inflict on our own species. The vast, ungainly mammal, crashing blindly round the planet, is us.'

2016

Britain's last lion tamer

The last lion tamer in Britain is waiting to meet me outside a pub called the Showman in the West Midlands town of Bloxwich. If I'm expecting a moustachioed impresario – charismatic, bullwhip-wielding and perhaps a little shifty – I'm confounded. With neat, slicked-back hair and a healthy glow, Thomas Chipperfield looks more like a young footballer.

Earnest, modest and recognisably belonging to the twenty-first century, he is an unlikely ambassador for what many see as the ultimate anachronism: big cats performing in a circus ring for paying punters. In the year that circus celebrates its 250th birthday, political parties are striving to outbid each other on animal welfare. Labour has pledged to outlaw wild animals in all circuses; the government has just committed to banning them in England by the middle of January 2020. Scotland prohibited them last year and Wales is looking to do the same. The issue would no doubt be on the agenda in Northern Ireland if there were a functioning assembly. A government consultation found that 94.5 per cent of the public favour outlawing wild animals in circuses, as happens in more than forty other countries.

Against this tide of public opinion stands Chipperfield, twenty-eight years old, who this year hopes to obtain a circus licence to enable him and his father to take his 'big beautiful boys' Tsavo and Assegai on the road in England again.

'Britain's last lion tamer? I owe that to the newspapers. It has a very romantic ring to it, but no, I prefer "big-cat trainer",' says Chipperfield. 'There are these pre-conceived notions of what animal circus is – this archaic Victorian practice with bullwhips cracking. The image of the lion tamer constantly prodding the lion in the face is not an accurate reflection of what animal training is today. The circus has evolved with every other animal-related industry.'

Chipperfield comes from a long line of animal trainers. His ancestor James Chipperfield displayed his menagerie at the frost fair of 1684 on the frozen Thames, nearly a century before showman and entrepreneur Philip Astley opened the first modern circus – a twelve-metre ring filled with jugglers, acrobats, clowns and equestrian stunt riders – on the marshes of London's South Bank in 1768. In the 1950s, Chipperfield's Circus packed out its 6,000-seat tent, featuring more than 200 animals, from elephants to polar bears. Chipperfield's great-uncle Jimmy pioneered the drive-through safari park.

Chipperfield was raised with wild animals, growing up in Ireland, where his father, Tommy, presented big cats in a circus. Bears, lions, tigers, baboons, snakes and alliga-tors were an everyday part of his childhood. He made his circus debut aged eleven, with two alligators. He trained them to jump on a box by the ringside and give the audience a pleasurable scare. Aged fifteen, he graduated to putting his head inside their open mouths.

He dropped out of his correspondence course GCSEs to concentrate on training big cats. 'I'm probably one of the least educated people you've ever spoken to,' he says. The circus, however, teaches its own lessons. 'It's an extraordinary . . . even to call it a world wouldn't do it justice – it's its own universe,' he says. 'When you're travelling in the circus, you're exposed to so many different people. I've worked with everybody from Cossacks to Shaolin monks.' It's given Chipperfield the wide-ranging reference points of an autodidact, and he cites everyone from psychologists and zoologists to writers such as Christopher Hitchens in his ceaseless debates with animal-rights activists.

Chipperfield obtained his lions from a private collector in 2011 when they were seven months old and the size of Alsatians. His dad has always supported his passion for the circus. 'The only thing he's said is: "You don't need male lions – they are hard work." Of all the big cats, they are the hardest. They are easy because they are so chilled but, because they are so chilled, they exhaust you working with them.'

He trains them daily. How? 'The long answer would be I've applied B. F. Skinner's theory of operant conditioning,' says Chipperfield. 'It's repetition and reward. The most effective way to encourage a behaviour is encouragement. Verbal praise is very strong. If an animal likes you, that can be more effective than a piece of chicken.'

YouTube videos of Chipperfield's method show him using both his voice and a piece of meat on the end of a stick. One, from six and a half years ago, shows him training his young maneless lions to sit on a raised seat. Another, from his 2015 tour, reveals his now splendidly maned lions lying down, rolling, sitting up and jumping, albeit with an occasional grudging rumble. Chipperfield holds a bamboo cane in his left hand and a riding whip in his right. The cane 'serves as an extension of my limb and if they are getting a bit cheeky they will bite that,' he says.

And they do. The whip isn't used to strike his animals, he says it's to draw them towards him in the way that a house cat will follow a dangling string. There's lots of verbal repetition, like a patient walker to their large, disobedient puppy. 'Good boy, Tsavo, good boy. Quick, here, Tsavo, good boy. On your place, good boy.' Circus training traditionally uses French and German commands, too, so there's, '*Allez*, Tsavo.' After a final man–lion kiss, Tsavo gets his reward of meat.

Has he ever hit a lion? 'The only way that would be remotely justifiable would be in a life-or-death situation, but that's not training. If I was in a position with a lion where I had to be physical, I've obviously made mistakes somewhere.' He doesn't punish them, either. 'If a lion is actively misbehaving, you don't go in all guns blazing, because it's not proportionate, it's not necessary and it builds up feelings of resentment that make it counterproductive,' he says. 'You work with them in a very slow, controlled way. You don't intrude on their space; you let them learn at a pace that's comfortable for them.'

He shows me photos of Tsavo and Assegai on his phone, the way a proud parent might of their children. They look magnificent. 'As Linnaean specimens, as physical specimens, they are perfect – they are big without being obese, their backs are straight, they don't have hunchbacks, and they are not cow-hocked or bow-legged.' Their personalities are quite different: Assegai, he says, is more reserved than Tsavo. 'I can still work with him inside the arena, but with Tsavo I can kiss him and hug him, I can stand next to him and scan his microchip. I'm working on Assegai but it's just taking more time; he hasn't come out of his shell in the way his brother has.'

Is he very attached to them? 'Oh yes. I work with animals because I like animals. Aside from the fact that I'm fascinated by their behaviour, I like animals' honesty. People always have agendas, they are quite self-serving, and by habit not upfront, whereas an animal will always let you know of their feelings. That's quite refreshing. There's that raw honesty.'

Chipperfield does not think that animal-rights campaigners are honest in their portrayal of wild circus animals. He argues that extremists are not interested in improving welfare, but seek an 'animal apartheid' whereby humans cannot even have animals as pets. 'Saying things like: "Circus animals perform unnatural or demeaning, degrading or embarrassing actions" – there's no evidence animals feel those emotions,' he says. 'If you were to analyse [an animal's] behaviour or try to empathise with them, you start from their point of view, not your own. Any animal trainer will tell you that. You have to understand how they are observing the situation, not how you observe it. That's important to take into account when talking about animal welfare.'

Eighteen months ago the group Animal Defenders International took photographs of the farm where Chipperfield kept his animals; it became a tabloid expose of 'cramped cages' with claims that the big cats' 'spirits [were] broken by their miserable living conditions'. But there was no suggestion the conditions were illegal. The upset that this caused his landlord and neighbours is the reason Chipperfield gives for politely declining our request to photograph him today with his animals. Chipperfield's lions are licensed under the Dangerous Wild Animals Act; an inspector checks their housing and welfare at least twice a year. 'But they come down more often than that,' he says. 'They can check at any time, and they do.' To put on a show, he must also obtain a circus licence, which requires several more inspections each year. Animal-rights activists say a piece of paper doesn't guarantee animal welfare. 'That's not a valid argument when you are scrutinised as much as a circus is,' responds Chipperfield.

When he moved to England in 2013, he and his father joined a circus that already held a wild animal licence.

Chipperfield's animal housing and show were then inspected: they satisfied Defra's inspectors. In 2015 he and his father toured Wales with their spin-off, An Evening with Lions and Tigers. But their application to tour England was turned down by Defra inspectors, who said their housing was too small. Chipperfield doesn't understand why the inspectors' view changed, but he has increased the space. 'Since then we've doubled the amount of space and we've only got three animals now,' he says. (He is also training a Bengal tiger called Altai.)

His enclosures are not as large as those in a zoo, but Chipperfield believes he provides more 'enrichment' than most zoos. 'Zoos focus on environmental enrichment and I do the same – a varied diet of raw meat, fresh foliage to play with, cardboard boxes – they love cardboard boxes – toys at their disposal. Even a different type of straw can provide subtle enrichment.' But, crucially, he argues, his animals get far more stimulus than zoo animals do.

Chipperfield is also a talented horse rider and trainer. Why not put on a show with horses and dogs, rather than wild animals with complex needs? 'We're very capable of meeting those complex needs and that's been determined by a number of scientific studies into animal welfare in circuses,' says Chipperfield. He cites an RSPCA study from the 1980s by Dr Marthe Kiley-Worthington, which found that the relationship between trainer and animal was the most beneficial human–animal relationship in any industry and that occupational illness among animals was less prevalent in the circus than in horse racing or zoos. Awkwardly, for a government seeking scientific evidence to ban wild animals in zoos, a 2007 Defra report concluded that animal welfare in circuses was no worse than any other captive environment. However, a scientific review for the Welsh government in 2015 judged that 'captive wild animals in circuses and other travelling animal shows do not achieve their optimal welfare requirements, as set out under the Animal Welfare Act 2006'.

We return to the question of whether a modern circus show could simply use domesticated beasts. Working with wild animals is 'a tradition, but I need more than that to justify that', acknowledges Chipperfield:

> I can't just say it's a tradition, because dog-fighting is a British tradition. What I do is a benign tradition. It doesn't have a negative impact on its subject. I feel it promotes a deeper understanding of the animals. Watching them work and showing their intelligence and abilities promotes a much greater appreciation of them. You go to a zoo and see beautiful animals in superb housing, but when you see them active, that changes things. It generates a passion for understanding and appreciating these animals much more than just seeing them lounging around.

But do people still want to watch lions in tents? One clip from Chipperfield's 2015 tour shows about ninety people in his modest 200-seater tent (he attributes quieter evenings that year to the Rugby World Cup). Whenever Chipperfield tours, he's pursued by animal-rights activists seeking to dissuade audiences, or venue owners from hosting him; he also receives death threats, and there's obviously no big money these days. It seems a melancholy prospect for one young man and his passion, if not his animals. Is he not disheartened by the public opinion against him? 'No,' he smiles. 'If nothing else, I'm stubborn.'

2018

Wolf Island:
can Åland learn to live
with its new carnivores?

Earlier this year, two unexpected guests crossed the sea to reach the largest of the Åland Islands, an archipelago of 6,700 mostly tiny isles between Sweden and Finland. The long, hard winter had frozen the Baltic more extensively than for many a year. A daring few among 30,000 Åland islanders drove their cars over the ice to Finland. In the other direction came two or possibly three wolves.

Europe's most feared carnivore was first seen padding over the sea ice by a ferry passenger in February. When islanders conducted their elk census during the March snows, they found wolf tracks heading west across the main island of Åland, a uniquely autonomous region of Finland. By the start of April a wolf had been sighted. By the end of the month, two were filmed together. In June a sheep was killed with ruthless precision, its skin covered in tooth marks – the work of a wolf, said experts. A few days later, a camera trap set over a carcass captured footage of the chief suspect returning to feed.

The Eurasian wolf is marching back into western Europe. It first flourished after the Soviet Union's collapse, slipping west into Poland, Finland and Germany and then wandering, recolonising densely populated landscapes where it had been absent for a century or more: northern France, Belgium, the Netherlands and Denmark. People with no memory of living alongside wolves are having to learn how to, because under European Union law the wolf is a protected species. Åland islanders exterminated their last wolf in 1883. But now they want to shoot wolves again, and they are prepared to challenge the EU to do so.

During endless summer days, these undulating islands look an improbable site for the wolves' latest conquest. Surrounded by bright blue water, most islands are minuscule, sun-kissed skerries, where stunted pines grow from crevices in the pink granite. They contain coves of grey sand, little wooden jetties and modest red wooden summer houses. But on the largest (50 km by 80 km) island there are also dark spruce forests, carpeted with blueberries. And, somewhere, a wolf or two.

Most people have retired to their summer houses but a few officials remain hard at work in the government building in the Åland Islands' tiny capital, Mariehamn.

'I am a lonely wolf here,' says Hanna Kondelin, laughing. Kondelin works for the island's environmental agency, overseeing its plan to tackle the wolves. Islanders, she says, are almost unanimously opposed to the wolves. The naturally secretive animals are now sighted almost every day. Are the wolves seen close to homes? 'It's impossible not to be close to houses and farms because this is a small-scale place,' she says. 'We don't have big forests like they do in Sweden and Finland.' She hears islanders criticising the government for inaction but she and her colleagues have spent 'many hours' drawing up a plan.

As a conservationist Kondelin admires the EU Habitats Directive, which provides legal protection for rare species, but it is now 'causing us quite a lot of headaches'. The Åland Islands must adhere to EU law and are thus legally obliged to protect their wolf population. Finland has run into trouble with the EU in recent years for permitting the seasonal killing of a significant proportion of its 150-strong wolf population. And now Åland's government wants to go further. It is proposing a system where islanders won't require a licence before shooting a wolf. Officials say a wolf can only be shot if there is an 'immediate' risk of an attack but, under its proposals, an islander could simply retrospectively claim a wolf threatened them or their live-stock. 'Our politicians are very much agreeing that wolves do not belong here,' says Kondelin. This autumn she hopes Finland's government will endorse Åland's plan. But couldn't this stance see the islands hauled before the European Court of Justice? 'It's even probable,' she says.

Alongside Kondelin is Robin Juslin, a bright young civil servant who heads up the island's hunting unit. 'In almost every household there is a hunter,' says Juslin. 'It's part of the subsistence lifestyle here that you rear your own meat and you hunt and fish.' But the European Com-mission took the islanders to court over Åland's spring shoot of 2,000 male eider ducks. Despite the court case, the islanders have restarted the spring shoot, and their dispute with the EU continues. 'People thought that the Commission would change their attitudes after Brexit and be more considered about local opinions, but it doesn't seem that way,' says Juslin:

> Now people in Åland are saying 'exit'. It comes up a lot in the wolf discussion. People in general favour the idea of the EU but the EU can't take into account the fact that we have had these strong traditions for hundreds of years, and haven't exterminated the bird population. They can't trust us to manage our own birds and wolves.

Juslin was visiting Denmark earlier this year when a video emerged of a wolf being illegally shot there. The Danish authorities, he says, 'have the same problems as everywhere else. Their government is controlled by the EU and can't do everything the way that they want. And they can't get local acceptance for the wolf.'

Beyond the tranquillity of Mariehamn, the islands stretch peacefully for miles. Pine forests grow on thick carpets of pale lichens; pine cones scattered on pink stone highways are undisturbed by cars. Small fields are squeezed between rocky outcrops; potatoes grow well in the sandy, grey soil.

Åland is a singular place. Islanders speak Swedish but in 1921 the League of Nations decided it would be part of Finland. Despite ties to Finland, Åland has its own stamps, its own internet domain (.ax) and its own flag, as well as more sunshine hours than anywhere else in northern Europe, a vineyard, a crisp factory and no McDonald's. It's within the EU but outside its tax border, and its economy is dependent on duty-free ferries. I take the ferry and people are drinking before 8 a.m. Disco dancing starts at 11 a.m. Many visitors to Åland only see the ferry terminal before hopping on the next ferry back to Sweden or Finland.

Åland's villages are little more than family farms. House martins dip over meadows beside pretty wooden windmills. By a big red barn, beside several long-dead Škodas half-buried in undergrowth, Berit Sjöberg's five sheepdogs lie obediently on the track. Sjöberg runs an organic farm with eighty ewes. This is her daily routine now: bringing her sheep from pasture to barn each evening because of the wolves. Like everywhere in northern Europe, small farms are going out of business or being agglomerated into large farms. Is it harder to make a living than twenty years ago? 'Twenty years!' exclaims Sjöberg. 'It's harder than last year.' This is her toughest season in farming: the grass hasn't grown during the north European drought, and now there are the wolves. 'I take the sheep inside every evening and put them out every morning. I thought it would be OK but I am quite tired. The sheep must be tired of this wolf situation too, because they are getting slower and slower every day. Only the dogs are happy.'

What do islanders think about wolves? Sjöberg puts her forefinger across her throat in a slitting motion. 'People who like the wolves and would like to have them will say that Åland is not the best place for the wolves,' she says. Conservationists argue that people will tolerate these carnivores if governments fund more shepherding, deterrents (such as big dogs) and wolf-proof electric fencing. But Åland's rocky terrain gives it paddocks that are small, wild and unfenceable. Ultimately, even if the government provides compensation for wolf kills, Sjöberg argues it never covers the cost of raising the sheep, or the value of its bloodline, or lost future productivity.

The wolf has been within 100 metres of Sjöberg's farm. 'I don't believe he will wait there and not take my sheep,' she says. Can't people learn to live alongside wolves, as they did in the past? 'Yes, maybe there were more predators in the past but there are more people now. We have to save the forest for the wolf but we can't have the wolf living like this, beside us.'

Near the village of Samuelstorp, where a wolf killed a sheep, Börje Jansson is tidying his open-sided wooden barn. 'I don't think the wolf belongs to Åland. It's too small,' he says. What should islanders do? His wife, Riitta, standing with their four-year-old grandson, is forthright. 'Shoot them,' she says. 'We haven't got the space. There is a house every 500 metres. There are no wild areas. I am scared when my grandchild is here and they attack our neighbour's sheep.' She thinks the wolf was here the previous day. 'Suddenly our two horses became uneasy. It must've been something, and then we had to take them in.'

The problem, say the Janssons, is that the EU's rules

are too broad for small and unusual places such as Åland. 'They can't make a rule and include every country because we're all so different, with different circumstances,' says Riitta. 'When the shooting season here starts in the autumn, if the wolves come, they are going to shoot it.'

Börje makes a grave face. 'It would then be murder,' he says. 'We can go to prison!' exclaims Riitta, eyes wide at what she sees as the ridiculousness of this situation. Is anyone in favour of the wolf? 'No, I don't think so,' Börje smiles. 'In Helsinki, maybe.'

Opposition to the Åland Islands' determination to shoot their wolves has indeed come from conservationists in Helsinki. 'There should be space for wolves on Åland, there are lots of roe deer for them,' says Sami Säynevirta of Luonto-Liitto, a Finnish wildlife charity. 'Killing a wolf should be a last resort. They should try other alternatives, like trying to scare a wolf away or building an electric fence. There should not be any exceptions for the Åland Islands.' Säynevirta suggests relocating the Åland wolves, ideally to Sweden, where ecologists are concerned that its wolf population is becoming inbred because the wolves' route from Finland to Sweden is blocked by Lapland. There are no wolves in Lapland because they are shot to protect reindeer-herding in the region.

According to Guillaume Chapron, associate professor in ecology at Sweden's University of Agricultural Sciences, our notion of the wolf as an icon of wilderness and best suited to wild areas is profoundly wrong. 'The reason we say the wolf is a creature of wilderness is that the only place where we couldn't easily eradicate them was in the wilderness. That was the only place they could survive. Then we made the emotional association – wolf equals wilderness. This artificially restricts the wolf, keeping it in areas where there are no people.'

In fact, says Chapron, we should consider the wolf to be like a carnivorous roe deer, or a big fox – it's an adaptable species that lives everywhere from Israeli deserts to the high Arctic. Wolf territories are dependent on food supply and the 750 square kilometres of the Åland Islands might be big enough for a few territories, according to Chapron. 'At the same time, I don't want to be more royalist than the king,' he says. 'If there were no people on these islands, we would have some wolves but would we really have more than two or three inbred packs? From an ecological point of view, it's difficult to imagine a thriving Åland wolf population. The future of the wolf here is probably regular solitary animals passing by in the winter.'

Chapron believes the relevance of Åland's struggle with the wolf is not whether its newcomers survive or are slaughtered but whether the islanders' approach becomes a template for the rest of Europe. Increasingly, he says, there is an assumption that predator populations have gone 'too far' and proactive measures must be taken before wolves damage our best economic interests. Germany's new coalition agreement includes a provision to ask the European Commission to review the protection of the wolf and bring about a 'necessary' population reduction. 'We don't want ideas from Åland recolonising Europe,' says Chapron. 'I don't see why we need to reduce the population size of the wolf. We are stuck on a very low baseline. We almost eradicated the wolf and now there's a modest recovery. Finally, we have a conservation success – predators are back. What's the first thing the politicians start to talk about? Reduce the population.'

Every islander I meet says the same thing: Åland is too small for the wolf. I'm sure I won't find a single pro-wolf islander. Finally, I reach the Åland Hunting and Fishing Museum near the faded wooden fishing sheds of Käringsund. Inside stands an enormous taxidermised elk, a wall of taxidermised eider ducks and a taxidermised wolf, commemorating the last beast shot on the islands. There's a net, too, that shows how the wolves were hunted to extinction here: a big hole was dug in the ground and covered by the net before a gang of islanders harried the wolves towards their trap.

'I think it's really interesting to find that people are still so afraid of the wolf, even though islanders haven't met them since 1883,' says the museum manager, Åsa Hägg. Amazingly, in this sea of dead animals, I find a wolf enthusiast. 'That's because I'm a biologist,' says Hägg. 'I think it's good that we get new species. Of course there are a lot of sheep farmers and I can understand their fear, getting sheep killed by the wolf.'

The last Åland lynx was shot in 1910 but in 2012 lynx were seen again on the island; a few now appear to be living here, preying on the island's thriving population of introduced wild roe deer. 'When the lynx came back, it was, "Oh God, it is going to kill all the roe deer,"' says Hägg. 'Now with the wolves it's, "Oh God, it is going to kill all the sheep."' She wonders whether her fellow islanders might live alongside wolves as Alaskans live alongside wolves and bears. But she fears they won't.

'I don't think a wolf population is possible with the farmers here,' she says. 'I have noticed the more we urbanise, the further we get from nature and the forest. In the past, they lived closer to nature and they knew it better. When we don't have knowledge about nature and the forest and the animals, we get more afraid.'

2018

*

DNA samples revealed that Åland's two wolves were siblings, born in the spring of 2017 north of Turku in south-west Finland. They were observed together on the islands in 2018. In 2019 only the male was seen. After he was reported to have taken a sheep, the government gave permission to shoot him. The wolf was killed in December 2019 and was found to have an earlier gunshot wound to his leg. The female was never spotted again, so was presumed to have been poached. The male is on display in Åland Museum. With global heating likely to reduce sea ice in the future, these wolves may be the last to naturally recolonise the islands.

2021

Requiem for the lost orcas

Two more public figures passed on last week: an impressive centenarian and community leader and a killer serving life imprisonment. They taught us about one of the planet's most intelligent creatures, and our own capacity for love and cruelty.

Granny, the matriarch of a wild orca population close to Vancouver and Seattle, may have been as old as 105. She was studied for forty years as researchers unravelled why orcas are one of only three mammals – with short-finned pilot whales and us – known to experience the menopause. Orca matriarchs, scientists learned, have a crucial role in guiding a pod, taking care of other females' calves, and even feeding adult males.

Granny was also a symbol of freedom during the most disastrous period of human–cetacean relations, dodging the 'capture kings' of the 1960s and 1970s who grabbed hundreds of killer whales and placed them in aquariums for our amusement.

Tilikum embodied this cruelty. Snatched from Icelandic waters aged two as recently as 1983, he was transported first to a Canadian marine park and then to SeaWorld in the US. One former trainer estimates this impressive alpha male was the largest cetacean ever to be held in captivity.

In one of the most carefully worded obituaries ever written, SeaWorld paid tribute to 36-year-old Tilikum's 'long and enriching life'. It was 'long' by the standards of captivity: analysis of 201 captive orcas found a median survival of just 6.1 years. And the 'enrichment' must refer to the human pleasure taken from inspiring encounters with this caged beast.

For Tilikum felt and also inflicted great pain. While in captivity, he was implicated in the deaths of three humans, including his trainer, Dawn Brancheau, in 2010.

One hundred million people have watched *Blackfish*, the documentary about Tilikum that takes the basic premise that if you were taken from your mother and reduced to a life chewing a concrete cage, you might become slightly psychotic. The film sparked a boycott of SeaWorld, and last year the 'theatrical killer whale experience' at its San Diego park closed. Orca entertainments continue at other SeaWorld parks, but the theme park operator has, crucially, ended its captive-breeding programme. Animal welfare groups want to release its orcas into sea pens, but there's no sign of that yet.

Granny's group of wild orcas number just seventy-one now, depleted by the capture kings, marine traffic and pollution. Britain's resident orca clan hasn't sired a calf for twenty years: scientists blame pollution. We are still far from making the wild a haven for these magnificent animals, as it should be.

2017

PART IV

Wild People

Attenborough's way:
the making of a British icon

In the late 1980s a meeting was convened at the BBC studios on Whiteladies Road in Bristol. Its participants – mainly amiable former public schoolboys named Mike – discussed the imminent retirement of a grey-haired free-lancer, who had been working with the BBC for almost four decades. 'We need to think about who is going to take over from David when this series is finished,' a junior producer, Mike Gunton, remembered his boss saying. David Attenborough was nearing sixty-five and putting the finishing touches to *The Trials of Life*, the third of his epic series about the natural world. These programmes had been broadcast around the globe. They had established a new genre, perhaps even a new language, of wildlife films. It was a fine legacy. Now it was time to go.

When Alastair Fothergill became head of the BBC Natural History Unit a few years later, executives were still worrying over the same question. The BBC director-general asked him to find a new David Attenborough. 'I remember thinking, that's not very sensible,' said Fothergill. 'He has always been this great oak tree under which it's been hard for a sapling to grow.' Today, Mike Gunton is creative director of the Natural History Unit. He still attends meetings on Whiteladies Road. But, three decades after the subject was first broached, finding the next David Attenborough is no longer on the agenda. 'We still haven't got an answer and I don't want one,' Gunton told me.

Attenborough was born on 8 May 1926, seventeen days after the Queen. And, like the Queen, he has become a symbol of stability in a turbulent world. It is hard to imagine a time before he was on our screens, affably engaging with sloths or giant turtles – partly because there wasn't. Television was invented the year after he was born, and only began to enter people's homes in the 1950s, when he was beginning his career. The first programme he made was watched by barely 10,000 people gazing at 405 flickering black-and-white lines on large boxes in living rooms in the south-east of England. This spring, his series *Our Planet* became Netflix's most-watched original documentary, seen by 33 million people in its first month. This autumn the BBC will broadcast *Seven Worlds, One Planet*, the nineteenth blockbuster series he has written and presented (add a zero and then some if also counting his pre-seventies series, short series and one-offs). The television executives who keep offering this 93-year-old freelancer bountiful employment agree that he is more powerful than ever.

In our fractured age, Attenborough is the closest we have to a universally beloved public figure. Last year, a YouGov poll found him to be the most popular person in Britain. The crowd at Glastonbury's Pyramid stage roared when he appeared on stage this summer. Viewers of *Love*

Island expressed outrage when one contestant declared she found his programmes boring. But Attenborough transcended national-treasure status some years ago. He is a truly global figure now. So many Chinese viewers downloaded *Blue Planet II* 'that it temporarily slowed down the country's Internet', according to the *Sunday Times*. The premiere of his new series, earlier this month in London, was broadcast live in South Africa and India, where rapt schoolchildren held up signs: 'Thank you for being you – Sir David A' and 'Sir David please come to India please'. As he moves from the White House to the World Economic Forum, urging presidents, businesspeople and the public to better protect the environment, he has come to be viewed, in a way he sees as overblown, as a keeper of humanity's conscience. 'That man who saves the world,' is how my seven-year-old daughter describes him.

'There will never be another David Attenborough. What makes him special, apart from all his personal qualities, is the timing of his life,' said Fothergill. When Attenborough began travelling the world in the 1950s, Fothergill noted, we were in a different geological epoch, the Holocene. Today, we live in the Anthropocene, an epoch defined by *Homo sapiens'* disruptive dominance of the planet. 'He's seen more of the natural world than any human being that has ever lived on the planet and he's also seen more change than anyone else. And he feels a responsibility.'

Despite the adulation, one charge has dogged Attenborough for decades. Critics argue that he has built himself a unique storytelling platform, only to fail to tell the most important story of all: the destructive impact of people on the planet. But one reason Attenborough has thrived on screen for seven decades is because he has always sensed how attitudes are changing, and moved with the times. For many years he maintained that his programmes must showcase the wonders of the natural world, and not speak of the human one. Now his newest series are filled with urgent messages about environmental destruction. Still, he resists the idea that he has changed; he prefers to say the public mood has transformed. After a lifetime of caution, almost despite himself, he has become a leading champion for action.

Attenborough fell in love with the natural world as a boy, exploring his neighbourhood in Leicester, looking for bugs, insects and amphibians. The middle child of three brothers, he grew up in a family of teachers. His father was principal of University College Leicester. His mother was a talented pianist. Education was revered. When I met Attenborough in the spring, he spoke of his boyhood passions – keeping tanks of tropical fish, venturing across northern England on his bike as a young teen, alone, in search of fossils.

To this day, Attenborough is still a collector – of tribal art, books and music – but although more than a dozen species are named after him, including a flightless weevil, *Trigonopterus Attenboroughi*, and a genus of dinosaur, *Attenborosaurus*, he is not an authority on natural history.

'Everyone thinks he's an amazing naturalist,' said the producer and writer Mary Colwell, who worked with him at the Natural History Unit in the 2000s. 'He isn't at all. He's a great storyteller. Everyone thinks he makes these programmes. He doesn't – but without him they wouldn't sparkle in the way they do.'

Attenborough agrees. 'Work and reputation get separated,' he said. Forty years ago he travelled around the world three times to make his groundbreaking series *Life on Earth*. He wrote the script, and every page of the accompanying book. 'But now I just write and speak the words. And people say: "What was it like when you saw that animal charging in?" And I say: "I wasn't there. Thirty cameramen worked on this thing." I'm given credit for things I don't do. I am grateful, but I'm also embarrassed.'

The only praise Attenborough will accept is for his skill as a storyteller. Robert Attenborough, David's son and an anthropologist at the University of Cambridge, remembered, as a teenager, 'watching him in the raconteur role as a host of a dinner party and admiring the skill with which he would tell a funny story. Sometimes they get slightly improved. That's something we used to tease him about. Of course he wouldn't do that, then or now, when making a serious point.'

Attenborough's storytelling has been honed over seven decades in television – and he is, above all, a TV man. After studying natural sciences at Cambridge, he married his university sweetheart, Jane Oriel, and ditched his boring junior publishing job for the glamorous new world of television. He started off behind the camera, after one of his first bosses decided his teeth were too big for a presenter. In 1954 Attenborough travelled to Sierra Leone with Jack Lester, London Zoo's curator of reptiles, to film a new series, *Zoo Quest*. The concept was simple: they would catch wild animals – their bounty from Sierra Leone included pythons, bird-eating spiders and their big prize, the bald-headed rockfowl – and bring them back to London to add to the zoo's collection. At the outset, Attenborough was the producer, director, sound man and animal-wrangler. He only ended up being the presenter because Lester was taken ill after the first episode.

Over the next few years, Attenborough's reputation grew. With his keen eye for the perceptions of his TV audience, he adapted cannily to a rapidly expanding industry. By the dawn of the sixties, as he admitted in his autobiography, *Zoo Quest* was looking 'increasingly antiquated'. He realised that it was time for a new approach. His next *Quest* series, filmed in northern Australia, eschewed attempts to bring animals home and instead depicted the cultural lives of Aboriginal peoples.

The trip to Australia inspired him to take a part-time postgraduate degree in anthropology, but he was tempted back to full-time TV work before he could complete it. In 1965 he became controller of BBC Two. At first he was considered lightweight, a youthful bit of eye candy, but he was soon hailed for his 'unexpected' success, as a *Daily*

Express profile put it. 'Everybody forgot I wasn't just a naturalist – I was always a trained TV man,' he told the paper in 1965. 'Hell, I love it. I watch everything. Straight home from the office – switch to BBC Two – see all my babies.'

As controller and then director of programmes for both BBC channels, Attenborough was a great innovator. In 1967 the government decided that BBC Two would be the first channel to switch to colour, and he set about exploiting this advantage. He put snooker on the channel and helped devise new forms of sport: one-day cricket and rugby league under floodlights. Programmes that emerged under his watch include *Dad's Army*, *Porridge* and *Monty Python's Flying Circus*. In 1972 he championed 'community programming' that included what has been described as the first sympathetic portrayal of transgender people on British television; he even suggested phone-ins to widen audience participation, years before they became a staple.

One of his lasting innovations was the all-you-need-to-know documentary, beginning with Kenneth Clark's *Civilisation*. Attenborough designed this epic, twelve-part series about the history of art and culture to showcase the glory of colour television. These monumental series became known as 'sledgehammers', and there followed uncompromisingly highbrow treatments of human evolution, economics and US history. But Attenborough believed the best subject for sledgehammer treatment was yet to come: natural history.

Attenborough's achievements at BBC Two made him a prime candidate for director-general. But he was tiring of the senior executive's life – desk-bound, constant meetings – and in the early 1970s he resigned. He yearned to be more creative, and had seen the thankless politics involved in the top job. 'The Archangel Gabriel couldn't do the DG's job,' he remarked to me.

Instead, he persuaded the BBC that he could create a *Civilisation*-style treatment of the evolution of plants and animals. *Life on Earth* was broadcast for fifty-five minutes on thirteen consecutive Sunday evenings in 1979. It 'started quietly', according to Mike Salisbury, a producer who worked on the programme. Despite the presence of a safari-suited Attenborough, binoculars around his neck, skipping between exotic locations, the early episodes often feel like a lecture with moving pictures. Our handsome presenter tries to make the best of diagrams of DNA, micro-organisms and 200-million-year-old fossils. 'A whole lot of worms have left this delicate tracery of trails in what was mud,' he enthuses in the Grand Canyon. Salisbury chuckled at the difficulty of bringing this to life on television: 'Fossils, for God's sake. They don't even move.'

But as its epic story slowly unfolds, the series warms up. The writing is often superb: 'Four million animals and plants in the world,' says Attenborough, 'four million different solutions to staying alive.' The penultimate episode, on primates, features the first memorable Attenborough 'two shot', where he appears alongside another animal. He joins a grooming session among mountain gorillas in Rwanda, and still has the presence of mind to whisper: 'There is more meaning and mutual understanding in exchanging a glance with a gorilla than any other animal I know.' Although some facts have changed – we now know there are more than eight million species – the series stands the test of time.

For old-timers at the BBC, history is divided into before and after *Life on Earth*. 'We hadn't realised what a game-changer it was going to be,' said Salisbury. 'By the end there were fourteen million people watching it.' The series established what television executives call the "blue-chip" natural history blockbuster. While the BBC has relinquished its dominance over most genres, it remains the pre-eminent maker of natural history programmes, according to Fothergill. So much of that 'is down to David', he said. Much imitated, these blockbusters are still a huge global export: the BBC will not reveal what profit, if any, these series make, but *Planet Earth II* and *Blue Planet II* were sold to more than 235 territories.

After the success of *Life on Earth*, Attenborough spent much of the 1980s completing a triumvirate of blue-chip behemoths, with *The Living Planet* exploring ecology and *The Trials of Life* revealing animal behaviour. From Natural History Unit veterans such as Salisbury to colleagues today, everyone paints the same picture of Attenborough 'in the field': a team player, energetic, curious, without vanity, funny, not suffering fools and preternaturally lucky. Everyone has a story about him joining a crew that has lucklessly staked out a target species for two weeks, only for that creature – whether Hungarian mayfly or polar bear – to suddenly hove into view. 'I don't like presenters on the whole. I don't think they are particularly nice people,' one producer told me. But Attenborough was different. 'He's not an ego on a stick. He doesn't need to be now.'

By the early 1980s Attenborough was recognised wherever he went. But he was not yet a global superstar. Until recently, when Attenborough's series were shown on US television, broadcasters would replace his narration with voices they thought an American audience would prefer. In 2010, when *Life* was broadcast in the US, Oprah Winfrey was the narrator.

Viewers tend to assume Attenborough writes every word he says on screen, while TV people think his lines are written for him. The truth is somewhere in between. Attenborough's scripts are written by production teams, but he is an unusually rigorous editor and rewriter. Even today, Attenborough rewrites each script to fit his own turn of phrase and checks for accuracy. When filming, according to Mike Gunton, Attenborough does not learn his lines precisely. 'He looks at it and comes back and says: "What do you think if I say it like this?" His turn of phrase – it's got such power. He has the same genes as his brother,' – meaning Richard, the Oscar-winning actor-director, who died in 2014. 'I've often said he's as good a performer as his brother,' Gunton said.

'You change the pace, you change the timbre, you change the mood, and the commentary has organic flow,' Attenborough told me. 'If the last sentence ended ten seconds ago rather than one minute ago, you start in a different kind of way. I don't think other people do that. It's a craft, and I quite enjoy it, actually.'

By his own admission, it took some time for Attenborough to realise just what a threat humankind posed to the environment. When he was younger, he said, people knew of species that had gone extinct, such as the Arabian oryx and the dodo, but 'you didn't perceive it as a major ecological problem. And in point of fact, let's be honest, if the Hawaiian goose disappears, the world doesn't actually judder in its revolutions.' It wasn't until *Life on Earth* that he came to see that species decline was systemic and 'actually the disappearance of the giant panda represented some major change'.

For most of his life, Attenborough's environmentalism has been the old-fashioned, off-screen variety. Ever since he was asked, as a bit of a joke, to open a visitor centre at a nature reserve by the village of Attenborough in Nottinghamshire, in 1966, he has given rousing speeches at hundreds of events for nature charities across Britain. It is hard to find a visitor centre at a Wildlife Trust nature reserve that does not feature a silver plaque declaring that it was 'Opened by Sir David Attenborough'.

To his critics, these good deeds do not make up for what they see as Attenborough's great failing as a broadcaster. Putting the case for the prosecution, the journalist George Monbiot has accused Attenborough of 'knowingly creating a false impression of the world' by making films that underplay humanity's impact on the planet and failing to identify the forces driving mass extinction and the climate crisis. Another environmentalist told me that Attenborough possesses irreproachable integrity, but his long silence on extinction and global warming in his television work has contributed towards a popular knowledge deficit.

Richard Mabey, a naturalist who worked in television before almost single-handedly reviving British nature writing, has long made a version of this argument. 'When *Life on Earth* came out in 1979, and *The Living Planet* five years later, I was concerned about the fact that this wasn't a place I recognised,' Mabey told me. 'What one saw was magnificent, but it was what one didn't see; no humans, no environmental degradation. It was like an idealised biosphere on another planet.' Once, in the early 1980s, Mabey bumped into Attenborough at a lunch. 'I asked him, genuinely curious, why this picture of the planet was so devoid of environmental strife? He said, very simply: "We wouldn't have got the viewers, they would have turned off." I was quite distressed.'

TV executives repeat Attenborough's argument today. A blue-chip series costs millions to produce and requires global funding. BBC programme-makers are terrified of being seen as 'political'. At the launch of *Seven Worlds, One Planet*, executive producer Jonny Keeling insisted that it's not 'preachy'. As Miles Barton, a long-standing Attenborough producer, put it: 'The more preachy you are, the lower the numbers are going to be.' The lower the numbers, the less money the series will make, the less funding for the next. Mabey understood this equation. 'Attenborough has power over the audience,' he said. 'I'm not sure he has power over the money men. My worry about him not including environmental disasters in his early series may have been less his personal choice than corporate pressure.'

As a young producer, it was drilled into Attenborough that private convictions must not be aired in public. He has always upheld the values of the liberal establishment – avowedly internationalist and anti-populist in his veneration of expertise – and taken the traditional BBC line on party-political neutrality. 'I'm not a political chap, I know about bugs,' he protested when asked about Brexit in 2017. (When pushed, he revealed that he voted to remain.)

Like most in the Natural History Unit, Attenborough has also long defended his work with a 'show the wonders and then people will care' argument. When we spoke earlier this year, Attenborough put it more bluntly: 'People ought to be concerned because they think the natural world is important. If they know nothing about the natural world they won't care a toss.'

To a sympathetic observer, the lack of campaigning

films in Attenborough's oeuvre might look like a canny political calculation about the most effective way to shift popular opinion over the long term. But it may just reflect his temperament. Attenborough praises more outspoken broadcasters, such as Chris Packham. 'Chris is to be admired, because he would sacrifice his career in the name of something that he thought was important. And more strength to his elbow,' he said. But that is not Attenborough's way. He acknowledged that he would 'probably not' ever risk getting banned from the BBC.

In public, he has always been reserved. Journalists have often noted his refusal to emote in interviews. This is not his private self at all, says his son. 'I regard him as an exception to all the rules of English maleness,' said Robert. 'In personal life, he's not shy with his emotions. I would not see him as a classic English male in that sense – he's a warmer, more expressive person than that.' When Attenborough's wife, Jane, died twenty years ago, 'his grief was intense and fully expressed', remembered Robert.

Even so, his public reticence and natural caution have made the final stage of his career all the more striking.

In November 2004, nearly twenty years after the phrase 'global warming' was first coined, Attenborough attended a lecture in Belgium given by Ralph Cicerone, an American expert on atmospheric chemistry. The graphs that Cicerone presented, showing the rise in global temperatures, finally convinced Attenborough, beyond any doubt, that humans were responsible for the changing climate.

Attenborough insists he was never a sceptic about man-made climate change; just cautious. Even after Cicerone's lecture, he still believed his job was to make programmes about wildlife. He worried that people would think he was setting himself up as an expert on climate science.

Attenborough's output changed, however. This distinction may mystify those beyond the Natural History Unit, but its film-makers distinguish between natural history and 'environmental' film-making. The former focus on animal or plant biology and behaviour; the latter address environmental issues. Attenborough's 2006 BBC two-parter, *The Truth About Climate Change*, was his first to address global warming explicitly. Three years later came *How Many People Can Live on Planet Earth?*, which reflected his long-standing concern over the rising human population. This year came a new Attenborough BBC documentary, *Climate Change: The Facts*. Next year, another, *Extinction: The Facts*.

When I interviewed Attenborough this spring, his Netflix series *Our Planet* had not yet been released. It was billed as a significantly more pressing appeal to save the world, and Fothergill, its producer, was keen to assert its environmental credentials. Attenborough, meanwhile, seemed equally keen to assert that it wasn't so different to his earlier work:

If you forget the flummery and the propaganda and the press releases, what does it do? It shows the most breathtaking sequences you've ever seen – beauty, wonder, spectacles filmed in a way that you never saw before, with drones and in fabulous colour, with surging music, and so on, and then at the end, it says it's all in danger. That's what they do. I'm not ashamed of that. I think it's a perfectly valid thing.

But the strange thing, when you sat down to watch *Our Planet*, was that it did not match Attenborough's billing. Each of its eight episodes began with him discussing the moon landing. 'Since then, the human population has more than doubled,' his voiceover continued. 'This series will celebrate the natural wonders that remain, and reveal what we must preserve to ensure that people and nature thrive.' The series returned, relentlessly, to this manifesto. It explained the importance of rainforest for a habitable climate, and almost no stunning sequence of wild animals came without Attenborough emphasising the precariousness of their continued existence. Likewise, in *Seven Worlds, One Planet*, the environmental messages are no longer restricted to an appeal at the end of each episode. The first story about the impact of climate change comes sixteen minutes into the opening episode. Throughout, there are sequences that highlight the human actions – climate change, pollution, habitat destruction, poaching – causing earth's sixth great planetary extinction.

This shift in Attenborough's work reflects a response by film-makers, and particularly the Natural History

Unit, to accusations that they have pulled punches in the past. Yet, as his protestations suggest, being 'environmental' has not come easily to Attenborough. 'I don't think he's naturally an environmentalist at all,' said one former colleague. 'He's not eloquent when it comes to environmentalism. But you can't take away his intelligence, his understanding of the zeitgeist and his integrity.' According to the source, Attenborough was initially reluctant to include the plastics story in *Blue Planet II*, worrying again that 'it would be a turn-off'. If that was the case – and senior BBC executives deny it – by the time the series was broadcast in 2017, Attenborough was fully behind the plastics episode. 'David really led on the plastics thing, talking about plastics before the series went out,' said the producer Miles Barton.

At ninety-three, Attenborough is more in demand than ever. Susan, his daughter, keeps a watchful eye on him and tries in vain to scale back his speaking engagements and charitable commitments. The BBC want him to narrate *Planet Earth III*, but he will be ninety-six when the time comes. Meanwhile, he devotes most of his stamina to appealing for radical action to tackle the climate crisis and biodiversity loss. In Poland, at the UN climate-change summit in 2018, he was chosen to represent the world's people in addressing leaders from almost 200 nations. At Davos, in early 2019, he questioned the wisdom of perpetual economic growth: only 'a madman or an economist' would cling to this notion, he argued.

Earlier this month, Attenborough launched *Seven Worlds, One Planet* with an exhausting round of interviews to journalists from six continents, while a police helicopter buzzed over Extinction Rebellion protests on the streets of London. At the premiere, when I asked if he was comfortable about his films inspiring Extinction Rebellion, he replied sharply: 'Extinction Rebellion doesn't have the monopoly of people who care about the planet. That's a section of people who care about the planet, but everybody should. We're citizens of the planet. We have the dominance of it and we ought to care about it.'

Attenborough has been supportive of school climate strikers, and likes to suggest that the planet now belongs in younger hands. He remains visibly fascinated by all kinds of life and social change around him, but instinctively cleaves to the role of his lifetime – as an interested observer, watching a new generation clamouring for environmental change. 'I've had my share of the platform. I'd be better off standing apart from it and trying to be as dispassionate as I can,' he told me last week. 'I'm old and they are young. They have their own techniques and their own ethos. It's their world, not mine, that's for sure.'

2019

The hermit of the Cotswolds:
Stephen Grendon

When he was six, Stephen Grendon was plucked from his school in rural Gloucestershire to play a young Laurie Lee in the television adaptation of *Cider With Rosie*. He could not understand how he would fit inside the box when he was told he would be on TV. Now he doesn't have one at all. 'There's the telly.' He points through the open window of his stone hut. 'If I hang a feeder out there I can sit and watch the birds all winter and all spring.'

Bespectacled and aged forty-one, the former child star is a modern-day hermit. He lives on an overgrown third of an acre tucked in a valley in the Cotswolds. He has called his hut Hermit's Corner. It measures 4.25 metres by 5.8 metres, has a corrugated iron roof, three stone walls and a fourth made of creosoted wood that frames his window. Last week he travelled to the high court in London to argue his right to stay in his home. But modern society does not really do hermits and Grendon lost his case. Now he faces eviction.

'I've always been interested in being close to the ground,' he says, sipping tea in the cool of his hut. He was raised nearby, the son of a solidly middle-class family, who grew their own vegetables, kept chickens and sparked his interest in self-sufficiency. His child acting faltered in the early 1970s after he played Boy Roger in *Swallows and Amazons* – '"It's a shark! It's a shark!" That was me.' He tried horticultural college and later married, but a house and bills induced an intense claustrophobia. 'I got into a panic, to a point where you freeze and can't do anything,' he says. Depression set in. He left his wife and two daughters and, in 1994, purchased his secluded plot by a wood from a pair of naturists for £1,000.

The hut was already there, although he lived in it without a window for years. He brought in an old wood-burning stove, a gas hob, a musty sofa and a set of drawers without a chest to slide them in. Shelves line the walls and are filled with fossils and pheasant feathers and a photograph of dew on grass. Mostly there are fading pink Ordnance Survey maps and books, which lean against a painted wooden bookend with 'D-A-D' written on it: *Grasses, Sedges and Rushes in Colour*; *A Guide to Snails*; *Celtic Art*; *The Mythology of the British Isles*; *The Teachings of Don Juan* by Carlos Castaneda. He keeps an old CD player to play his reggae, ska, punk and dance albums.

Grendon does not completely cut himself off from the world, but he finds it helpful to meditate about 'the madness we're in' for two hours each morning after listening to Radio 4. 'People think about hermits being reclusive or religious. Some hermits had no contact with people, but others were stationed next to crossroads on pilgrims' routes. The Greek god Hermes is the god of communication,' he explains.

For a decade he has treated his depression himself, by living simply and recording every bird, snail and dragonfly that crosses his path. 'I've got a fairly analytical mind. When I got here I wanted to identify everything in my garden – the plants, the birds, the frogs and the more obvious insects. It all goes into a filing system.' He writes every species he identifies on an oblong piece of card. Several hundred are stored in a wooden box.

From May to September Grendon sleeps outside, lying on an old carpet draped over two wooden pallets under an orange tarpaulin. By his bed is a Collins book of birds and a grubby yellow bowl with a small mirror, an old razor and soap on a dish. Firewood is stacked in one corner of his plot. There is a cherry tree and raspberries, blackcurrants and strawberries. Apples and plums are ripening. A birdbox hangs from a damson tree. Eleven jam jars stand in the sun waiting for the gooseberries he is stewing in a large cauldron.

A contemporary hermit makes some concessions to modernity. Grendon has a mobile phone and electricity (which he pays for). But he does not have plumbing or a toilet. A spring pops up in the hedge bordering his land. This is his running water and fridge: a carton of cream is propped under the trickle to keep it cool. He would like a composting toilet but still digs a small hole in a wild corner of his land at dawn and covers it with soil at dusk. He survives on £80 income support each week. A few friends and a mental health visitor call on him.

There is much about Grendon's life which is sad. His children used to love coming to visit him in the wilds, he says, but he has fallen out with his ex-wife and can't see them. His depression, however, has been better this year. He has been busier, building a beautiful dry-stone wall to shield his front door from the lane.

He keeps a nature diary, recording the temperature, rainfall, wind direction and how fast the spring is flowing. Monday's entry is written in capitals: 'HEATWAVE.' Tuesday's is: 'EVEN HOTTER TODAY.' In other years when he felt good, he has sketched plants and insects in intricate colour. He can tell his bad years by how few moth species he has made note of. Last year, there were barely a dozen; this year, there are scores. Two weeks ago, he cycled to the bookshop in Cheltenham eleven kilometres away and picked up a new guide to moths. 'It cost thirty quid and I've probably had my money's worth already,' he says.

Grendon frets about losing his temper in the world outside Hermit's Corner. Little things can trigger a terrible 'righteous anger' he has had since childhood. Something awful must have happened to him, he thinks. Here, among the purple thistles visited by bees and peacock butterflies, he can 'lose his worries'. Whether he has chosen or been driven to the balm of life outside an ordinary home, he can see virtue in it:

I sometimes wonder, 'Am I an escapist? Am I just running away from society?' No, I'm living what I believe in. I'm not consuming much from this planet Earth and I took this to court because I know it's not just me that this is about. I've been depressed and not very motivated but if you gave many people a third of an acre they would scrape a living together from it and they would be happier than on benefits in a town.

Our overconsumption is 'a collective burying of heads in the sand,' he says. 'I could turn that "Am I an escapist?" argument around: you're the escapists. These big motors that people go around in – it's like a blasphemy on the face of the earth. There are people without water and without food and we carry on with our shop, shop, shopping.'

After living quietly for several years (Grendon claims the farmer up the lane and the neighbour in a cottage 300 metres away didn't even notice he was there), Hermit's Corner came to the council's attention. In an area of outstanding natural beauty, Grendon was living against the rules. An enforcement notice was issued against him in 2004 because he did not have planning permission for its 'residential use'. Grendon argued that Cotswold district council could not remove him because his building had been a dwelling – he had lived there – for at least four years. A planning inspector disagreed. An appeal was rejected.

So Grendon went to the high court, which heard he

valued 'the simplicity of his unconventional lifestyle'. Mr Justice McCombe, however, upheld the planning inspector's rejection. Grendon's home 'simply did not have the physical attributes of a dwelling house, even with the claimant's modest requirements', he ruled.

Now the modern-day hermit must find a new way to legally prolong his stay or find a new home. He still hopes that, with legal help, he could apply for planning permission under 'exceptional circumstances', which would involve declaring that only he could live there and he could not pass it on to anyone else.

He understands that there have to be planning laws but argues there should be a law to allow truly low-impact dwellings, like his own. He has lived here lightly and yet he has no right to be here, whereas someone could perfectly lawfully chop down all the trees and install polytunnels on his plot, which would far more drastically transform this wild corner of the Cotswolds.

And Grendon fears for his health if he is forced into the straitjacket of mainstream society. 'I would end up being a cost to society – in prison or a mental institution. I've saved the authorities money – the council don't need to find me a flat. It feels as if they would prefer me to be completely reliant on them than go off and do my own thing and try to look after myself.'

2006

*

Unexpectedly, in 2008, Cotswold District Council allowed Grendon to continue to live at Hermit's Corner, on the understanding that the dwelling was for him alone and the site could not be developed or sold as a house. Around that time, a series of low-impact, self-built, environmentally friendly dwellings in Wales were given planning approval and the Welsh government introduced the 'One Planet' development policy. This formally allowed people to build low-impact developments on rural land where normal houses would not be considered, as long as they met stringent environmental, economic and social criteria. Small, sustainable alternative communities have grown up but it continues to be extremely difficult to live like Grendon, or build a truly sustainable, low-impact home, even in Wales. Many politicians continue to seek to use planning laws to thwart those who want to eschew a conventional house and our neoliberal way of life.

2021

The man who saves species: Carl Jones

The last surviving bird of prey on Mauritius seemed doomed. In 1974 there were only four Mauritius kestrels left in the wild and attempts to breed them in captivity were failing. Extinction was 'all but inevitable', in the words of Norman Myers, one of the world's leading environmental scientists.

Carl Jones, a biologist who arrived on the island in the 1970s as an idealistic 24-year-old, remembers his employers, the charity that became BirdLife International, instructing him to 'pull out elegantly' and leave the kestrel-saving to Mauritius government officials. 'That actually meant closing it down, because the Mauritians didn't have the resources or capacity for doing it,' he says.

What happened next on the island of the dodo is a source of inspiration in an age of extinction. Since 1970 humanity has wiped out 60 per cent of mammals, birds, fish and reptiles, according to WWF, and one in eight bird species are threatened with global extinction. But Jones rescued the kestrel from oblivion, increasing its numbers a hundredfold, before going on to save more species than probably any other individual. Now the chief scientist at Durrell Wildlife Conservation Trust, he has preserved many plant species and nine animals, including four other bird species that numbered fewer than twelve known wild individuals: the pink pigeon, the echo parakeet, the Rodrigues fody and the Rodrigues warbler. The 64-year-old has won the Indianapolis prize – the conservationists' Oscars – but he is not an international celebrity, perhaps because his thinking challenges the conservation establishment.

There are few better guides to the Anthropocene – the era of the sixth mass extinction, in which we live – but Jones sighs at that phrase. 'We definitely have to be aware of what's happening, but we can do a lot to reverse these trends. All species are saveable,' he says. Even obscure insects? 'I'm sure you can find examples where they are not saveable. I know this is very clichéd, but you've got to start with solutions, otherwise you do nothing.'

He is still infuriated by Myers' argument for wildlife triage – prioritising species more likely to survive at the expense of desperate cases. 'Where does it end?' Jones says. 'You can't save rhinos? You can't save elephants? There's no room in the modern world for Californian condors? The worst is: "We don't have enough money." How much money is there in the world and how much is wasted on trivial things? It's such a defeatist argument.'

How do you save species? 'It's very easy. It's no secret at all,' says Jones. We meet at the remote Welsh farmhouse he shares with his partner, his two children, a black-chested buzzard-eagle called Igle and countless skulls, remains and taxidermised animals, from giant tortoises and a huge grizzly bear to a polecat's penis bone. 'They talk to you after a while,' he says of his treasures. 'A specimen is a repository for an infinite amount of information. You've got to live with your specimens, your animals. They've got to be part of your life.'

Jones embraces E. O. Wilson's concept of biophilia, the human need to live intimately with other species. He has done so all his life and it has honed his hands-on approach to saving species. His fascination with animals began in his earliest moments – soothed by an owl's hoot in his cot – in rural Carmarthenshire, Wales. As a boy, Jones rescued injured wild creatures – badgers, owls, kestrels – and bred raptors in homemade cages. 'I knew that breeding birds was something very special. When I learned about the plight of the Mauritius kestrel, I thought: "I can do that."'

Jones challenges the classic conservation wisdom that we must first precisely understand the reasons for a species' decline and then restore its habitat. Instead, he argues that scientists must tweak the limiting factors on a species' population – food, nesting sites, competition, predation, disease – with practical fieldwork. 'If there's a shortage of food, you start feeding. If there's a shortage of nest sites, you put up nest boxes. You don't need endless PhD students studying a species for twenty years.' Conservation science, he argues, is often too remote. 'Do you sit back and monitor a sick patient or do you treat them and see what works? A lot of species have been studied to extinction.'

In Mauritius, he used traditional captive-breeding methods developed by his heroes – the conservationists

Gerald Durrell and Sir Peter Scott – 'cosseting them in captivity and encouraging them to reproduce'. He added new scientific methods to manipulate the birds' productivity such as 'double-clutching', removing a kestrel's eggs and hand-rearing the young to encourage females to lay a second brood.

Controversially, he also applied these techniques to wild birds, spending hundreds of hours camping beneath wild kestrel nests. 'The most important thing when you start to work with a critically endangered species is to know that species with great intimacy,' he says. He trained wild Mauritius kestrels to take white mice; supplementary feeding encouraged them to lay more eggs. 'By stealing those eggs and putting them in incubators, I could get them to lay second clutches. When I'd hatched eggs in captivity, I put some of the youngsters back in the wild and I fed the wild parents so they could look after them.'

Then, when he discovered that mongooses were raiding nests, he designed mongoose-proof nest boxes for safer wild breeding, trapped mongooses around nest sites and, if he encountered a mongoose during his fieldwork, killed it with his bare hands. His bosses were 'very sceptical', he says: 'Traditional conservation is all about preserving animals and being hands off. Here I was doing completely the opposite.' But his methods worked.

Jones worked on Mauritius throughout the 1980s and 1990s and still spends three months there each year. He used similar hands-on techniques to rescue the pink pigeon (now numbering 400 wild birds) and the echo parakeet (now 750) and worked with islanders on Rodrigues, 600 kilometres east, to restore lost forests, helping the Rodrigues fody and the Rodrigues warbler increase in number to 14,000 and 20,000 respectively. Some rarities still require 'supportive management', says Jones: the number of Mauritius kestrels has declined recently, although he is confident the population can be boosted with more nest boxes.

Many conservationists view 'single-species' conservation as an old-fashioned luxury in the twenty-first century. Jones argues that this is completely wrong. 'Working with species is a key to unlock all the problems that you see in the system,' he says. Restoring a species revives an actor that performs a function – grazing or scavenging – within an ecosystem. 'When you save an individual species you end up looking after the whole system.'

Jones's species-saving has led to the restoration of whole systems. Round Island, a once-verdant islet near Mauritius inhabited by unique reptiles including the Round Island boa and Gunther's day gecko, was reduced to a moonscape by goats and rabbits released by sailors. These invasive mammals were removed to allow the flora to recover. Surprisingly, however, native plants found nowhere else in the world then started to decline. Jones decided to put the Aldabra giant tortoise, from the Seychelles, on to Round Island. 'Everybody thought it was the worst idea in the world. They said: "You can't do this. Extinctions on islands are caused by exotic animals and you want to put exotic animals on islands!"' Jones stressed that he would be restoring the ecological role of extinct giant tortoises. Now, 600 tortoises roam Round Island and native plants such as the ebony tree are thriving again thanks to the tortoises' grazing and seed dispersal.

Jones thinks small islands are where we can begin to revive species. How would he revive Britain, one of the most nature-depleted countries in the world? After decades working overseas, the Durrell Trust is planning collaborative projects to revive British wildlife. Restoring 'ecological functions' with proxy species is an idea whose time has come: Konik horses are already used widely on nature reserves to mimic the grazing of extinct wild horses. One extinct European species is the great auk; Jones thinks a penguin species could be a proxy. 'We should seriously assess the ecology of the great auk to see whether or not there is an appropriate penguin we could release in the northern hemisphere as its ecological replacement. We could reactivate the lost ecological interactions of the great auk. It's a wacko idea, but it's a lovely idea.'

Jones advocates slow, consensual rewilding and hopes eventually to reintroduce extinct wildcats to Wales. 'If we bring wildcats to Wales, we'll do it very gently. We're not going to thrust it down farmers' throats. We'll do it by showing that wildcats won't have any profound effects on farming practices and might even be beneficial, reducing rodent numbers and medium-sized predators such as foxes.'

Small islands could be ideal laboratories for larger carnivores. 'I'm not necessarily saying we should put wolves and bears back into the Highlands, but we could certainly be thinking about putting them on some islands and large fenced areas.' He admits this is not perfect, but 'it's a way of getting them back into people's consciousness, about seeing the beneficial impact that these species can have on systems'.

He would like to use captive breeding to save the turtle dove, which could be lost from Britain within a decade. Big conservation charities, he argues, are 'very risk-averse' and hide behind landscape-scale conservation schemes.

'While you're doing big landscape stuff, the species can disappear and you can say: "Oh well, you know, these things happen,"' he says. 'There's a great reticence to do hands-on conservation in Britain. Think about your dying patient. You get in there and start looking after them, rather than standing back and watching them through binoculars.'

2018

Badger rhapsody: Brian May

The shrubbery rustles and shakes, then Brian May falls out of the rhododendrons, dusts himself down and stumbles towards five fox cubs at play in a clearing. In the landscaped gardens of his historic home in the Surrey hills, the Queen guitarist looks every inch the semi-retired rock star: huge curly hair on gangly frame, black trousers, immaculate white Pumas and a dangerously unbuttoned white shirt.

May has a plethora of projects to promote – every Queen album is being digitally remastered to celebrate the band's fortieth anniversary this year; next month he will tour the country with Kerry Ellis, who starred in his musical *We Will Rock You*; he has just played guitar on a new Lady Gaga track and a documentary he has made about the history of 3D will be broadcast on Sky. But instead, the 63-year-old musician and astrophysicist is crooning softly to the fox cub he has clutched to his chest.

In the state-of-the-art animal rescue centre May has built in his garden, the guitarist behind Britain's biggest-selling album (*Queen's Greatest Hits*) is currently nursing back to health 140 hedgehogs and half a dozen abandoned fox cubs. He is also fast becoming the public face of the campaign to stop a cull of badgers; proposed by the authorities to answer the concerns of farmers who are convinced the animals are infecting cattle with bovine TB.

Multimillionaire rock legends often dabble in fast cars, metal detecting or saving rainforests. Is May worried his anti-cull campaign will be dismissed as just another rock-star hobby? 'Hobby, hmmm,' he murmurs, treating the word with a quiet disgust:

> There aren't many people from rock music or entertainment who put the time in that I have . . . this has become a huge part of my life. I don't care what people say. I'm not doing it to make money. I'm not doing it because I want to be famous. Even if it was a 'hobby', why would I have that hobby? It could only be because I care about animals. This concerns us all. It's not just something that concerns farmers.

May, who simultaneously channels the ethereal other-worldliness of a long-term resident of planet rock with the precision of a professional scientist, came to this passion through blogging. He began his 'soapbox' before blogging was fashionable and although gentle and softly-spoken in person, he lets off steam online: his rants on subjects such as a review of Mika's album by the *Guardian*'s Alexis Petridis have led him to be dubbed the world's grumpi-est rock star. His intention, he says, is to discuss import-ant issues 'so if you want to call it being grumpy, yeah, but it's being concerned and trying to raise awareness of things which need to be fixed'. There are 'joyful' posts about music, astronomy and 3D on the soapbox, but May is most profoundly anguished about cruelty towards animals. The blog 'changed my life completely because it's a two-way communication', he says. 'I started talking about animals with people on the soapbox.'

May has never been an ordinary rock star. Helped by his father, he built his own guitar, Red Special, as a child. He abandoned his PhD on zodiacal light for fame with Queen but returned four years ago and completed it. He is a great friend of astronomer Sir Patrick Moore, with whom he has written *Bang!*, an accessible history of the universe.

His love of animals has been less well documented but 'it's always been there', says May a little defensively, highlighting his Queen song 'White Man' as an example. He promised himself 'if there was ever an opportunity in my life to make a difference for animals I would take it'. That opportunity came when someone contacted him online about a proposed cull of hedgehogs on the Scottish island of Uist. May was 'aghast' and successfully fought to have the hedgehogs transported to the mainland instead. 'When David Cameron started saying that if he got into power he would try to repeal the hunting act, my ears really pricked up and I thought if I can make a difference with hedgehogs maybe I can alert people to the possibility of going back into what I regard as something very barbaric,' he says.

May, who is married to the actor Anita Dobson, and has three children from his first marriage, and three grandchildren, has set up a charity, Save Me, which rehabilitates injured wild animals, and is campaigning against the badger cull and any repeal of the hunting ban. Dobson is supportive but does not get involved. 'Everybody has to work on their own passions,' says May very quietly.

> So many people have said to me, foxes are just like rats, who gives a shit? And then you say, so a rat isn't worthy of some consideration? Rats are so like human beings, it's frightening. And it's human beings who are relegating them to 'vermin'. It gives people the feeling that they don't have to treat animals with any kind of consideration, and to me that's wrong.

May, who has long been an 'imperfect vegetarian' but does not now eat meat or fish, 'certainly wouldn't' engage in direct action, but thinks that animal rights has become a dirty word because its image has been 'deliberately manipulated' by opponents who incorrectly characterise hunt saboteurs as violent. Hunting and killing animals for pleasure 'boggles my mind', he says. 'A decent life and a decent death – that's what I ask for myself, and that's what I would ask of any creature.' Ultimately, he believes animals have rights – both moral and legal – and wants to challenge 'the mentality that says human beings are the only creatures on this planet who matter':

> I don't really love badgers because they are furry and good-looking. It's not about that. They are appealing,

there's no doubt, they are like little bears, especially when they are young. To me they are fascinating and rather mysterious because they have been in the British isles longer than humans and they have their own social ways, not all of which are understood by us.

I can't help but have a sort of awe for all wild creatures who have survived even the awfulness of what we have done to the world. We are the vandals in this world, there's no doubt about it.

Despite being the first wild animal to be given legal protection in Britain, in 1973, the illegal 'sport' of badger-baiting and digging still goes on, and this year killing badgers is set to be sanctioned by the government – which wants to authorise farmers to trap and shoot them to reduce bovine TB. May is convinced this is the Conservatives' political sop to the countryside lobby because, locked in coalition, they lack the numbers to repeal Labour's hunting ban. 'It's a panacea that is being offered to farmers, look we are doing something, we are on your side, we're going out and killing things,' he says.

Bovine TB led to the slaughter of 24,899 cattle in England last year, costing £63 million. Farmers insist the disease is a genuine crisis, and argue it has increased with a burgeoning badger population and that disease hotspots correspond to high badger populations, particularly in the West Country. May insists that it is still unproven that badgers pass TB to cattle (it is proven that cattle transmit it to badgers) and unproven that a cull would help.

He quotes the conclusion of a ten-year culling trial in which 11,000 badgers were killed: culling cannot meaningfully contribute to the control of TB.

After travelling to Cardiff to unsuccessfully plead with the Welsh assembly to reverse its own separate decision to cull badgers in Pembrokeshire, May admits he 'got into a lot of trouble' for suggesting farmers should abandon cattle farming in bovine TB hotspots. 'There was a nasty little piece' in the farming press that said telling farmers they should not farm cattle is

> like telling Brian May he can't play guitar and they said some people would welcome that. Ha ha, lovely. But there was a time when Queen was very uncool in Britain and what we did was play elsewhere. I actually took my family and my little boy went to school in LA partly because of that, so it's not such a ridiculous suggestion.

He believes bovine TB can be solved with vaccination – of badgers and cows. But the vaccination of cows is tricky: EU legislation forbids the export of vaccinated cows because it is difficult to distinguish between a vaccinated cow and one carrying bovine TB. In contrast, the vaccination of badgers is 'eminently doable', argues May. 'All the research has been done.' A badger vaccine is currently being trialled in Gloucestershire, although the coalition cancelled five other trials put in place by Labour. The National Trust recently announced plans to vaccinate badgers on its land in Devon.

May once said he stopped voting Conservative because of the party's attitude towards wild animals. Now he says he is 'very close' to the group Conservatives Against Fox Hunting, 'who have the courage to stand up against the party line' but relates to the Green Party more than any other. Did he vote Green at the last election? 'You can't ask me how I voted! It's a secret vote. The truth is, I'm really not political. I just care about the animals. That's my party. I'm a party that cares about changing attitudes to animals.'

May has all the accoutrements of a multimillionaire rock star – assistants running around, a stable full of gold discs and, incongruously, huge pink stems of rhubarb freshly picked from his organic garden – but says he scarcely gets time to enjoy the good things in his life. He has suffered depression, particularly after the deaths of his father and Freddie Mercury, and seems prone to pessimism, even bemoaning his follicular majesty when he has his photograph taken with his foxes. 'It's disappearing now,' he murmurs despondently, mussing his luxuriant curls. 'The hair has seen better days.'

Long nights awake debating with badger lovers and haters on the web can get 'depressing', he admits, especially when he is confronted with videos of animal cruelty. 'It's a thing you have to fight, being depressed about it. It's very uncomfortable to see into the minds of people who are so full of violence. Some mornings, I find it hard to deal with.' He pauses. 'I get over it.' He shrugs and laughs at himself for the first time.

2011

*

In 2020 the Conservative government finally came round to Brian May's way of thinking, signalling that it would phase out the badger cull and tackle bovine TB with vaccines for badgers and cattle. The caveat is that the government will continue to allow culling until at least 2025 with at least 40,000 badgers being culled across an area of England the size of Israel. Nevertheless, May's animal-rights principles are increasingly influential in Conservative echelons, with anti-cullers firmly backed by the prime minister's wife Carrie Johnson. Although the badger cull debate has been polarised for a decade, May has for a number of years quietly supported farmers who are tackling bovine TB through improved biosecurity, testing and badger vaccination.

2021

Udderly surprising: Rosamund Young

'I'll see who is in the mood for talking,' says Rosamund Young, strolling across a steep field on the Cotswold escarpment. 'Hello, are you busy? You're very nice, yes you are. Don't walk off.' Young pauses, empathising with Celandine's shyness. 'She doesn't like being photographed any more than I do.'

'She won't know she's being photographed,' harrumphs Graeme Robertson, the photographer. Or will she?

For Celandine is a pale, horned and handsome cross-breed cow. And Young has written *The Secret Life of Cows*, a book based on tending generations of cows on her family farm, which challenges casual assumptions. If given liberty, cows form intense friendships. They communicate with people, invent games, babysit, forecast the weather and open closed gates. They can even self-medicate, choosing to eat certain plants when poorly. Most profoundly, Young has realised that this herd species is notably individual. Each one of her 113 cows has a name.

Up here on Kites Nest Farm, the only sound is the gentle tearing of grass and the contented puffing of bovine breath. So I don't quite realise that I'm the one being interviewed. By the cows.

When we sit down later, in the kitchen of her gorgeous

old farmhouse, Young reveals that the cows are her character judges. On the hillside, Dot eventually poses for some pictures for Robertson.

'The cows know he's a nice person. If he wasn't they would walk off,' says Young. 'You can be charmed by a person, but a cow can't.' Three times her cows have reacted badly to visitors, although one unfortunate woman had simply worn strong perfume. (One of Young's smaller revelations is that cows hate artificial scent.)

Young, sixty-four, has lived on a farm since she was twelve days old, when her father obtained a tenancy on a council farm with no electricity or telephone. But she's not exactly a cow whisperer. 'If I've got someone with me I'll tell them what the cow is thinking, just like Johnny Morris [the presenter of 1970s TV show *Animal Magic*]. It's a bit of an affectation,' she says with typical self-effacement.

In reality, she has no truck with cheap tricks. 'Some farmers will always scratch the top of a cow's tail and the cow goes into ecstasies. I don't like doing that. It's using your power to make them like you. If a cow doesn't like me, that's fine.' Mostly, she communicates non-verbally, placing a hand on them. 'You don't need to talk. It's the presence, or feeling calm.' And cows talk back to her: they may push, moo or simply seek her out, standing outside her kitchen window if they have a problem.

When Young was thirteen, she brought some young cows back to their main herd after a summer in a distant grazing field and remembers noticing how one stood intently 'talking' to her mother. 'I thought, crikey, they've missed each other,' she says. 'We didn't know they even knew each other because that calf had been taken from its mother at birth.'

Young has noticed more than most, perhaps because she is deeply rooted in one place. She has never had a passport and is stressed about her first ever trip to a book festival. 'Going anywhere is monumentally worrying.'

The Secret Life of Cows was originally published by a small farming press in 2003. It was rediscovered when a Faber sales rep spotted a favourable reference in Alan Bennett's diaries. Young has never met Bennett, although he sent her an appreciative postcard. 'He bought the book because he thought it was a stupid title and read it thinking he'd hate it, and he didn't,' says Young. 'I love being called an author. It's an enormous compliment, but I think I'm a ghostwriter for the cows.'

Young has been so bound to her farm partly because she has devoted most of her life to caring for her chronically sick mother. 'She got very severe reactions to any food that wasn't organic,' says Young. 'When we grew our own wheat, milled our own flour, had our own milk, cheese and butter, I could keep her fairly pain-free and happy. That made me more aware of the power of food to make people well.' Since her mother's death six years ago, she has farmed in partnership with her brother, Richard, and now also her partner, Gareth Williams.

The Youngs have been organic since 1974. The animals

stay in family groups – or sometimes not, for she reveals some mothers fall out with grandmothers over how to raise a calf. Their pastures are full of 'weeds' because they have realised that cows seek out different plants for a balanced diet. If injured, a cow will often eat willow.

Cows fed solely on grass may not sound radical but intensively farmed cows are stuffed with maize or soya beans. 'Cows need grass, they don't need cereals. They are ruminants,' says Young, firmly. Cereal-fed cows produce less healthy meat, too: factory-farmed beef has a much lower proportion of healthy omega-3 fats than grass-fed beef, for instance.

'I would just say, in general terms, the better you get to know an animal, the more use you can be to it.' For instance, because she can safely get close to her cows, she can check one for mastitis without spending an hour putting it in a crush and calling a vet.

That's pragmatic, but Young's intimate understanding of her cows is also very moving. On one occasion, two cows gave birth to dazzlingly white calves within twenty-four hours of each other. 'The first calf walked over to greet the new arrival and stared at him as if looking in a mirror. They became devoted and inseparable friends from that minute,' she writes. 'The White Boys lived in a world of their own in the midst of a large herd but oblivious to it. They slept each night with their heads resting on each other. They were magnificent: tall, gentle, independent, kindly, though not over-friendly, noble.'

The Secret Life of Cows may be full of life but it is coy about death. 'I cheated in a way,' says Young. 'I didn't know how to go into . . .'

Most of her calves' good lives end, aged two. What happened to the White Boys? 'Oh, they got eaten. They went together, in a horsebox. I drove them to the abattoir and they got killed within seconds of each other.'

Young believes good meat is part of a balanced diet and Britain's climate and geography make meat production the only truly sustainable land use on its grasslands. Her slopes are too steep to grow crops and vegan diets dependent on imported soya beans from ex-rainforests don't appear to be sustainable. At times, however, she sounds rather like animal rights philosopher Peter Singer. Cows, Young writes, 'should be given the wherewithal to succeed as animals, not as some inadequate servants of man'.

Shouldn't she be vegetarian? 'Being a vegetarian doesn't do anything for animal welfare. If you become an abattoir owner and make sure animals are killed well then you're doing something for animal welfare, but just giving up meat you're not.'

She would much prefer on-farm slaughter but this is barred by the EU. Young devised the concept of mobile slaughterhouses – a hi-tech trailer that could visit farms – but the two that were constructed proved unviable because of expensive regulations, including the need for an on-site vet who billed at £100 an hour. 'The young animals that go to be killed, the two-year-old boys, I would guess most of them don't know what's going to happen. Most. The older cows know more. Some of them think, "This isn't right, why am I not at home? That smells funny."'

Young breaks off and says she really must prepare to leave for her book festival debut. She mocks her own nerves with a laugh. 'It's almost as though I'm going to be slaughtered tomorrow and I'm never coming back.'

2017

The animal whisperer: Eva Meijer

Fagan the horse is enormous, nervy and then, suddenly, inexplicably calm when Eva Meijer strokes his neck and whispers in his twitching ears. Meijer, a Dutch philosopher, novelist, visual artist and singer-songwriter, is visiting the splendidly acronymed Faith (For Animals In Trouble, There's Hope) animal rescue centre in Norfolk.

Our photographer is hoping to obtain a portrait of Meijer talking to the animals, Dr Dolittle-style, for this interview about *Animal Languages*, her fascinating, accessible new book about how animals communicate, and what this means for their place on a human-dominated planet.

Meijer does not disappoint, crooning to the camera-shy horse. 'Fagan was wonderful. He is someone I'd like to get to know,' she sighs. 'People say animals cannot speak. Of course they speak. They speak to us all the time. The only thing is that we don't really listen. Listening is really important, not just for their sake but for ours because there is a limit on how far we can use the planet and its natural resources.'

Meijer is part of a growing movement of academics and mostly younger people examining how to redefine humans' relationship with other animals. She grew up in the Netherlands with cats, a neighbour's pony and a guinea pig, Dotje, who lived for an astonishing thirteen years. When she became vegetarian at eleven, she regretted not having done so earlier. Loving animals 'was just something that was there and was natural', she says.

It was only when she began to study philosophy that she saw that animals were almost completely absent from western thought. And when they appeared in science, they were treated solely as objects. This clashed with what she knew to be true from her own experience – that animals had agency, emotions and deeply communicative lives. When a human rides a horse, for instance, she says: 'There is a lot of communication going on.' Research shows that the heartbeats of rider and horse synchronise.

While the ancient Greeks saw humans as part of a greater whole with other animals, Christianity and the Enlightenment set people apart from mere beasts. Descartes believed animals had no soul. In recent decades, however, the list of things that 'only humans are capable of' has become steadily shorter. Thinking, empathy, expressing emotions, grammar, generalised reciprocity (doing something for someone unknown, or without expectation of a return favour) – science is beginning to show that other animals can do it all. Understanding how animals communicate can unlock these insights.

Meijer reveals fascinating research into how animals communicate. Jays and crows choose particular gifts they believe will appeal to their partners, and so have a 'theory of mind' – they can see things from another's point of view. Prairie dogs use chattering calls to describe different intruders – not only a human, but how large he or she is, the colour of their clothes and whether they are carrying an umbrella or a gun. Many mammals can learn human words, produce new sounds or acquire other languages: orcas, for example, can imitate the cries of dolphins.

One consciousness-shifting example of animals' inner lives given by Meijer is that wild elephants have a call for humans that also means danger. When we see humans anew via the language of animals, it is not a pretty sight. This is what Meijer would call an anthropocentric idea (hey, let's find out about what animals think of us), but it is a useful awakening. 'It is also a bridge from studying animals as objects to noticing they are subjects – they are thinking about us, they are speaking about us,' says Meijer.

For her, learning more about animal language should herald a decisive shift towards rights for animals. In academia (one of Meijer's many jobs is as a research fellow at a Dutch university), she senses a shift in biology and ethology, but also in philosophy and animal rights:

Because our society is deeply anthropocentric, that still reflects back on science as well, but I do think it's changing. It's something that's self-confirming because when you begin studying animal culture and you find out that all these animals have cultural knowledge that they pass on, it changes your image of what animals are. I think we are living in quite an exciting time.

There is a 'political turn' in animal-rights philosophy, driven not only by influential thinkers such as the Australian moral philosopher Peter Singer, but by the growth of factory farming and more general environmental and spiritual anxiety. More people are replacing shopping by seeking more fulfilling connections with nature and animals.

Animals cannot vote but, actually, Meijer supplies numerous examples where they do something pretty similar. Red deer decide to move en masse when about 60 per cent of their herd stands up. Where and how could we begin granting political rights to animals? Presumably we will apply anthropocentric ideas of intelligence to animals and grant limited rights to, say, chimpanzees or dolphins first?

'That's a typical human way of going about things,' says Meijer. She argues it is useful to have an 'ideal situation' – rights for all animals from bees to jellyfish – and work towards that, but also consider different relationships with different animal groupings.

The political philosophers Sue Donaldson and Will Kymlicka suggest there are three communities of animals: wild animals that are 'sovereign' and self-governing; wild animals, such as pigeons, that coexist with us in cities and could be considered 'denizens'; and domesticated animals.

'It's clear that certain animals want to have relations with humans for now, although it might be different if we stop confining them,' says Meijer. 'These are species we domesticated as humans, so we took something away from them. We should actually affirm their membership of our societies because, de facto, they are members – they live in our houses, they sleep in our beds,' she laughs. 'But that's absolutely not recognised.'

How would Meijer begin to change our relationship with, say, dogs? She says she would stop the pursuit of pedigree dogs and different breeds. 'Let them perhaps choose their partners,' she says. 'The whole system of owning animals is very problematic – selling them and making them pregnant.'

Meijer's own dog, Olli, is a stray rescued from Romania. Olli is vegan. 'There are a lot of vegan dogs. They like vegetables. One of Olli's favourite foods is pumpkin. When the first pumpkins come in during the autumn, he's like: "Yes!"' If he sniffs out, say, a dead rat, Meijer will let him eat what he finds. 'They are not ethical vegans,' she says of her pets. 'But I don't want pigs or cows to be killed to feed my dog because that's just simply unnecessary.'

What about if a dog's freedom to roam infringes a ground-nesting bird's freedom to safely rear chicks? It is also difficult to imagine how animals could be granted significant freedoms when there are so many humans. We are, ultimately, competing for resources with other species.

'Ideally there would be fewer humans,' says Meijer. But she also argues that we tend to see human–animal interactions in terms of conflict. 'It's a challenge for us as a species to live with others who are different from us. We're not very tolerant. And maybe in some stage of our evolutionary process that was necessary, but we're now in a very different stage where we can choose to have different types of relations with these animals.'

We seem a long way from granting animals meaningful rights and yet Meijer identifies plenty of progress, from the electoral success of the Party for Animals in the Netherlands (moving from two seats in the Dutch parliament in 2006 to five in 2017) to pensions for police dogs; animal sanctuaries are undertaking 'some kind of interspecies negotiations about how the place should look'; while academics such as Barbara Smuts are not simply more alert to anthropocentric assumptions about the nature of 'intelligence' or 'morality', but are exploring whether animals can co-determine their research questions.

Meijer sees hope in history, too. A century ago, she points out, women were considered undeserving of political rights. 'People get upset and say you're comparing women to animals, but that's not the case,' she says:

> Because society is absolutely human-centred and change seems so far away, it's good to go back to other situations in history that felt similar. Humans throughout history have been able to change their collective opinions about some social groups. There's lots of reasons to feel pessimistic, but we're here now so we should make the best of it. Also, animals are generally really nice and they are willing to forgive us.

2019

Diary of a young naturalist:
Dara McAnulty

It is a challenging time to be sixteen and, like his peers, Dara McAnulty must currently endure a form of house arrest that means not seeing friends and no GCSEs. Unlike other locked-down teens, McAnulty is also dealing with the harsh mischance of having his first book, *Diary of a Young Naturalist*, published during the coronavirus crisis. He was supposed to be touring festivals but every date is cancelled. 'I feel like my being is suffering from a slow puncture,' McAnulty tweeted in March. 'I honestly feel like my world is falling apart right now.'

When we meet via a video call a month later, his mood has lifted. Lockdown is tough. His mum, Roisin – who McAnulty likes to have by his side, discreetly, during interviews – contracted coronavirus quite severely; meanwhile, he feels 'trapped' and is 'bouncing around the house like a ping pong ball'. Mercifully, over the road from their modern housing estate is a wood where he takes his daily exercise. 'If I didn't have it, I would be utterly insane,' he says. 'The ground there is alive with peacock butterflies,' and that morning, he saw a red squirrel 'so that makes the day', he grins.

There is a genuine buzz around his debut, a combination

of nature book and memoir, a warm portrait of a close-knit family and a coming-of-age story. Robert Macfarlane has hailed his 'extraordinary voice and vision'; Chris Packham has become a friend; Steve Silberman, author of *NeuroTribes*, called him 'inspiring'. The teenager's environmental activism has led to comparisons with Greta Thunberg.

McAnulty is autistic, and it would be easy to file his book alongside Packham's *Fingers in the Sparkle Jar*, which gave a vivid insight into the naturalist's Asperger's, but Dara has his own style. Simple, gorgeous sentences unfurl, one after another. Of a hot summer's day, he writes: 'Dragonflies are whizzing, grasshoppers are trembling in the grass, and swallows are everywhere.' Or: 'The valley sings, heaves and rests.' There are original, imaginative descriptions too – caterpillars move 'like slow-motion accordions' and a goshawk chick looks 'like an autumn forest rolled in the first snows of winter'.

He lives with his dad, Paul, mum and younger siblings, Lorcan and Blathnaid, in a small rented three-bedroom house in Castlewellan, Northern Ireland. As a young child, Dara loved to bang on about black holes to anyone who would listen, and was diagnosed as autistic when he was five. In fact, Roisin, Lorcan and Blathnaid are also autistic; only Paul, a conservation scientist, is not. The teenager describes his family as 'as close as otters'. They are also punk-lovers, chaotic and 'pretty formidable, apparently'.

McAnulty exudes energy and laughs a lot. His voice,

however, belongs to an older man, and his writing is often
unexpectedly wise too. When I ask about literary inspiration, he answers immediately: Seamus Heaney. 'You can
reread his poems again and again'; there are 'all these different compartments like bubbles. You pop them one at a
time and there's no centre to it. There's this saying about
a brain: if a brain was simple enough to understand, we'd
be too stupid to understand that brain. That's almost the
same as Seamus Heaney's poems because they have such
complex connections.'

He also enjoys reading Ursula K. Le Guin, is currently 'neck-deep' in his umpteenth rereading of *The Lord of
the Rings*, and is fond of Agatha Christie for her focus on
people's hidden motives. 'That's been quite important to
me because I try my best to learn about humans so I can
make acceptable social interactions.'

A teacher once told McAnulty he would never be able to
string a paragraph together. He was miserable – 'and miserable is an understatement' – at a succession of schools,
including Oscar Wilde's alma mater, Portora. The bullying
(he didn't know how to make small talk about Minecraft)
intensified as he became a teenager. The noise and clutter
of classrooms made them the worst environment for him.

McAnulty learned that being in nature helped:

I can't speak for all autistic people, but I feel things
more intensely. In a shopping centre there's all of
those different noises coming from different angles

– my brain can't process them quickly enough, and everything goes completely crazy. Being out in nature, the sounds are quite level and I find it easier with muted colours. Everything just works. It's not oppressive.

He wrote from a young age, on scraps of paper. 'One of my ways of processing the world is writing things down,' he says. Then social media helped him find a path. Aged twelve, he began a blog about nature and joined Twitter. 'Four years ago I wouldn't have been able to talk to you right now,' he says. 'Twitter opened my world to like-minded people. You'll always find someone who is willing to talk to you about mycelial networks. It's given me so many opportunities to connect with people and not feel so isolated.'

As McAnulty wrote, and also took his first steps in environmental activism – campaigning to end the perse-cution of birds of prey – his blog gained readers and ad-mirers. Three years ago he appeared on *Springwatch* and was befriended by Packham. Adrian Cooper and Gracie Burnett, the husband-and-wife team behind tiny indepen-dent publisher Little Toller, spotted his writing and began talking to his family about a book.

Diary of a Young Naturalist tells the story of McAnulty's year from spring equinox to spring equinox, from his fourteenth to fifteenth birthday. It was a difficult time. His family moved from one side of Northern Ireland to the other and he had to cope with changing schools and losing his cherished wild heartlands, a forest called Big Dog. 'When I was younger, I remember moving from a school I absolutely hated. Even though I wanted to get out of that place with every single fibre of my body, still, in the back of my mind, I was going: "I don't want change."'

The move from Big Dog precipitated a breakdown, where McAnulty ended up screaming in panic in his garden. His struggles that summer were not helped by the rise of social-media trolling (the downside of forging those positive connections). 'Removing' himself from Big Dog 'was devastating, as if it killed a part of me. Then I went up into the Mournes' – the mountain range close to his new home – 'and everything became fine again.' Was his recovery as simple as that? 'No, but it definitely helped discovering a new place and building up a new connection with the land. I slowly crawled my way back into some semblance of a calm state of mind. Exploring was a really big part of that, trying to find new places to root myself.'

Writing was followed by a seven-month edit with Cooper and his parents. 'All my family got together, trying to coax this book into something that was manageable,' says McAnulty. But Roisin says she wouldn't want people to think his writing was overly shaped by others. 'Although it has been edited sensitively and beautifully, the first draft was actually incredible.'

Rewriting was a mixed blessing for McAnulty, forcing

him to 're-experience' memories both traumatic and joyful. 'I uncovered things about myself along the way. It's like reading a book for the second time. I had to drag myself back through that thorn bush. But I understood myself all the better because of it.'

After his breakdown, he started at a new school. Despite huge anxiety, in the book he finds kindred souls and a nurturing environment. 'It has been the best school I've had,' he says. He still has to flee lessons at times but 'I have, dare I say it, friends now, for the first time ever. I've had the best luck in the world . . . I managed to land myself in a year group that was basically made up of nerds.'

McAnulty plans to take biology – his first love – alongside maths, chemistry and politics at A level. He is currently writing a picture book for younger children and anticipates a career in conservation science. Activism takes up an increasing portion of his time. He runs a project to satellite-tag birds of prey, an eco-group at school, and is prominent in his generation's call for action over the climate and biodiversity crises. Although the British government last year became the first major economy to make a legal commitment to 'net zero' carbon emissions by 2050, these are still only words, he believes, and his generation is becoming impatient. 'We see a problem and we need to fix it. So when [politicians] don't fix it and seem to be making excuses we get angrier and angrier.'

In the meantime, McAnulty keeps his family, and the simple glories of the natural world, close. His favourite time is dusk, when 'the night sky seems to chase the sun out of the sky and you can't really see the sun's light but you know it's just underneath the horizon,' he says. 'At that time, the energy in the air is so charged. That's when the bats begin to come out, and you feel such a rush.'

2020

*

Dara McAnulty's *Diary of a Young Naturalist* won the Wainwright Prize in 2020.

2021

The bard of rural England:
Ronald Blythe

The track down which Ronald Blythe first walked in 1947 sinks into a valley on the border between Suffolk and Essex and ends at Bottengoms Farm. Everything in the rambling garden is blazing on an oddly hot autumn day. The runner beans are plentiful, and three roses throw competing scents into the air. A recently vacated folding chair shows that Blythe has just taken his lunch outside. It is a deeply peaceful scene.

Bottengoms Farm is the star of Blythe's latest book, *At the Yeoman's House*. 'It's a kind of poem, the book, isn't it?' he says diffidently. A book about your home might be considered a narrowing of horizons that comes, quite naturally, with old age. Blythe, who is eighty-nine, has lived a geographically restricted life. He has never left East Anglia for more than a month at a time. His writing, however, is vivid and outward-looking, part social history, part memoir. In the new book he spins all kinds of tiny stories and vivid recollections from these sturdy, independent dwellings built by yeomen – countrymen above a farmer but below a gentleman – in the sixteenth and seventeenth centuries.

Blythe is best known for *Akenfield*, his stark account of village life in Suffolk, which was published to instant acclaim in 1969. He thinks of himself primarily as an essayist and poet but has written two novels and many short stories, has edited editions of Thomas Hardy and Henry James, and inspired a generation of nature writers, including Richard Mabey and Roger Deakin, who became close friends. This year has also seen the publication of *At Helpston*, a collection of lucid essays about John Clare (he is president of the John Clare Society), and every week for two decades he has written his 'Word from Wormingford' diary for the *Church Times*. He continues to accept speaking engagements across the country. While Penguin and Faber have recently republished his classic works, it is perhaps surprising that only small publishing houses are publishing his new writing.

We sit in his garden and gaze at an ash tree instantly recognisable from *At the Yeoman's House*. 'The last plough horses drank in its shade about three o'clock every afternoon, hurrying when it came into view. John Constable often walked past it, and probably sketched it. He had a passion for bark,' writes Blythe. 'Now and then pairs of magpies dive snowily from a particular bough like Olympic youths, white and perfect, to seize crusts.'

Blythe was born in Suffolk. His family has lived here for centuries; even his surname comes from its river Blyth. He thinks his mother, who 'read all the time', is responsible for his love of books. He devoured French literature and wrote poetry. He did not go to university but does not feel that he missed out. 'I was brought up with all these very cultivated people, botanists and artists. None of them went to university.' Working as a reference librarian in Colchester library, he met Christine Nash, wife of the painter, John Nash, and was first invited to their home, Bottengoms Farm, in 1947.

There was a run of spectacularly good summers in the late forties. 'It was Provence, or even Paris, in Suffolk,' he writes, as he was thrust into a glamorous, rather bohemian world. He became friends with Sir Cedric Morris, who taught Lucian Freud and Maggi Hambling and lived nearby with his partner, Arthur Lett Haines. 'I was a poet but I longed to be a painter like the rest of them,' says Blythe. 'What I basically am is a listener and a watcher. I absorb, without asking questions, but I don't forget things, and I was inspired by a lot of these people because they worked so hard and didn't make a fuss. They just lived their lives in a very independent and disciplined way.'

Christine found him a cottage near Aldeburgh, and Blythe was introduced to Benjamin Britten. They became friends and he edited festival programmes for Britten while wrestling with his first novel. One day he returned home and found a note pushed under his door inviting him for a drink at Britten's house. It was from E. M. Forster. 'How he knew I was there I don't know.' Blythe met Forster a number of times; they would go shopping together for groceries, and Blythe helped Forster write an index for his biography of his great-aunt, Marianne Thornton. One evening, Imogen Holst took Blythe and Forster to see

Gustav Holst's one-act chamber opera, *Savitri*.

This must have been thrilling for a meek Suffolk lad, who did not smoke, barely drank, never took drugs and house-sat for the Nashes. 'It was rather frightening, really. All I did was work. I suppose in a way I wanted to be thought of as a writer by them. I was a very quiet sort of boy, with a bike,' he says. 'I was overwhelmed by the grandeur of these people. I didn't tell Forster I was writing a novel. I didn't dare. But he was just an old man who was charming, and I expect he found me attractive.' Blythe's first, Forster-inspired novel, *A Treasonable Growth*, was recently republished by Faber Finds. Another book republished by Faber, *The Age of Illusion*, a social history of life in England between the two world wars published in 1963, led to an editor at Penguin asking Blythe to edit a series of classics for the Penguin English Library. He began with Jane Austen's *Emma*, and chose one of his heroes, William Hazlitt, for his next volume.

Writing an introduction to *Far from the Madding Crowd* helped to complete the profound grasp of country life that came to underpin *Akenfield*. 'I had a deep knowledge of agriculture and the church in the countryside and education and natural history, without realising it,' Blythe says. He feared that his first-person voices of horsemen, pig farmers, blacksmiths, headmistresses and gravediggers – some taped, some remembered and recounted – was not what his publishers wanted. 'I just put these people together in Charsfield, where I was the church warden, and all the things one had heard or seen since boyhood came together,' he says. His subjects' speech was 'all genuine', although he 'can't think why' he gave them names he found on tombstones.

Blythe had no idea *Akenfield* would have the impact it did. Fifteen million people watched Peter Hall's film of the book, shown simultaneously on TV and in the cinema, in which Blythe had a cameo as a vicar. His portrait of village life captured a hitherto barely noticed revolution in the countryside: *Akenfield* marked the end of an essentially feudal pattern of farming by hand and horse that had endured for millennia. Within the lifetimes of the people he wrote about, physical hardship, poverty, deference and communities centred on the land and the church had been pushed aside by the juggernaut of industrial farming.

Akenfield didn't make waves because the countryside had previously been a literary backwater. 'There was an enormous amount of excellent country writing, like Adrian Bell and Henry Williamson. But I think the realism of *Akenfield* had a harsher note,' he says. Although Blythe never laboured on the land, *Akenfield* gave voice to those who did. 'If you read John Clare, he makes you realise that they weren't just lumpen creatures, even if they couldn't read and write. They had dreams and visions which we don't know about.' Have we lost something because we lack people labouring on the land like Clare, who could write about it in a more intimate way? 'Hardy never worked on the land but he was among people who did. I actually haven't worked on this land but I've seen the land ploughed by horses,' Blythe says. 'So I have a feeling and understanding in that respect – of its glory and bitterness.'

Upstairs at Bottengoms, on lopsided floorboards, is Blythe's desk. He writes by hand every morning, sometimes in the garden, and then types it up. He does not use a computer and has never driven a car. 'Hopeless, you see,' he says. Blythe is generous about contemporary nature writers, including Mabey, Deakin and Mark Cocker.

Mabey, who first met Blythe in 1969, has studied his prose to figure out how it works. 'It is bewitching to trace how the narratives wind effortlessly this way and that, joining reading and first-hand experience, compressing past and present so that an event or an insight from a thousand years ago is as real as yesterday's,' he writes in the introduction to *Aftermath*, a big book that is a small sample of fifty years of Blythe's writing. He winds his way towards his target and yet does not ramble, writing with great exactitude and economy. His 'genius is to so faithfully reflect this wonderfully connected muddle that what is some of the most beautiful and precise prose in modern English reads like conversation', Mabey writes.

Blythe loves writing but is less comfortable discussing how he does it. 'I don't know how to describe it. When I'm writing I'm in a kind of dream,' he says. 'It's a bit like looking at your own profile in the mirror. You shrink from it.' He is firm about one thing: he is not a nature writer, nor a country writer but a writer who lives in the country. This undercuts Mabey's belief that Blythe is a 'first-class naturalist' but reflects the breadth of Blythe's passions. He is 'heavily influenced by George Herbert and a lot of Christian poets and also just by simple village worship', but turned down the chance to become a priest; he is a writer and could not run a parish, he says, although he takes services as a reader and is a canon of the cathedral in Bury St Edmunds. He is not saddened by the loss of the church as the central organising factor in village life; the church, he says, has 'always gone up and down' and its buildings 'are beautifully kept, ancient and full of treasures. It's part of the pattern of life, prayer and music and great language.'

Blythe describes his writing as the work of 'a solitary man who is serene and not bitter and who loves nature and poetry and has a circle of friends, but mostly is by himself'. He has never lived with anyone. Has he ever been lonely? 'No, I don't know what it means.' His writing contains many lucid personal insights and yet his interior life – his loves, his joy and his pain – is never directly mentioned. 'There are writers whose books are intensely autobiographical, about their bodies, and sex, and things like that. I think that's perfectly all right. I haven't done that, no.' He falls silent. Passions and sorrows must flow into writing, and he has written of love in his fiction. 'My emotional attitudes and sexual attitudes are more apparent in stories,' he says, diverting the conversation to praising Colm Tóibín's 'explicit' short stories. It feels impertinent to press him again on his intimate life, but he picks up the thread. 'I imagine if you went through a lot of [my] books you'd find almost everything, but not explicitly so. I suppose I use everything that's happened to me emotionally for writing. That's all one has, really, isn't it?'

His reticence, he agrees, is in part a generational predisposition, 'a matter of taste and feeling', but it may be more than that. Blythe adores Virginia Woolf's writing, and briefly met Vanessa Bell at Aldeburgh. Mrs Dalloway said that love and religion would destroy the privacy of the soul. 'A lot of people in my stories say things like that,' Blythe says. I start to mention that one small anecdote about his love life was revealed in a biography of the crime writer Patricia Highsmith. 'I slept with her,' he interjects. In the book he was quoted as saying that she breached the boundaries of their friendship by exploring him physically, on one or two occasions. 'Well, it wasn't my fault really,' he says. 'She lived four miles from me and she came over every week for several years. I admired her enormously. She was a very strange, mysterious woman. She was lesbian but at the same time she found men's bodies beautiful. And I think she found me beautiful. But it was ridiculous, really. She also drank like a fish, which I don't do.'

So she got him drunk? 'We weren't at all drunk, no, no, no. I was just staying the night. I've got piles of letters from her and I admired her,' he says. They discussed writing, and Blythe enjoyed her droll humour although he felt 'a terrible darkness' in her preoccupation with psychopaths. After a few years living in Suffolk after falling in love with a married woman from London, Highsmith continued her peripatetic existence, moving to France, Switzerland and Italy.

In the 1970s Blythe nursed John Nash, and wrote *The View in Winter*, a prescient look at old age, which he considers one of his best books. When Nash died, Blythe inherited Bottengoms. This autumn, the village school has not reopened its doors for the first time since 1870, he remarks lightly. There has been a hollowing out of village life, a kind of disenchantment, which he has captured in his writing. At the entrance to Bottengoms there are two thirty-year-old ashes, which stand in striking contrast to the tree Constable knew. 'Like most of today's villagers, they have no notion of toil or myth,' he writes. 'They shiver in the wind and throw out boughs with a calculated aim, which is to be beautiful. "Welcome home, useless farm-dweller," they say. "You are one of us. When did you grow corn and turnips in this paddy-field? When did you cry when the harvest was a wash-out?"'

Does the state of the countryside, preserved, perhaps, but denuded of its vigour, fill him with melancholy? 'No. I think the countryside looks wonderful today, don't you think? The excesses of the 1960s and 1970s after prairie farming took over, with all the chemicals and the burning of the stubble, is in the past.' But he also notes that few people actually look at the fields any more:

There is often very little true life. People lead the lives they might lead in Birmingham or anywhere in a remote village, with the same TV and fitted carpets and supermarkets – it's an identical life and they go and get the same things. They make gardens and join in traditional village events but it's not as it used to be. It can't be.

Friends have suggested alternative homes but, Blythe says, 'I just tumbled into these places and stayed. I like routine and solitude, and the kind of order of reading and writing and thinking and drifting.

'I won't pretend that it's some great romantic thing. It's simply the countryside. I take it very much for granted. I'm not infatuated with it or anything like that. It's a normal place to live.' Then again, he seems to agree that a still life in a still place must do something to you:

If you go for walks with a friend in the countryside, that is a lovely experience. But if you live as I live in the middle of nowhere by yourself, that's another experience. There's nothing mystical about it, but it makes me dream. If you're in this house, surrounded by fields every day, something happens to you. I don't know what it is.

2011

*

Like many admirers of Ronald Blythe – 'Ronnie' to his friends – I kept in contact and returned to Bottengoms to watch badgers in his wood as part of my research for *Badgerlands*. I saw Ronnie in his home in the summer of 2020 when he was nearly ninety-eight and still incredibly courteous, smart and interesting. His short-term memory was slipping away but he was excellently cared for by a circle of dedicated friends, whom he called his 'dear ones'. Bottengoms is to be given to the Essex Wildlife Trust after his death.

2021

PART V

Saving the Planet

Tuvalu:
the South Pacific nation
in danger of vanishing

The dazzling white sand and dark green coconut palms of Tepuka Savilivili were once much like those on dozens of other small islets within sight of Funafuti, the atoll capital of Tuvalu. But shortly after cyclones Gavin, Hina and Kelly had paid the tiny Pacific nation a visit, islanders looked across Funafuti's coral lagoon and noticed a gap on the horizon. Tepuka Savilivili had vanished. Fifty hectares of Tuvalu disappeared into the sea during the 1997 storms. The tiny country's precious twenty-six square kilometres of land were starting to disappear.

Five years on, the government of Tuvalu has noticed many such troubling changes on its nine inhabited islands and concluded that, as one of the smallest and lowest-lying countries in the world, it is destined to become the first nation sunk by global warming. The evidence before their own eyes – and forecasts for a rise in sea level of up to 88 cm in the next century made by international scientists – has convinced most of Tuvalu's 10,500 inhabitants that rising seas and more frequent violent storms are certain to make life unliveable on the islands, if not for them, then for their children. A deal has been signed with New

Zealand, in which seventy-five Tuvaluans will be resettled there each year, starting now. As the vast expanse of the Pacific Ocean creeps up on to Tuvalu's doorstep, the evacuation and shutting down of a nation has begun.

With the curtains closed against the tropical glare, the prime minister, Koloa Talake, works in a flimsy Portakabin at the lagoon's edge on Funafuti. Tuvalu's largest island is a crowded, uninhabitable-looking line in the ocean, smaller than Hampstead Heath in London. You are never more than 150 metres from the sea and the air has a permanently salty tang. Talake, who sits at his desk wearing flip-flops and bears a passing resemblance to Nelson Mandela, likens his task to the captain of a ship: 'The skipper of the boat is always the last man to leave a sinking ship or goes down with the ship. If that happens to Tuvalu, the prime minister will be the last person to leave the island.'

Talake realises that his government cannot simply order people off the islands, but must balance the continued development of the country – embracing sealed roads, telephones and the Internet – with the precautionary evacuation of the most vulnerable. The prospect of rising seas or tropical storms engulfing their nation has left Tuvalu's deeply Christian people grappling with a fear of the ocean, a belief that God won't flood their land, and anxiety that their culture might not survive transplantation to a developed western nation such as New Zealand.

The highest point on Tuvalu is just four metres above sea level. From the air, its islands are thin slashes of green against the aquamarine water. From a few miles out at sea, the nation's numerous tiny uninhabited islets look smaller than a container ship and soon slip below the horizon. On a map, the islands are pinpricks south of the equator, only visible because the international dateline does them the courtesy of swerving east to avoid them. A Spanish explorer spotted an island in the sixteenth century, but it was another 200 years before storms pitched the first missionary on to Tuvalu's coral atolls, which were named the Ellice Islands and subsumed into the British Empire.

Hardly any tourists take the 22-seater plane from Fiji that touches down at Funafuti twice a week (travel agents think you're having a laugh when you quote the airport code: Fun). For the rest of the week, islanders sleep on the runway at night (where they can enjoy a cooling breeze), and pigs, bicycles and games of football and rugby traverse the airstrip by day. Eight of Tuvalu's nine inhabited islands have no cars or Internet. Daily life on Tuvalu revolves around the ocean. It is the islands' garden, washroom, swimming pool and slaughterhouse. As dawn quickly rises on the island, men and women stand neck-deep in the sea, eating fish and bits of coconut, or periodically raising pans they are silently scrubbing beneath the surface of the water. At midday, a father and son heave four pigs into the lagoon for slicing up; the pigs' slashed-open bellies turn the water red and their entrails drift off on the ocean. At dusk, islanders gather on motorbikes to watch the sunset from the low concrete jetties jutting out into the lagoon. Children slide down algae-covered boat ramps into the water and a man clutches a fish the size of a dog to his chest.

The Pacific Ocean brings relative prosperity. Tuvalu sells licences permitting the US, Japan and others to fish in its 900,000 square kilometres of territorial waters. Money is bringing change – and lots of motorbikes. Most islanders stand with one foot in the cash economy and one in the traditional realm of subsistence farming and fishing. Extended families live together, with some members tending a small pen of pigs or dropping a line from a boat to fish for their suppers, while others bring in a wage by working for the government, or go overseas to study at the University of the South Pacific in Fiji. Education is greatly valued, and the island's only ship spends much of its time ferrying young Tuvaluans to the second-largest island Vaitupu, where girls and boys board at the country's only secondary school.

Many of the nation's young lads then join the maritime training school, a thriving government enterprise that teaches modern shipping lore. Employment agencies snap up the young Tuvaluans, who are renowned for their knowledge of the ocean, work ethic and strength. At any one time, more than 600 Tuvaluan men are labouring on container ships at sea. The money sent home by family-minded Tuvaluan sailors has trebled to more than A$4 million (£1.5 million) in the past three years.

Islanders still fish around Tuvalu in small wooden boats and every year several go missing, drifting to oblivion after losing sight of their low-lying land. 'Personally, I am very worried about sea-level rising, because I don't want to be caught. Drowning is a dreadful death,' says Talake, motioning with his hand to indicate the waters rising above his neck.

Tropical storms have also long frightened the islanders – and now global warming appears to be bringing more each wet season. Talake vividly recalls Hurricane Bebe, which destroyed 800 homes on Funafuti in 1972:

At 5 p.m. I was at the airstrip up to my knees in water. Kids were paddling about in canoes. In the evening, when the wind turned west and began blowing really hard, the police came round telling people that the eye of the hurricane was coming. A few metres from our house, the water was up to our hips. At 9 p.m. we headed for high land with our kids. Another couple had got there before us and were hiding there under bamboo mats. They felt sorry for us and offered us shelter. We were lucky to survive. If the water really rises and you cannot find anything to hold on to, the current will take you away and then you die. So we worry about getting to that stage.

Like many Pacific islanders, Tuvaluans are open and easy-going – as you have to be in the tropical humidity – and don't give the impression of being easily worried. They know all about the outside world. Many on Funafuti have travelled further and wider than westerners, working on ships around the world, getting an education in Fiji, or visiting relatives in New Zealand. Most are keenly aware of the likely effects of global warming and sea-level rise thanks, not least, to island radio (which alternates days of traditional Tuvaluan and Pacific Island songs with Britney Spears and Billy Ocean).

Iopu Iupasi leans against a palm by a pigpen in the shade of his backyard. He worked at sea for twenty-two years before turning to traditional life. He fishes for snapper, yellowfin tuna, marlin, swordfish, and, at night, takes a torch and what looks like an oversized butterfly net to pluck flying fish out of the air on the pitch-black ocean. He has noticed the erosion on the islands such as Tepuka Savilivili. 'I look at the small islands – before, they were big ones, eh? Now it is all gone, so I think I believe in sea-level rise.' He points to the rough coral shoreline, where his backyard ends. 'My beach here used to be about four metres. Now it is nearly coming up to the house. We used to have sea walls, but it is useless. They don't work.'

Sam Vaiku stands under a blue plastic canopy where he is building a wooden fishing boat. Aged seventy, he attributes his huge muscles to hard work and toddy – fermented and mildly hallucinogenic coconut milk – which he drinks in moderation at mealtimes. He has also noticed a loss of trees on the small islands around Funafuti where he fishes. But he has faith that the islanders will be spared.

Tuvalu is one of the most Christian countries in the

world. Early missionaries reported how ready the placid Polynesian Tuvaluans were to convert compared with the 'difficult' Melanesian peoples of Fiji and Papua New Guinea. While there is a neat mosque on the island, more than 97 per cent of the islanders are Christians. 'There is a strong belief in the story about Noah's Ark, and God's covenant that he will not flood the earth again,' says Paani Laupepa, the assistant secretary of Tuvalu's environment department. 'We are trying to explain the scientific facts to Christian people. It is coming through slowly.'

The Reverend Pitoi Etuati retreats into his sparse, white-washed church to escape his young children. Like most people on the island, he lives in a simple two-roomed house. His church is a large hall, with matting woven from pandanus leaves for his 1,000-strong congregation to sit on. Unlike many Tuvaluan clergy, he understands that, while the seas may not rise to cover the islands in his lifetime, 'it is going to happen, if not in our time, then in the future':

Conservative Christians would say I am not a faithful pastor because I am giving up now. But we cannot think that, because we are Christian, God will do everything for us. You have faith, you work and accept. It might be God's ways to inform us that there will be a time when this island sinks, so we have to push our government to make arrangements so we can be refugees, if not in our time then for the coming generation.

While Tuvaluans debate issues of faith, scientists in the region continue to argue over whether Tuvalu is yet experiencing rising sea levels. The National Tidal Facility (NTF), based at Flinders University in Adelaide, recently published figures from its tide gauge on Tuvalu that recorded no rise in average tide levels since record-keeping began in 1993. The findings were used by the Australian government in November last year to justify its rejection of Tuvalu's request that it admit a small number of islanders every year as 'environmental refugees'. (To add insult to injury, the Australians later informally asked Tuvalu whether it could find room on its twenty-six square kilometres for boat people refused entry into Australia. Tuvalu politely turned down the request.)

Perched on the prow of a small wooden boat, Hilia Vavae, director of Tuvalu's meteorological office, heads across the lagoon, eventually spotting a forlorn sandy dome. It is all that is left of Tepuka Savilivili, the islet that vanished after the 1997 storms. Today there is nothing living left on the few metres of sand, only several odd flip-flops and a rusty tin. Further south is Vasuaafua, an island of nine coconut palms clinging to a scrap of sand. Vavae points to a small sand cliff: 'Erosion,' she grimaces. Two years ago, the island was buttressed by several hundred metres of beach.

Vavae's meteorological office is huddled next to the airstrip on Funafuti. This is where research meets the reality of climate change. Vavae has a picture on her wall from the highest tide last year, in which she and her staff are standing on their office doorstep, up to their ankles in water. She quietly explains that NTF's scientists have misrepresented their data. 'Their analysis of their information is correct, but it is inappropriate,' she says. 'You need to look at the extremes – examining average sea levels doesn't reflect the impacts that the small island states are facing.' It only takes one high tide to permanently wash away fragile soil or kill the precious vegetation that holds small islands together. Tuvalu's highest tide gets higher, its low tides lower, and so NTF's 'average' stays the same. There is another, less well publicised tide gauge on Tuvalu – also focusing on tidal averages – run by the University of Hawaii's sea-level centre, covering a much longer period, from 1976 to 2000. It has recorded a 2.2 cm rise per decade in average sea levels.

Vavae has plenty more evidence of global warming in the twenty years she has been working in the met office. Higher tides are flooding the island more frequently. 'In the mid-1980s it was only February. Now it is November, December, January, February and March,' she says. One or two serious cyclones used to hit Tuvalu every decade. In the 1990s the islands faced seven. Floods and storms cause more erosion. Several outer island farmers report that their crops of *pulaka* – swamp taro, a traditional accompaniment to fish – have yellowed and yielded less in recent seasons, a probable sign of rising salinity.

Like the government, and the scientists at the

Intergovernmental Panel on Climate Change, who predict a sea-level rise of up to 88 cm in the next century, she believes the islands will not simply be swamped by water. It is far more likely that the ferocity and frequency of storms and high tides will simply make Tuvaluan daily life untenable.

Regional analysts in Sydney scathingly refer to the South Pacific as a 'basket case'. The island nations are characterised by government corruption, corporate exploitation and, with a population explosion in most Pacific countries, ethnic tension over increasingly scarce land. The economy of Fiji, the Pacific's hub, has yet to recover from the disastrous coup in 2000, triggered by tension between indigenous landowners and Fijian Indians. Papua New Guinea's rainforests are being plundered as the government struggles to maintain law and order. The Solomon Islands lie ruined by civil war, while Nauru is a virtually bankrupt detention centre for 1,118 migrants unwanted by Australia.

Against this backdrop, the Tuvaluan government is a beacon of sanity. The only national tax is a A$10 (£3.60) annual levy on the islanders, but the government raises funds through a trust fund it created in 1987, which has grown from A$27 million (£9.9 million) to more than A$60 million. There are rumblings of discontent: four PMs in the past three years have left many local people murmuring that ministers put self-interest above the general good. Aid agencies privately expressed misgivings after the government made an uncharacteristically large withdrawal from its trust fund last year to cover ambitious spending programmes. Tuvalu's government counters: 'It is a good thing to keep on developing,' says Talake. 'If you reduced development because of the rising sea level, you would be discouraging or frightening your own people.'

A government-funded road sweeps from one end of Funafuti to the other, awaiting surfacing, and the new A$14 million (£5 million) government office will become the island's tallest building – three storeys – when it is constructed with money donated by Taiwan later this year. A new hospital is planned: there are three HIV-positive Tuvaluans, but diabetes and heart disease are more serious problems, as naturally large islanders gradually replace their traditional fish diet with all the corned beef and fizzy drinks their wages can buy. It may not live to see its centenary as an independent nation, but the country is still determined to develop politically as well as physically: a referendum is planned this year to see if Tuvaluans want to discard the Queen as head of state and become a republic.

In choosing independence and its own name, Tuvalu also had a strange stroke of financial fortune. When country code top-level domain names were shared out, most countries got a mundane '.uk' or '.fr'. Tuvalu was granted the eminently marketable '.tv', and sold the right to license it for US$50 million (£35 million) to American entrepreneurs. In a separate deal, Tuvalu is now guaranteed an annual payment of US$2 million per year 'in perpetuity'. Virtual Tuvalu could now outlive real Tuvalu.

The next stop on the Tuvaluan government's international campaign is the commonwealth heads of government meeting in Brisbane on 2 March. A new member of the old colonial club, Tuvalu will use its 'maiden' speech to tell Tony Blair, the Queen and leaders from the other fifty-three commonwealth nations about the ocean tides creeping up Tuvalu's narrow beaches.

But no amount of sympathy, aid or dot.com cash could construct a viable sea defence system for the islands. Funafuti is little more than a flimsy sea wall, a wafer-thin curving strip of land shielding the coral lagoon from the six-kilometre depths of the South Pacific. What happens if Tuvalu does lose its land? Does it lose its sovereignty over that area? Who gets access to Tuvalu's territorial oceans? How can exiled Tuvaluans benefit from this distant patch of water? 'This is unprecedented stuff,' says Greenpeace's Angenette Heffernan. She predicts that under-resourced Pacific countries will have to lobby to change the UN law of the sea to ensure that if they lose their land, at least their waters are protected.

Tuvalu's resettlement plan begins this year. Priority will be given to those who don't own any land on Tuvalu or who live in particularly vulnerable areas. Panapase Nelesone, the government's chief secretary, says they will not allow their most educated or skilled citizens to take up the offer of a home in New Zealand. 'We don't want to train our people and then send them away again. We need them here.'

Standing chest-high in the turquoise water off one of Funafuti's outer islets, Cliff O'Brien, twenty-five, looks shocked when I ask if he would leave Tuvalu for New Zealand. His great-grandfather was an Irish missionary who landed on Tuvalu and married a local girl. Cliff, too, has travelled the world, working as a seaman, but, like many young Tuvaluans, remains ferociously loyal to the islands. 'This is my home. I have no choice. Of course this is where I want to stay, but if the islands go under we will have to try and preserve Tuvalu sometime else, in another country. We want to keep our island and maintain our relationship with the land. Land is very important to us.'

But, in increasing numbers, people have been drifting away from the islands. 'Every year you see four or five families going,' says Iupasi. 'It is very slow, but they are moving out. Most of our people just go to New Zealand for a weekend then stay.' They are drawn to Auckland, the largest Polynesian city in the world, and hope their cultural affinity with Maoris and other Polynesians living there will help preserve some Tuvaluan traditions.

One person is definitely departing: despite his analogy of the Tuvaluan PM being the skipper of a sinking ship, Talake wants to retire to New Zealand, where his two sons are now living. 'I am going there to be with someone who loves you and looks after you well,' he says. There are no pensions in Tuvalu, even for a prime minister.

'Tuvaluans do not like the western style of living,' says the Rev. Etuati. 'There are no old people's homes where we dump our parents. It is very hard to leave your father or mother because you are the person to care for them. If you go to New Zealand, you can send money back, but people also like to sit beside their parents. It's the Pacific way.' He has advised his congregation not to go to New Zealand. 'I've been there and I don't like to live in these places,' he says. 'Time is money there. I like to live my life here and I want to be buried with my ancestors.'

Other Tuvaluans, too, insist that they are not yet ready to give up a lifestyle where they can still survive on the sea and, if they own land, can evade the slavery of the wage economy. 'I was thinking of migrating because of the rising seas,' says Iupasi, who recently visited his brother and sister in New Zealand:

> I think everybody is thinking of migrating. But every year I prefer to stay here. The rent is too much in New Zealand. You have to work there. It's *palangi* [white 'European'] life there: you have to pay your rent, then you sleep. You have to be wise about using your money. It's not like here. Most of the time here, you have plenty of friends. Over there, if you don't have a car, you just stay in the house. You are isolated.

One Tuvaluan who has moved abroad, Puasina Bott, returns regularly, partly to visit her thriving shop, TV Varieties Store. She loves her home, but finds the communal life on the island difficult. 'If I am here any longer than two weeks I feel obliged to give A$2,000 here, A$200 there, to the first cousin of my sister, who is considered a very close relation. People come and ask for money, and it is expected of you to give it if you can. It is the Pacific way.'

She brought up three daughters in Melbourne with her Australian husband, but took them back to Tuvalu every eighteen months when they were young. 'As a Tuvaluan woman, I did relate Tuvaluan culture to them, so it is not too hard for them to adjust when they come back here,' she explains. 'They are used to their grandparents kissing them all over, not just a "mwwwup" on the cheek, and they know how they should behave in front of other Tuvaluans. I brought the girls up in two cultures.'

Iupasi is confident that most of the 1,000 Tuvaluans in New Zealand 'are still maintaining the culture over there'. But the next generation?

I know that after three, four, five years there, most of the young ones don't think about the Tuvaluan culture any more. They prefer going out; it is better than going to the *fateles* [traditional island celebrations of dancing and drumming]. They take on the *palangi* ways. They go there because they want the easy life, then they find it is not so easy. You're not happy with your life there. It is not your life.

Some doubt that Tuvaluan life could survive, anyway. 'Our identity as Tuvaluans will not just disappear when

297

we go to other countries because of global warming,' says the Rev. Etuati. 'It has already started to disappear because of the influence of modernisation. Most of our people are exposed overseas in education. Change is coming now.'

2002

*

In the two decades since I visited, Tuvalu has become a cause célèbre of the climate crisis. Tuvaluans are used to being dropped in on by writers of books, diplomats and dignitaries – UN secretary general António Guterres visited in 2019. But the tiny nation's woes only periodically come into focus in the wealthy west. Limiting global heating to 2°C won't be enough for Tuvalu: their prime minister took to the stage of the 2015 UN Climate Change Conference to appeal for 1.5°C. 'Let's do it for Tuvalu,' said Enele Sopoaga. 'For if we save Tuvalu, we save the world.'

Despite the loss of young people to New Zealand, the islands' population has grown, to 12,000. Islanders report that flooding is an increasing occurrence. During the highest measured sea levels, 46 per cent of the central inhabited area of Funafuti is below sea level. Latest estimates suggest the islands will become uninhabitable around the middle of this century. The nation is likely to cease to exist in a physical form by this century's end.

2021

Sheffield's war on trees

When Jenny Hockey was woken by two policemen hammering on her door at 5 a.m. last Thursday, her first fear was that some disaster had befallen her children or grandchildren. But as chainsaws revved in the dark and the officers ordered her to move her car, a disaster was about to befall her street trees. There is often a moment in long-running disputes when one side performs an action so preposterous that its case is forever discredited: so it was with Sheffield's Labour council and its dawn raid to destroy eight trees in Rustlings Road, where Jenny Hockey lives.

A seventy-year-old emeritus professor, she felt unable to stand 'feebly watching' as these mature limes were hacked down, so she stepped past a protective barrier with another pensioner in peaceful protest. Both women were arrested and spent eight hours in a cell. Hockey fears she could face a six-month jail sentence.

The bleak stumps, on which locals have lain flowers, are perhaps not as distressing as the council document published at 4.25 a.m. last Thursday morning: its independent tree panel found that seven of the eight trees were in good condition with a good life expectancy. Ah, experts.

There is something rotten in Sheffield and it's not the

36,000 mature street trees in this uniquely green city. Contrary to council claims, an independent survey in 2007 found that just 1,000 required replacing. Instead, 4,000 so far have been chopped down by Amey, who are four years into a 25-year PFI contract to manage Sheffield's roads.

This contract is disastrous for trees because, like big old buildings, big old trees cost more to maintain. A newly planted tree is far cheaper over the 25-year contract. If a PFI deal were signed to manage Buckingham Palace, it would be demolished.

This is no parochial dispute. Enfeebled local authorities have signed secret PFI contracts (even the local MP Nick Clegg can't see Sheffield's unredacted version) across the land.

The myopic mathematics involved fail to account for the financial contribution a mature tree makes to flood alleviation, air quality, climate-change amelioration and property prices. That's before we consider trees' impact on mental and physical health. And is it irrelevant that local people find these trees beautiful?

Sheffield says it must engage in sensible husbandry, and trees will be replanted, but poor Jenny Hockey must see her name in the news. The people responsible for this controversy in Sheffield – from councillor Bryan Lodge to Sheffield city council chief executive John Mothersole to Amey chief executive Andy Milner – should be named too. They won't feel shamed but they should.

2016

In praise of breathing:
the case for Sheffield's street trees

In 1985 Neil Kinnock made his most famous speech, attacking 'the grotesque chaos of a Labour council – a *Labour* council – hiring taxis to scuttle round a city handing out redundancy notices to its own workers'. He was talking about Liverpool, but last Friday I visited Sheffield and heard an echo of Kinnock's oratory from another lifelong Labour man. This was Richard Hawley, the singer-songwriter, who castigated his Labour council for creating a situation where pensioners are prosecuted under anti-trade union legislation for peacefully opposing the felling of trees by a multinational corporation.

Two pensioners, Jenny Hockey, seventy, and Freda Brayshaw, seventy-one, will appear in Sheffield magistrates court on Thursday. Hawley was speaking at the launch of a new competition to find people's favourite trees in Sheffield.

This contest, organised by campaigner Rob McBride, is a riposte to the city council, which signed a 25-year private finance initiative contract with Amey to manage its roads that is now causing the felling of thousands of Sheffield's 36,000 street trees. The fact that Hawley's fellow judges include Jarvis Cocker and Nick Banks from Pulp,

Chris Packham and myself might lend credence to council supporters' best defence: luvvies from leafy districts are opposing a Labour administration seeking to help the poor.

But every furious local I met votes Labour, including Hawley, the least luvvie person imaginable. As he said:

> This hasn't got anything to do with politics. I'm a lifelong dyed-in-the-wool Labour voter. I was on picket lines with my dad. I don't view protesting against the unnecessary wastage of trees as all of a sudden I've become fucking middle class. Chopping down shit that helps you breathe is evidently wrong. We're not talking about left or right. We're talking about the body. It boils down to something really simple. Do you like breathing? It's quite good. It's called being alive. What we exhale they inhale and what we inhale they exhale. The end.

It wasn't quite the end because Hawley continued to wax lyrical about the ubiquity of nature in his home city, such as the kestrel (the bird, not the can, someone joked) he watched perched on a tower block that morning. 'People in the north have struggled massively because of cuts. I do understand how difficult it is. When we've got families who can't afford this or that, a tree doesn't seem that important. But to me, having lived here all my life, your environment has got to be everything,' he said. 'I've got two words. "Asset." "Problem." How did an asset become a problem? This is a fucking beautiful asset.'

He was such an inspiring speaker, I offered to ghost-write a column for him. But becoming a celebrity campaigner isn't his style. As he explained: 'People think it's a thin strip between artist and celebrity. It isn't. It's the fucking M1. Once you step across, you can't go back.'

2017

＊

As tree-felling, direct action and court cases continued, Sheffield city council was chastised by the Forestry Commission and the Information Commissioner's Office, as well as numerous politicians, celebrities, tree experts and local people. Eventually, in 2019, the council began to work constructively with local people seeking to save cherished street trees. Cynics would say that by then many mature trees had been felled but at least 'condemned' street trees could now be saved with kerb repairs, which had previously been deemed 'impossible'. The council's handling of the furore was scathingly criticised by the Local Government Ombudsman in 2020 but calls for an independent inquiry into the saga were brushed aside.

2021

Fast train coming:
walking the line of HS2

West Ruislip to Great Missenden
Ron Ryall, wearing an oil-smudged blue boiler suit, was fettling a cream Morris Minor in his low wooden workshop on a lane where the suburbs of West Ruislip give way to scrapyards, dog kennels and horse paddocks. A strong whiff of solvents filled his shed and the rain battered on the roof. Ryall was born in a council house on this lane and started his car bodywork repair business there in 1962; it remained, he said, his own little world.

Earlier that day, in an August downpour, I had set out to walk the route of the first phase of HS2, the new high-speed railway that, when it is completed in 2026, will stretch from London to Birmingham. I wanted to follow at 3 mph the path the trains will take at 225 mph, to see how they will transform the middle of England. Stepping out from West Ruislip station, where HS2 will emerge from a tunnel under north-west London, I crossed Breakspear Road South. Cars sluiced past noisily on wet asphalt. A forbidding fence stopped me exploring Newyears Green Covert, the first of fifty-nine ancient woodlands (more than 400 years old) which will be blighted, or even obliterated, by this first phase of HS2, according to the

Woodland Trust. I had to press myself into brambles on a single-track road to avoid lorries destined for a municipal tip. The rain had penetrated my waterproof, and I was grateful for the chemical embrace of Ryall's workshop.

Under the current plans for the route of HS2, one pillar of a viaduct whisking high-speed trains over the Colne Valley will go through Ryall's living room. 'It's going to wipe my house out,' he said, giving me an intense look from behind wire-framed, aviator-style spectacles. 'But do you know the thing that really bites?' he pointed to his home, which was not visible behind an overgrown hedge. 'It's Grade II-listed. Queen Elizabeth I visited it in 1601. Cecil Kinross, who won the Victoria Cross at Passchendaele – he was born there.' Four generations of Ryall's family live in the house – his mother, his aunt, Ryall and his wife, their son and daughter, and their grandchildren. He recently restored the property, the pedigree of which meant that he required approval from the planning authorities for every detail. 'We took ten years rebuilding it – they were arguing about the colour of the roof tiles – and within six weeks of finishing it, they said they were going to bloody bulldoze it.'

His workshop will be erased by the new line too. 'This isn't a hard-luck story. I've got everything I could possibly want. I've worked all my bloody life for that – from a council house to a mansion. I'm quite proud of what I've done. It's just this "well, we're taking it" attitude. Everybody feels sorry for you.'

'I don't,' interrupted his colleague Mick, who was removing the dents from a Vauxhall. 'He's always fucking moaning.'

Ryall laughed. He had been to Westminster to petition MPs about changing the route. Anyone affected by HS2 can address concerns to a select committee of six MPs, who can ask HS2 Ltd, the government-funded company that is developing the railway, to tweak its plans. 'I love my country but I fear my government,' he said, fishing some sheets of A4 from his pocket with a flourish. It was a British Library factsheet about Britain's constitution. 'We haven't got one! And we should have. It's all going wrong. This is wrong – what they are doing with ordinary people.'

HS2 will be the first mainline railway built between British cities since the Great Central linked London and Sheffield in 1899. During the twentieth century Britain built roads, not railways, and other countries swooshed past us: the Japanese with their 198 mph Shinkansen, the French with their 200 mph TGVs and the Chinese with their 268 mph Maglev. So when the government announced HS2 in 2010, it emphasised that 250 mph trains will cut London–Birmingham rail journeys to forty-nine minutes, saving thirty-two minutes. Critics questioned the need for modest time-savings and deplored the rising cost of HS2 to a predicted £56.6 billion, nearly ten times the price of the 109-kilometre HS1 between the Channel Tunnel and London. In response, HS2 Ltd reduced the top speed of the trains, and placed less emphasis on shorter journey times in its publicity announcements. Instead, HS2's supporters have argued that a new south–north connection will ease a looming capacity crisis on the railways and boost the economy beyond London. The West Coast Mainline from London to Glasgow via Birmingham and Manchester cannot carry many more trains: the solution is the most expensive piece of infrastructure ever built in Britain.

This glamorous project enjoys the cross-party support of the Conservatives, Labour and the Liberal Democrats. Phase one, 192 kilometres from the capital to Birmingham, is minutely mapped out. A bill is expected to be passed by parliament in 2017, granting powers to begin construction. Spades will hit the soil the following year.

Misbourne Valley to Wendover

Railways are well liked and environmentally friendly, passenger numbers are soaring and HS2 is as popular with Westminster politicians as it is with Chinese investors. I expected to find opposition as I explored how HS2 will change the middle of England but, as I walked on, I was surprised by the depth of the disconnect from Westminster thinking. To many residents, HS2 has come to symbolise a country run against the interests of the many and in the interests of the few.

On the second day of my journey, I met Jacky Statham standing by a stile in drizzle on the side of the Misbourne valley, above her home in the village of Great Missenden.

The route of HS2 will pass a few kilometres from her door. Asked what she felt about HS2, she said: 'Absolute horror. Despair, horror, depression, anxiety. They are lovely big expensive houses round here. We have to be careful not to say, "My house used to be worth £3 million, now it's worth £2 million," but there are a lot of normal people here too, like me.' The Chilterns is a place of beech woods whose residents tolerate the slow trains on tracks laid by Victorians into Marylebone station. Following the route of HS2 there was easy. 'Stop HS2' and 'Bury HS2' posters were fixed to lampposts, banners hung between fine trees over country roads. In response to a well-organised campaign, it has been agreed that the line will be buried in a sixteen-kilometre tunnel beneath the chalk hills, emerging by the village of South Heath.

The valley was filled with traffic noise from the busy A413 and a line of pylons crackled in the damp. 'Where we are standing is the heart of an Area of Outstanding Natural Beauty designated by law, unless the government dictates that they can completely destroy it. Max, stop it,' she said, as one of her Norfolk terriers leapt at my legs. 'It's like the partition of India – they just got a blue crayon out. It should be in a tunnel to the other side of Wendover. Once it's done it's – pardon my French – buggered for ever.'

The beech copses that hugged the hillsides smelt of foxes and were filled with pheasants. They reminded me of the illustrations in *Danny the Champion of the World*,

Roald Dahl's romantic children's story about a boy and his poacher father. (It was not until I walked into Great Missenden and saw a museum decorated with the words 'Swizzfigglingly Flushbunkingly Gloriumptious' that I realised this was where Dahl lived.) The footpaths I followed became swamped with knapweed, bramble and nettle. I reached a field of old tractors and rusty bits of machinery. This pleasantly dilapidated farm will be wiped out as HS2 crosses the valley on another viaduct. A yellow JCB was running in the yard and inside a dusty barn I found a dusty farmer wearing a bright blue jumper.

'There's still a lot of this around here,' he said, tugging on an imaginary forelock when I asked him about HS2 (though he declined to give his name). His grandfather and father were tenant farmers and obeyed strict rules: they were not even allowed to shoot a rabbit for dinner and, as a boy, he would not walk up his landlord's drive with hands in pockets. He had been 'daft enough' to buy seventy hectares in his thirties and was still going, aged sixty-eight, with beef cattle and arable land. And HS2? 'A pain in the arse. You can't plan anything.' Farmers plan five, ten years ahead and this complaint was repeated along the route.

What about the consultation process? He felt it had not included the little people: HS2 Ltd 'haven't really met anybody – only those that want a free lunch, the Hooray Henrys'. And so he had not petitioned parliament. Instead, he had simply received official HS2 letters addressed 'to the owner'. Over the last five years, he said, no one had bothered to discover his name. 'We haven't seen anyone with a collar and tie yet, with money in his pocket, who can tell us what to do.'

This farmer was nurturing his land to pass on to his son. 'That's what's farming is about. Well, what we think farming is about.' He gestured to the lovely patchwork countryside around us. 'We've made it. The peasants have made it.'

Stoke Mandeville to Finemere

At Wendover, thirty kilometres into my walk, the Chilterns vanished and the Vale of Aylesbury lay ahead, flatter fields of heavy clay soil that clung to my walking boots. HS2 will pass close to the modest housing estates of west Aylesbury and at a more respectful distance from Waddesdon Manor, a French chateau built on a wooded hill by Baron Ferdinand de Rothschild in 1874. It was uncanny how HS2 appeared to be so straight but subtly avoided stately homes, churches and (most) golf courses. It could not, however, miss the estate belonging to Christopher Prideaux, whose family have farmed a patch of the old royal hunting forest of Bernwood, in Buckinghamshire, for 500 years.

Prideaux and his wife live in a low-ceilinged farmhouse to which they moved so their son and his family could reside in their spacious old hall. Prideaux was smartly turned out in a blue checked shirt, red tank top and mustard cords, but drove me around his 560 hectares in a middle-aged Subaru estate with tattered newspapers in the footwell. HS2 will pretty much divide his land down the middle. One of his two tenant farms will cease to be economically viable. He will lose farm buildings and a lodge. 'In an estate agent's patter, it's "a fine rural location" and all that sort of garbage,' he said. The new line will pass shudderingly close to the hall, which is listed as Grade II* – a highly protected category of building. 'It's an architectural mix-up of Elizabethan, Jacobean and William and Mary. Everybody's had a go at it,' he said, which did not really do justice to the gracefully proportioned house. He then added: 'It's one of the three or four most important houses on the line between London and Birmingham.'

Residents within 60 metres of the line can sell their property to the government for its 'unblighted' value. Even if Prideaux does not sell up, he will be compensated for HS2: there will be money for lost acreage, lost production and also 'injurious affection'. Which means? 'In my best Australian, total buggeration.' Prideaux scoffed at the theory shared by some local people that big landowners secretly favoured HS2 because they will make millions. But then, he reflected, 'everybody's situation is different and so it's easy for HS2 to play divide and rule. If you're an elderly landowner with no particular successors you might say, "I'll roll over for a cheque."'

Prideaux, a former high sheriff of Buckinghamshire, was not rolling over. He was lobbying MPs and petitioning parliament. 'Cameron is a young man in a hurry. Major infrastructure projects are not things to be done in a hurry when we are a little country.' He had a touching faith in the democratic process and was looking forward to a Lords' debate on the economic case for HS2, scheduled for the following month.

We sat in the Subaru, Prideaux discussing HS2's destruction of his huge blackthorn hedges, a relic of the hunting forest, and the rare butterflies and bats that depend on them. Environmental consultants employed by HS2 have been scrambling to understand what wildlife it threatens, and what 'mitigation' – the planting of replacement hedgerows, woods or other habitats – can be undertaken. Prideaux watches Bechstein's bats, a particularly rare species, feeding in Grendon Wood, the inspiration for Shakespeare's *A Midsummer Night's Dream*.

After Prideaux dropped me off in a neighbour's muddy farmyard, I climbed a hill into Finemere Woods, an ancient woodland owned by Berkshire, Buckinghamshire and Oxfordshire Wildlife Trust. At the top was a scrawny oak with a creviced scar – part of the mouse-sized Bechstein's main roost. HS2 will divide these roosts from the bat's feeding grounds on Prideaux's land. Tim Read, a young ecologist with a bouncy stride, took me on a tour of the wood. 'There's also brown long-eared, Natterer's, pipistrelles,' he said. An infrequently used freight line taking Londoners' rubbish to landfill had become 'a great little highway for bats' alongside the wood, he said. But high-speed lines do not permit wooded embankments. Trees – and deer and badgers – are a menace to fast trains.

So a concrete and steel-fenced barrier will be built along the length of the track, through the middle of England.

I walked on, refuelling with blackberries from the hedgerow, following the route as it swept past a vast new incinerator, several quarries and landfill sites and a wealth of handsome working farms. Everyone I came across criticised HS2. Phil Jenkins was planting lavender outside his 1930s semi in Calvert Green; the line will pass within metres of his home. 'These bloody – excuse my French – trains. It's just for rich men,' he said.

'It's vanity, isn't it?' said Mike Roberts, taking down banner adverts around the immaculate recreation ground in the village of Twyford, the cricket season over for another year. 'Maggie had her tunnel, Blair had his war and Cameron wants his train. It's a legacy.'

'I don't think we're being Nimbys. If we thought it was necessary we'd be for it,' said Pauline Harkin, the tenant at Blackgrounds Farm, a low farmhouse and a cluster of pigsties converted into stables where the only sound was the atonal chirp of sparrows. This year, Harkin had erected a box and attracted barn owls to nest in her barn:

You almost feel cruel enticing them in knowing that in a couple of years they'll be gone. There's no light pollution here, you can see every single star in the sky. They do not understand what they are about to destroy. The sound of birds singing in the morning is amazing here. Once it's gone, it's gone for ever.

Newton Purcell to Hunningham

The Victorians would have enthusiastically endorsed HS2. The Great Central, which opened in 1899, was the brain-child of Sir Edward Watkin, an indefatigable Victorian entrepreneur, and might be considered Britain's first high-speed railway. It duplicated existing routes from Sheffield to London but was a superior piece of engineering: gentle curves and gradients and only one level crossing. Most notably, it was wide enough to take continental trains, for Watkin had a much bigger idea: why not connect England with continental Europe via a tunnel under the Channel? He dug two kilometres beneath the cliffs west of Dover, where he invited dignitaries, including the archbishop of Canterbury and the Prince of Wales, to champagne receptions in the tunnel shaft. But Watkin's scheme was torpedoed by a hostile press and generals who feared a French invasion.

Watkin would surely be gratified to find HS2 shadowing the skeleton of the Great Central, through north Buckinghamshire. I tried following the old line. Many disused railways have been turned into green footpaths, but this had been abandoned and enveloped in hawthorn, sallow and elder, with the occasional fly-tipped fridge thrown from a bridge. I waded through teasels, thistles and rosebay willowherb. Finally, I was confronted by impenetrable dereliction: great mounds of brambles and nettles. I crawled through spiky blackthorn scrub to escape: the wildest place I encountered in central England was an old railway.

We may think of England as an urban country, dominated by people and roads, but HS2's route through the
middle – Buckinghamshire, a smidgen of Oxfordshire,
Northamptonshire and Warwickshire – has been plotted
along a largely unpopulated fieldscape. Each field is like
a room: mostly wheat or pasture but occasionally barley,
oilseed rape, maize or broad beans. Industrial agriculture
may have replaced rural workers with big machines but
a great grid of hedges survives, like capillaries, giving life
to the land. Filled with long-tailed tits or goldfinches or
cackling green woodpeckers, many are as thick as houses,
a coalition of holly, rowan, hazel, dogwood and bramble,
with oaks permitted to grow into grand trees.

I trudged for hours on footpaths without seeing anyone. Over virtually every field in the Vale of Aylesbury
soared a red kite, the handsome hawk that was extinct in
England forty years ago. Occasionally I spotted an agricultural contractor in a pickup. Within half a mile of a village, I met one person walking a dog. Finally, at 11.30 a.m.
on my third day of walking, close to Stoke Mandeville, the
rarest species of all: three children, actually playing in the
countryside.

On a hilltop beyond the Northamptonshire village of
Culworth, I stopped to admire the valley formed by a
nameless tributary of the River Cherwell. HS2 will cut
past a historic battleground, Danes Moor, below. The only
buildings visible across eight kilometres of wheat and pasture were three barns, one of which was a ruin. There were

no houses, no pylons, no roads and no people. It was a landscape sculpted by humans but there were no straight lines, and a kind of alchemy in the mix of fields, hedge-rows, copses; it had evolved at a gentle pace, and plants and animals survived alongside our exploitation of its fertility. So much of England possesses this grace and silence. But it has no voice.

High-speed rail was intended to close up these spaces between us. In turn, they will become less peaceful, less attractive to people and emptier than ever. But perhaps this land was ripe for developments such as HS2 because most of us had already vacated it. By the time I crossed into Warwickshire, I was wearying of the desolation. In the absence of people, communication was via signs: 'Beware of the bull', 'Beware driven golf balls', 'Thieves beware, Selecta-DNA advanced forensic marking is used in this area'. If strangers were not permitted to enjoy the countryside, why would anyone beyond local residents care enough to stop HS2 dividing it? So when I heard someone cheerily singing along to bhangra in his allotment on the edge of Southam, I followed the tune. Kamaljeet Bhandari, an associate specialist at University Hospital Coventry, was tending to his runner beans. 'Oh yes, it's coming just over the back there. I'm all for it,' he said. Pardon? 'If we want to be competing with the first world, then we have to have it. I travel a lot. You go to China or Japan and you'd be amazed [by the railways]. People complain but the problem is, you get old – you want everything to stay the same.'

Suddenly Bhandari produced a carrier bag and filled it with beans for me. He liked walking too. Shouldn't we move more slowly? 'Speed is normal. There's one constant in the world and that's change. Do you want fast Internet? Of course you do. Do you have a computer for a phone? Everybody wants fast from day one.' He hated the dominance of London; how he had to go there to see a good play. But won't HS2 make the capital even more domineering? 'Many people wouldn't think twice about applying for work in the north if they only have a 45-minute journey.' Do we really need to shave half an hour from a London–Birmingham journey? 'If you say that, we should have carts instead of cars.' He laughed. 'I don't know whether I'll be alive to see it. I'll be too old to get on it. It will be too fast for me to catch.'

Warwickshire is densely wooded, its earth ochre and its houses red brick, not stone. I followed where HS2 will cross the pretty Leam valley and dive through the middle of South Cubbington Wood. This ancient woodland was a tangle of honeysuckle and hawthorn; its most charismatic resident a huge pear tree. Reputed to be the second-largest in the UK, it boasted five trunks, three colours – green leaves at head height, yellow further up, red at the top – and no pears. Last week it was named the Woodland Trust Tree of the Year after 10,000 people voted for it. It will be felled to make way for the new railway.

I had arranged to meet Ed Green, chief executive of Warwickshire Wildlife Trust, by the tree. Like a number of conservationists, he agreed that HS2, if planned well, had the potential to benefit the environment, providing a natural corridor through the intensively farmed English countryside. 'We've got climate change pushing species further north, but their habitats have been destroyed and broken up. HS2 is an opportunity to build a piece of ecological infrastructure, a wildlife corridor that allows species to move up through that landscape,' he said. Green sought a constructive relationship with HS2. He had offered HS2 Ltd his Wildlife Trust's skills and surveying expertise. He had petitioned the HS2 committee of MPs and, ultimately, hoped to persuade them to tunnel under South Cubbington Wood. While the golf course at nearby Kenilworth had been reprieved, this woodland was still earmarked to be sliced in two.

'What is HS2's ambition?' said Green. 'It's just to get trains from Birmingham to London as quickly as possible. The cost of being as ambitious for the environment would be a fraction of 1 per cent of the railway. It's a philosophy – that the environment is a barrier to this sort of thing.'

South Cubbington to Kenilworth

Beyond Cubbington Wood, I approached a busy A-road and spied a huge chestnut-coloured creature inside an aviary. One large leather glove lay on a garden gatepost. I walked through the gate and knocked on a door, which opened to reveal a white-bearded man with a gravelly voice. Bob Edwards has led an interesting life: ladies' hairdresser, car-sales manager, repossession agent – 'I've had a gun in my nose' – and, for sixteen years, falconer. He flies Tweed, Richard and Bomber, three South American Harris hawks, and his passion for birds began at school, where he befriended a crow. 'Corvids are very smart. Most birds of prey are,' he said. 'We're the ones who are dumb because we've allowed ourselves to be controlled by TV, electricity, motor cars. They are wonderful things but we've lost contact with the real world.'

What did he think of HS2? 'It's probably necessary,' he said, but he was upset by how HS2 Ltd has treated those affected by it. Edwards' home and business won't be destroyed by the line – although it passes close enough to diminish his quality of life – but his birds could be. The field next door will store soil excavated during construction. Edwards fears this long-undisturbed earth will release aspergillus spores, a fungal mould that kills raptors. He also flies his hawks every day on his neighbouring 500-acre farm, through which HS2 will speed. 'My birds don't understand a 200 mph train. They will pursue their quarry – a rabbit or pheasant – unaware of the potential danger. Effectively, I've got to move.'

Before I finished my walk, the House of Lords debated the economic case for HS2. Torrential rain fell on the queue of people waiting outside parliament to go through security. Before listening to the debate, I ducked into the oak-panelled Walpole Room, where the HS2 committee were listening to petitioners. Political sketch-writers have mocked these discussions for resembling an obscure provincial planning meeting but this, surely, was democracy in action, where citizens could discuss their homes, hopes and livelihoods.

A farmer, Wendy Gray, gave evidence. She lived in the Chilterns and described the area as 'refreshment' for stressed urbanites. She expressed fears about the construction's impact on her business, local roads, noise and barn owls. She suggested that HS2's mitigation could include new chalk grassland. She was polite and deferential and tried to entertain the committee by brandishing a plastic bag containing a regurgitated barn owl pellet.

The panel of MPs – all men, all of late middle age – barely glanced up. Only the chair, Robert Syms, looked engaged. Attending to endless petitioners must become repetitive. HS2's barrister, James Strachan QC, was listening closely, however, and addressed specific points with a lawyer's care to make no rash promises: HS2's noise would be less than traffic on the A413; HS2 were working with the RSPB to 'mitigate' for barn owls; and, 'If there's a need for chalk grassland, that's the sort of thing that can be put into these areas to compensate.' Wendy Gray was allowed to respond: 'It's very difficult to be reassured on an unknown quantity,' she said.

As the committee meeting rolled on, the House of Lords debate was under way. Older versions of 1980s and 1990s politicians – Lord Carrington, John Prescott – tottered in and out of the chamber. At first, their debate drifted far from the concerns of the people I had met.

Lord Desai spoke about 'using animal spirits' to decide in favour of HS2. Lord Mitchell wondered whether high-speed travel was relevant because we would soon connect via holograms of ourselves. Labour peers from the north tended to favour HS2; others argued that the Manchester–Leeds electrification was more important. Lord Truscott revealed that the expected cost of construction per mile for HS2 is up to nine times higher than France's high-speed lines. Lord Mitchell wondered if driverless cars would confound forecasts of ever-rising rail passenger numbers. The Bishop of Chester quoted from Ecclesiastes.

'My worry is that the proponents of HS2 have made the terrible business mistake of falling in love with their investment,' declared Lord Wolfson, a Conservative peer and Next chief executive who, at forty-eight, was by far the youngest-looking person in the chamber. 'The alternative to HS2 is not another grand project, it is myriad small, high-return projects that would deliver benefits in the near future: bypasses, flyovers, underpasses, commuter line upgrades, carriage improvements, platform improvements and more . . . projects that would serve the many rather than the few.'

Berkswell to Birmingham
My walk ended on the autumn equinox, as it had begun: in the rain. Another disused railway line near Kenilworth was now an urban 'Greenway': the companionship of cyclists and dogwalkers was welcome after my discomfort

on the deserted, brambled-choked footpaths of rural England. This tree-lined path will be noisily overtaken, and partially rerouted, by HS2. The countryside was wooded but the city's proximity was revealed in the packaging (Carling, Capri-Sun, Cadbury's Fingers) thrown onto verges. Planes descended into Birmingham International, as long-bodied and ponderous as cormorants rising from the ornamental lake by Berkswell Hall.

I arrived on the edge of Birmingham. Security guards at a haulage depot eyed me. White-shirted motorists turned to stare as they sped by in executive saloons. A pedestrian is a rare sight in these parts. To the east lay the A452; to the south, the A45; to the west, the M42. Between all these connections was an island of rough meadows with a buzzard calling overhead. I found myself on a country road featuring half a dozen cottages, with porches and greenhouses. This unexpected oasis was the site of the projected Birmingham Interchange, an overhead monorail transferring passengers to the National Exhibition Centre and the airport, billed by Lord Adonis in the Lords' debate as a '145-hectare site with the potential for 20,000 new jobs and thousands of homes'. It could become 'a major enterprise zone', Adonis, the former transport secretary now employed by HS2, told the Lords debate excitedly. But it needed 'strong leadership' because there were 'major unresolved green-belt issues'.

These included what to do with residents. A 79-year-old woman was polishing her small car (she didn't want to give her name). Her life had been uprooted more than forty years ago by 'the road people'. Now it was the turn of 'the railway people'. 'We were moved here to make way for the M42. Now they are moving us again.'

The woman's home will be surrounded by a car park for HS2's Birmingham Interchange. She attended a local HS2 meeting but felt patronised and ignored. 'They have security at the door. There were five or six men in beautiful grey suits. The men don't want to know. They just talk to other men.' Eventually she had collared the 'understudy engineer' who traced a finger down a map, and declared: 'You're about 200 metres away from the station.' That was the end of the conversation.

Eventually, I found a crossing over the M42 to the National Exhibition Centre (NEC), which advertised itself as the best-connected spot in Britain. The ultimate logic of our multiplying means of connecting with each other is that the countryside becomes a void between roads, railways and runways.

We need connections, of course: I trotted through the NEC, seeking its train station to take me home. I found a footpath around a cavernous new mall and supercasino, the quiet middle of England a vanishing memory as I trod over plastic grass on a temporary floating bridge that spanned an artificial lake.

2015

*

HS2 continues to be built, and campaigners continue to oppose it, with direct action against the construction including treehouse camps and tunnels dug into chalk by activists, including veteran anti-roads campaigner Dan 'Swampy' Hooper. Construction is underway on the next leg, from Birmingham to Crewe, with the government committed to an extension to Manchester. In late 2021, the government abandoned plans for the leg to Leeds. This has pleased some environmentalists opposed to the line, which calculations show will be a net emitter of carbon during its lifetime. The cost of HS2 continues to rise: the latest government estimate after scrapping the Leeds leg is between £72 billion and £98 billion (at 2019 prices); critics argue it will be double that. In 2020 Ron Ryall lost his home. A wide swathe of Cubbington Wood was cleared for the line. The Cubbington pear tree was chopped down.

2021

A Berlin Wall for wildlife

A public inquiry begins today into the most destructive new road in a generation. The six-lane M4 through Newport is a little twisty and vulnerable to traffic jams, so the Welsh government wants to flex new borrowing powers to fund a £1 billion-plus 'relief' road.

This twenty-kilometre motorway will carve through the Gwent Levels, dividing and destroying an ancient wetland that is one of the last strongholds for the shrill carder bee and the new home, as of last summer, to Wales's first breeding cranes for 400 years. The road will wreck four sites of special scientific interest, and create a 'Berlin wall for wildlife' across the marshes for otters, water voles and rare dragonflies.

I had assumed the bad old days of ripping up nature reserves for motorways were long gone, but the scale of wildlife destruction on the Gwent Levels is bigger than both the Newbury bypass and Twyford Down, which triggered mass protests in the 1990s.

The justification is 'resilience'. The south Wales economy supposedly grinds to a halt when the M4 at Newport is jammed. Are we so rich (in borrowed money) that we can duplicate motorways?

Credit to the Welsh government for one positive piece

of policymaking. Two years ago it appointed a commissioner, Sophie Howe, with a legal duty to advise ministers on whether projects offer a good deal for future generations. Last week Howe concluded the road was not a good deal. 'Building roads is what we have been doing for the last fifty years and is not the solution we should be seeking in 2017 and beyond,' she said.

Will the Welsh government listen to its own commissioner? Cynics fear the public inquiry is a foregone conclusion. It isn't – if enough local people join Howe and other campaigners in telling politicians they don't want this divisive road.

2017

*

The Gwent Levels turned out to be a rare victory for wildlife verses road-building. In 2019 the Labour-led Welsh government announced it was scrapping the scheme, to howls of outrage from business leaders and Conservatives. Despite the UK's commitment to net zero emissions by 2050, at the time of writing (2021) the government is still wedded to what it billed in 2020 as 'the largest ever investment in English strategic roads' – a £27 billion road-building programme over five years.

2021

Once there were swarms of butterflies in our skies ...

On a bright spring day, the chalky slopes of the Chilterns smell of warm thyme. Tiny purple violets bloom underfoot. For miles beyond, the Vale of Aylesbury unfolds in a tapestry of newly minted trees, yellow fields and the spires of village churches. This great vista of the English countryside seems gloriously immutable, unchanged since Victorian times, when Walter Rothschild would set out from Tring Park, his country house in the valley below, to throw his net at our summer butterflies and place them in his extraordinary zoological museum.

Not everything, however, would please the eye of Victorian lovers of nature. An easyJet plane casts a shadow across the downland. The air is filled with the complaint of two diggers, quarrying chalk from the bottom of the hill. But what would really make Rothschild weep is what is missing: the sky and the steep meadows dotted with the white flowers of wild strawberry are almost bereft of butterflies.

A casual eye might not notice it. Butterflies are still a conspicuous symbol of our summers, much celebrated by everyone from Wordsworth to Nabokov. On the Chilterns, a male orange tip patrols a hedgerow, two peacocks spiral into the air in a territorial dogfight and a speckled wood jinks its way through the trees. This scattering of a few common species is pitiful, however, compared with the riches that once adorned our countryside in summer. Near contemporaries of Rothschild wrote of skimming hundreds of purple hairstreaks from the trees or catching a hundred Lulworth skippers in an hour. In 1892 S. G. Castle Russell took a walk through the New Forest: 'Butterflies alarmed by my approach arose in immense numbers to take refuge in the trees above. They were so thick that I could hardly see ahead and indeed resembled a fall of brown leaves.' A few centuries earlier, Richard Turpyn recorded a probable mass migration to or from Britain in his *Chronicles of Calais* during the reigns of Henry VII and VIII: 'an innumerable swarme of whit buttarflyes . . . so thicke as flakes of snowe' that they blotted out views of Calais for workers in fields beyond the town.

Swarms of butterflies have long disappeared. And a relentless decline may now become terminal for some of our best-loved species. Following the wet summer of 2007, last year was a disaster for butterflies: the lowest number was recorded for twenty-seven years. Of Britain's precious fifty-nine resident species, twelve experienced their worst ever year since the scientific monitoring of butterfly numbers began in 1976.

I began a less than scientific monitoring of butterflies in a little notepad when I was eight, helping my dad count the tiny brown argus on the Norfolk coast where we spent our summer holidays. Finding this darting, chocolate-brown gem ignited an awkward passion for butterflies that I kept well hidden during my teenage years. Dad and I would go on expeditions to discover, and photograph, rare species: we would sit in a wet meadow in Cumbria waiting for the marsh fritillary to emerge, or hover by piles of horse manure in the woodlands of Surrey, hoping the majestic, haughty (and turd-loving) purple emperor would descend from the treetops for us. Twenty years on, some of the nature reserves we visited have lost their precious rarities. If trends continue, another couple of bad summers could kill off some species for ever.

Numbers of the delicate wood white were down by 66 per cent last year on dismal 2007; its population has slumped by 90 per cent over the long-term recording period. The Duke of Burgundy and the high brown fritillary are most at risk of extinction. The high brown survives in just fifty small sites: at one spot in Dartmoor, there were 7,200; in 1995 last year, there were just eighty-seven. Nationwide, numbers have fallen by 85 per cent over ten years. 'This run of bad weather has really pushed those species to the brink in many areas,' says Martin Warren, the chief executive of Butterfly Conservation.

Butterflies find it difficult to fly, feed and mate in bad weather but these figures are not just a seasonal blip caused by freakishly soggy summers. The collecting of British butterflies has ceased to be acceptable and yet butterfly populations have still plummeted. Far more devastating than unscrupulous collectors of old has been industrial

agriculture and the loss of 97 per cent of England's natural grassland and wildflower meadows; planting conifers
or letting our broadleaved woodlands become too overgrown for woodland flowers; and the sprawl of motorways and urban development.

To this deadly cocktail has been added a new poison:
climate change. In theory, a gentle global warming should
benefit almost all of Britain's butterflies. Creatures of
sunshine, most of our butterflies are found in southern
England where many are at the limit of their natural range;
as our summers become hotter, these butterflies should
thrive and spread further north. There are a few winners
already: the beautiful comma is moving north and the rare
silver-spotted skipper has done well thanks to hotter summers. Britain may also be visited more regularly by exotic
species that were once rare migrants.

The fate of one much-loved native shows that this
happy outcome, however, will not come to pass for most
species. The small tortoiseshell is the Labrador of the butterfly world: cheerful and content to live close to humans.
Its caterpillars devour ubiquitous nettles. As an adult
butterfly, it feasts on suburban flowers and hibernates in
garden sheds, pitter-pattering against our windows when
spring comes round again. Thanks to climate change, it
is spreading north and is now seen for the first time in
remote parts of Scotland. Unfortunately, so too is *Sturmia
bella* (how the person who named this ugly brute could
call it beautiful is beyond me), a species of parasitic fly.

This nasty fly was recorded for the first time in Britain in Hampshire eleven years ago. By last summer, it had reached Merseyside thanks to a modus operandi every bit as gory as the *Alien* films. It lays its microscopic eggs on patches of nettles where small tortoiseshell caterpillars feed. These unwittingly eat the fly's eggs, which become tiny worms inside the caterpillar, bursting out of their bodies just when the small tortoiseshell is beginning its miraculous transformation into a butterfly inside its chrysalis.

Last year was the worst ever year for small tortoiseshells, its population slumping by 45 per cent compared with 2007, despite thousands of migrant small tortoiseshells arriving from Europe in September. In southern and central England, it appears to have been virtually wiped out: during my afternoon roaming the Chilterns last week, I saw ten peacocks and twelve yellow brimstones and the odd rather more elusive species, such as the grizzled skipper, but not a single small tortoiseshell.

Is *Sturmia bella* wiping it out? Where the fly finds small tortoiseshell caterpillars, their mortality rate is 61 per cent, according to research by Dr Owen Lewis, an ecologist at Oxford University who is studying the impact of the fly. As with many declining species, there is seldom just one cause and the case against *Sturmia bella* is not yet conclusive. In most instances where new predators arrive, the attacked species eventually adapt to elude them. Other research suggests that, before the last two wet summers, the dry summers of a warming world also hit small

tortoiseshell caterpillars: low moisture reduces the nutri-
tional quality of nettles.

'Whichever way you look at it, it's linked back to the
climate,' says Tom Brereton, head of butterfly monitoring
at Butterfly Conservation. Climate change, he says, is a
particular problem for our butterflies because our countryside is so fragmented. Decades of ploughing up grassland and ripping out hedgerows means that more than half
our butterfly species are now confined to small islands of
land. When the climate makes the current sites unsuitable,
butterflies will no longer be able to fly elsewhere and find
new sites. 'If you had an intact countryside, butterflies
should be going through the roof, but the species can't
move through the countryside like they once would have
done,' says Brereton. 'Habitats are too fragmented. There
are vacant suitable habitats in parts of the countryside but
the butterflies won't necessarily find them.'

Our largest and most charismatic native butterfly, the
swallowtail, was once found across the fens of East Anglia
and beyond until the draining of these wetlands for arable
agriculture caused its extinction. It is now confined to the
Norfolk Broads. When global warming causes the Broads
to be inundated with sea water – widely expected within
a hundred years – the swallowtail will die unless it is relocated by humans to suitable inland sites. These new sites
will have to be meticulously created to cultivate a single,
rather neurotic wetland plant used by this notoriously
picky species.

Conservationists playing God like this has already happened. The last species to become extinct in Britain was the large blue in 1979. Despite heroic scientific endeavour, the full complexity of this butterfly's weird lifecycle was not understood until it was too late. When tiny, the large blue caterpillar throws itself on to the ground and secretes a tantalising scent, which tricks ants into carefully taking it into their underground nests, whereupon the nasty caterpillar devours ant grubs until it is fully grown. Its dependence on ants was known; but not that it relied on a very particular species, which in turn needed a very specific kind of rough grassland to survive. So, in the 1980s, conservationists brought stock from Sweden and successfully re-established the butterfly on a small field on the edge of Dartmoor. Dad and I were ticked off by a warden when we found this secret meadow, still known only as Site X. The large blue has since been successfully reintroduced into other areas.

With this kind of ingenuity, could we turn the whole country into a giant butterfly farm? Could we save every species by reintroducing them to tailor-made nature reserves or boosting populations with specimens from abroad? 'We might do it for a few species, but it's not the basis for a conservation strategy,' says Warren. 'What about all the other insects? We want to get the habitats right and butterflies will tell us if we are getting it right, and then we'll be getting it right for biodiversity as a whole.'

Amazingly, despite all our knowledge, we still get it wrong. The pearl-bordered fritillary was known as 'the woodman's friend' because it would faithfully follow foresters around broadleaved woods as they coppiced or cut down patches of trees, attracted to the flowers that blossomed in the freshly cut glades in subsequent years. Like many butterflies, it became inextricably linked to the way we managed our landscape, but has undergone a dramatic decline in numbers since this traditional way of 'harvesting' our wood died out.

While conservation management has reintroduced coppicing – which is rarely economically viable because of the falling demand for wood fuel and is now often carried out by volunteers on nature reserves – pearl-bordered fritillaries have continued to die out, often because the work has not been carried out on a big enough scale. Even Monks Wood, a national nature reserve and the site of a celebrated government research station that has been the source of much of our scientific wisdom about butterflies, has lost twelve of its forty species of butterfly since 1954, including the pearl-bordered fritillary.

The decline of butterflies is 'not all farmers and climate change', as Brereton puts it. Some of our rarest butterflies have been inadvertently decimated by conservation efforts. Matthew Oates, the National Trust's adviser on nature, takes me to the beautiful Rodborough Common in the Cotswolds, to see the first Duke of Burgundy butterflies of the year. The delicate beauty of this small, fritillary-like butterfly belies its pugnacious urge to scrap with every other insect that comes near as it suns itself on the steep sides of the common. 'The Oates motto is "never underestimate a butterfly",' says Oates, a jovial polymath who brings his scholarly training in poetry to bear on butterfly conservation. If climate change brings better summers, he points out that some species will become more capable of travelling across our decimated landscape to look for new sites. 'But I am seriously worried for Burgundies. The figures are very alarming. What's messed it up in the last twenty years is conservation management.'

Before climate change, another man-made event, the introduction of the rabbit-killing disease myxomatosis in the 1950s, caused the decline of many grassland butterflies, which relied on large rabbit populations to keep the grass short and full of flowers. Conservation plans saw a widespread reintroduction of grazing to help rare plant species and butterflies such as the Adonis blue. But the Duke of Burgundy requires longer, rougher grassland and a certain size of cowslip plants; overgrazing has caused its population to plummet. Now it exists in such tiny colonies it could easily disappear. 'The track record of conservation management on this butterfly is bloody awful,' says Oates. 'I really think we could lose it.'

We are belatedly getting better at conserving the right kind of land for fragile, complex and, frankly, contrary butterfly species. Butterfly Conservation had one conservation adviser a decade ago; today, thirty advisers help landowners manage 1,000 precious sites. Once the bête noire of conservationists, the Common Agricultural Policy now offers some funding – although not enough – to encourage farmers to manage their land for conservation. 'It's by no means all doom and gloom but getting enough done in enough areas is the problem,' says Warren. New demand for eco-friendly wood fuel from the sustainable harvesting of broadleaved woods would help too, recreating our traditional woodland system in which flowers and butterflies could thrive.

Climate change, however, makes it all much more complicated. As well as new predators, new diseases may destroy native trees, flowers and insects that butterflies depend on. Invasive weeds could crowd out butterfly food plants. Grass and bracken – with which many rare fritillaries have a delicate relationship – are already growing back more vigorously than in the past. Tangled woodland will need clearing more regularly. 'A lot of conservation management won't necessarily work in the future,' says Brereton. 'With climate change, species are changing their habitats and their requirements are changing as well. It can be fatal to manage for what a butterfly needed twenty years ago. We need to keep on the ball with understanding what species need because their requirements are changing as the earth warms up.'

Just as I kept my passion for butterflies hidden for fear of ridicule at school, so the butterfly hunters of old were often derided for such a whimsical, frivolous pursuit.

Butterflies may be pretty but they seem inconsequential ornaments when compared with majestic eagles or pragmatically functional insects such as worms or bees. Every century, butterflies have become extinct in Britain. Why should we care if we lose a few more?

For a start, butterflies are an excellent indicator species: if butterflies are suffering then so too are thousands of less well-monitored insects. (Thanks to the scientists who set up butterfly monitoring in the 1970s and the 1,500 volunteer butterfly recorders who count numbers every summer, we have excellent data showing their decline.) It is insects that pollinate many flowers, help matter decompose and protect other species by preying on pests. Plants, birds, rodents and big, greedy mammals – such as human beings – depend on them. 'There is a good moral case for conservation but there is a pretty good selfish, economic case as well,' says Warren:

> With the economic downturn, people think saving butterflies is pretty low down on our list of priorities, but human beings and the natural world are linked very closely. If the natural world goes to pot, sooner or later we will go to pot. Butterflies' decline probably indicates a rapid decline in invertebrates in general. If the British situation is true across the world, we are heading for a sixth great extinction event. There have been five in the history of the planet and this one will be man-made.

Oates has another reason for saving our butterflies. Each species, in its own way, is part of the cultural identity of our landscape. Butterflies are a 'conduit into natural beauty', he explains. 'They take us on voyages of discovery to some of the most beautiful landscapes in this country.' Many of our earliest memories of summer will involve a vivid image of a butterfly. If we seek out butterflies, they can lead us into a natural world from which we are increasingly estranged by our material, technological and suburban existences. 'We underestimate the importance of beauty and wonder in our lives at our peril,' says Oates. 'As much as I love football, it's no substitute for the real thing.'

After a day failing to see a single small tortoiseshell in the land where thousands once roamed – chased by the nets of obsessives such as Walter Rothschild – I head to a cool stone cupboard in Harrow School where a fraction of the 2.25 million butterflies and moths gathered by Rothschild are stored in mahogany cabinets. This amazing collection of foreign butterflies with iridescent wings of purple, green and gold will be auctioned by Bonhams at the end of May. Beautifully preserved, they look as if they could have been flying last week. This glittering hoard is a melancholy reminder that we are only a hundred butterfly generations from summers of plenty. In time, these dried, dead beauties may be the only butterflies we can gaze upon in wonder.

2009

*

We are much more aware today of the rapid global invertebrate decline which presages a sixth great extinction event, which Martin Warren warned about in this feature. With two-thirds of Britain's fifty-nine native species of butterfly still declining, butterflies remain a useful indicator of what's popularly called 'insect Armageddon'. Some scientists dispute this populist phrase – we lack precise data on insect declines for much of the world – but the patterns of flying insect decline in Britain are mirrored in other countries where industrial agriculture reigns.

Neonicotinoid pesticides implicated in post-1990s insect declines have been banned across the EU but in 2021 the British government announced an exemption for sugar-beet farmers, potentially allowing the pesticide's return, although it was not used during that year.

The high brown fritillary continues to struggle but conservation action has decisively improved the fortunes for the Duke of Burgundy, which is thriving again.

After I wrote this story, I was reprimanded by a reader for calling the parasitic fly implicated in the decline of the small tortoiseshell a 'nasty fly' and an 'ugly brute'. The reader was right – I was wrong. I feel embarrassed by these words now: of course parasitic flies are every bit as beautiful as butterflies and are no worse or better than any other creature seeking to make its way in the world. The only species worthy of such moralistic judgement is, of course, *Homo sapiens*.

2021

Beware celebs bearing trees

The upturned spade, the beneficent smile and the tender sapling gently lowered into a well-watered hole – blessed are the tree-planters. For the planter, careers are built on such fine photo opportunities. For the planted, the blessing of being shoved into soil belonging to a naive new owner is often rather more mixed.

Last week we learned that the Cox's Orange Pippins, planted in 2009 on land acquired by Greenpeace and celebrities including Emma Thompson and Alistair McGowan to stop Heathrow's third runway, had expired in a tangle of rank grassland. Nick Clegg had planted one tree; David Cameron had adopted another.

The trees died because our attention span is closer to that of a mayfly than a mighty oak. A cynic might claim they had served their purpose: 100,000 people signed up as beneficial co-owners of Greenpeace's orchard, the third runway was supposedly defeated, and the charity and its celebrity backers quietly sold the lease back to a local landowner for £1.

Beware the celebrity bearing saplings may be a better aphorism for our times, with Madonna also criticised for receiving generous tax breaks for creating a tree nursery that will screen her new mansion in the Hamptons.

In 1953 Jean Giono – the man more responsible than any other for our modern love of tree-planting – wrote *The Man Who Planted Trees*, a tale of his encounter just before the First World War with a shepherd, Elzéard Bouffier, who roamed a barren patch of France, poking acorns into the dusty soil. When Giono visited the shepherd at the end of the Second World War, he found the countryside transformed – alive with oaks and a newly vigorous local community too.

It is often forgotten that Bouffier was a figment of the imagination of a writer who wanted to 'make trees likeable. Or more specifically make planting trees likeable.'

But planting trees must not be a cheap substitute for real environmental commitment, as Richard Mabey warns in an introduction to a new edition of Giono's tale: 'Tree-planting has too often become an easy escape clause, a cheapskate forfeit for fossil-fuel abuse, a PR gesture by dubious corporations, a panacea for environmental ills that would have been better prevented than compensated for.'

2015

*

I like to think this little riff was prescient. Today, more than ever before, tree-planting is championed by politicians, celebrities and big business who embrace the alluring but dangerous idea that we can plant our way out of the climate crisis. We can't.

2021

From the melting frontline:
a chilling view of a warming world

It is calving season in the Arctic. A flotilla of icebergs, some as jagged as fairy-tale castles and others as smooth as dinosaur eggs, calve from the ice sheet that smothers Greenland and sail down the fjords. The journey of these sculptures of ice from glaciers to ocean is eerily beautiful and utterly terrifying.

The wall of ice that rises behind Sermilik fjord stretches for 2,400 kilometres from north to south and smothers 80 per cent of this country. It has been frozen for three million years. Now it is melting, far faster than the climate models predicted and far more decisively than any political action to combat our changing climate. If the Greenland ice sheet disappeared, sea levels around the world would rise by seven metres, as 10 per cent of the world's fresh water is currently frozen here.

This is also the season for science in Greenland. Glaciologists, seismologists and climatologists from around the world are landing on the ice sheet in helicopters, taking ice-breakers up its inaccessible coastline and measuring glaciers in a race against time to discover why the ice in Greenland is vanishing so much faster than expected.

Gordon Hamilton, a Scottish-born glaciologist from

the University of Maine's Climate Change Institute, is packing up equipment at his base camp in Tasiilaq, a tiny, remote east-coast settlement only accessible by helicopter and where huskies howl all night.

With his spiky hair and ripped T-shirt, Hamilton could be a rugged glaciologist straight from central casting. Four years ago he hit upon the daring idea of landing on a moving glacier in a helicopter to measure its speed.

The glaciers of Greenland are the fat, restless fingers of its vast ice sheet, constantly moving, stretching down into fjords and pushing ice from the sheet into the ocean, in the form of melt water and icebergs.

Before their first expedition, Hamilton and his colleague Leigh Stearns, from the University of Kansas, used satellite data to plan exactly where they would land on a glacier.

'When we arrived there was no glacier to be seen. It was way up the fjord,' he says. 'We thought we'd made some stupid goof with the co-ordinates, but we were where we were supposed to be.' It was the glacier that was in the wrong place. A vast expanse had melted away.

When Hamilton and Stearns processed their first measurements of the glacier's speed, they thought they had made another mistake. They found it was marching forwards at a greater pace than a glacier had ever been observed to flow before. 'We were blown away because we realised that the glaciers had accelerated not just by a little bit but by a lot,' he says. The three glaciers they studied had abruptly increased the speed by which they were transmitting ice from the ice sheet into the ocean.

Raw power

Standing before a glacier in Greenland as it calves icebergs into the dark waters of a cavernous fjord is to witness the raw power of a natural process we have accelerated but will now struggle to control.

Greenland's glaciers make those in the Alps look like toys. Grubby white and blue crystal towers, cliffs and crevasses soar up from the water, dispatching millennia of compacted snow in the shape of seals, water lilies and bishops' mitres.

I take a small boat to see the calving with Dines Mikaelsen, an Inuit guide, who in the winter will cross the ice sheet in his five-metre sled pulled by sixteen huskies.

It is not freezing but even in summer the wind is bitingly cold and we can smell the bad breath of a humpback whale as it groans past our bows on Sermilik fjord. Above its heavy breathing, all you can hear in this wilderness is the drip-drip of melting ice and a crash as icebergs cleave into even smaller lumps, called growlers.

Mikaelsen stops his boat beside Hann glacier and points out how it was twice as wide and stretched 300 metres further into the fjord just ten years ago. He also shows off a spectacular electric blue iceberg.

Locals have nicknamed it 'blue diamond'; its colour comes from being cleaved from centuries-old compressed ice at the ancient heart of the glacier. Bobbing in warming waters, this ancient ice fossil will be gone in a couple of weeks.

The blue diamond is one vivid pointer to the antiquity of the Greenland ice sheet. A relic of the last Ice Age, this is one of three great ice sheets in the world. Up to three kilometres thick, the other two lie in Antarctica.

While similar melting effects are being measured in the southern hemisphere, the Greenland sheet may be uniquely vulnerable, lying much further from the chill of the pole than Antarctica's sheets. The southern end of the Greenland sheet is almost on the same latitude as the Shetlands and stroked by the warm waters of the Gulf Stream.

Driven by the loss of ice, Arctic temperatures are warming more quickly than other parts of the world: last autumn, air temperatures in the Arctic stood at a record 5°C above normal. For centuries, the ice sheets maintained an equilibrium: glaciers calved off icebergs and sent melt water into the oceans every summer; in winter, the ice sheet was then replenished with more frozen snow. Scientists believe the world's great ice sheets will not completely disappear for many more centuries, but the Greenland ice sheet is now shedding more ice than it is accumulating.

The melting has been recorded since 1979; scientists put the annual net loss of ice and water from the ice sheet at 300–400 gigatonnes (equivalent to the ice sheet losing 300–400 cubic kilometres each year), which could hasten a sea-level rise of catastrophic proportions.

As Hamilton has found, Greenland's glaciers have increased the speed at which they shift ice from the sheet into the ocean. Helheim, an enormous tower of ice that calves into Sermilik Fjord, used to move at seven kilometres a year. In 2005, in less than a year, it speeded up to nearly twelve kilometres a year. Kangerlussuaq, another glacier that Hamilton measured, tripled its speed between 1988 and 2005. Its movement – an inch every minute – could be seen with the naked eye.

The three glaciers that Hamilton and Stearns measured account for about a fifth of the discharge from the entire Greenland ice sheet. The implications of their acceleration are profound: 'If they all start to speed up, you could have quite a large rise in sea level in the near term, much larger than the official estimate by the Intergovernmental Panel on Climate Change (IPCC) would project,' says Hamilton.

The scientific labours in the chill winds and high seas of the Arctic summer seem wrapped in an unusual sense of urgency this year. The scientists working in Greenland are keen to communicate their new, emerging understanding of the dynamics of the declining ice sheet to the wider world. Several point out that any international agreement forged at the UN climate-change conference in Copenhagen in December will be based on the IPCC's fourth assessment report from 2007. Its estimates of climate change and sea-level rise were based on scientific research submitted up to 2005; the scientists say this is already significantly out of date.

The 2007 report predicted a sea-level rise of 30–60 cm by 2100, but did not account for the impact of glaciers breaking into the sea from areas such as the Greenland ice sheet. Most scientists working at the poles predict a one metre rise by 2100. The US Geological Survey has predicted a 1.5-metre rise. As Hamilton points out: 'It is only the first metre that matters.'

Record temperatures

A one-metre rise – with the risk of higher storm surges – would require new defences for New York, London, Mumbai and Shanghai, and imperil swathes of low-lying land from Bangladesh to Florida. Vulnerable areas accommodate 10 per cent of the world's population – 600 million.

The Greenland ice sheet is not merely being melted from above by warmer air temperatures. As the oceans of the Arctic waters reach record high temperatures, the role of warmer water lapping against these great glaciers is one of several factors shaping the loss of the ice sheet that has been overlooked until recently.

Fiamma Straneo, an Italian-born oceanographer, is laboriously winding recording equipment the size of a fire extinguisher from the deck of a small Greenpeace ice-breaker caught in huge swells at the mouth of Sermilik fjord.

In previous decades the *Arctic Sunrise* has been used in taking direct action against whalers; now it offers itself as a floating research station for independent scientists to reach remote parts of the ice sheet. It is tough work for the multinational crew of thirty in this rough-and-ready little boat, prettified below deck with posters of orang-utans and sunflowers painted in the toilets.

Before I succumb to vomiting below deck – another journalist is so seasick they are airlifted off the boat – I examine the navigational charts used by the captain, Pete Willcox, a survivor of the sinking of the *Rainbow Warrior* in 1985. He shows how they are dotted with measurements showing the depth of the ocean but here, close to the east coast of Greenland, the map is blank: this part of the North Atlantic was once covered by sea ice for so much of the year that its waters are still uncharted.

Earlier in the expedition, the crew believe, they became the first boat to travel through the Nares Strait west of Greenland to the Arctic Ocean in June, once impassable because of sea ice at that time of year. The predicted year when summers in the Arctic would be free of sea ice has fallen from 2100 to 2050 to 2030 in a couple of years.

Jay Zwally, a Nasa scientist, recently suggested it could be virtually ice-free by late summer 2012. Between 2004 and 2008 the area of 'multiyear' Arctic sea ice (ice that has formed over more than one winter and survived the summer melt) shrank by 1.54 million square kilometers, an area larger than France, Germany and the United Kingdom combined.

Undaunted by the sickening swell of the ocean and

wrapped up against the chilly wind, Straneo, of Woods Hole Oceanographic Institution, one of the world's leading oceanographic research centres, continues to take measurements from the waters as the long Arctic dusk falls.

According to Straneo, the rapid changes to the ice sheet have taken glaciologists by surprise. 'One of the possible mechanisms which we think may have triggered these changes is melting driven by changing ocean temperatures and currents at the margins of the ice sheet.'

She has been surprised by early results measuring sea water close to the melting glaciers: one probe recovered from last year recorded a relatively balmy 2°C at sixty metres in the fjord in the middle of winter. Straneo said: 'This warm and salty water is of subtropical origin – it's carried by the Gulf Stream. In recent years a lot more of this warm water has been found around the coastal region of Greenland. We think this is one of the mechanisms that has caused these glaciers to accelerate and shed more ice.'

Straneo's research is looking at what scientists call the 'dynamic effects' of the Greenland ice sheet. It is not simply that the ice sheet is melting steadily as global temperatures rise. Rather, the melting triggers dynamic new effects, which in turn accelerate the melt.

'It's quite likely that these dynamic effects are more important in generating a near-term rapid rise in sea level than the traditional melt,' says Hamilton. Another example of these dynamic effects is when the ice sheet melts to expose dirty layers of old snow laced with black carbon from forest fires and even cosmic dust. These dark particles absorb more heat and so further speed up the melt.

After Straneo gathers her final measurements, the *Arctic Sunrise* heads for the tranquillity of the sole berth at Tasiilaq, which has a population of fewer than 3,000 but is still the largest settlement on Greenland's vast east coast. Here another scientist is gathering her final provisions before taking her team camping on a remote glacier.

Invisible earthquakes

Several years ago Meredith Nettles, a seismologist from Colombia University, and two colleagues made a remarkable discovery: they identified a new kind of earthquake. These quakes were substantial – measuring magnitude five – but had been invisible because they did not show up on seismographs. (While orthodox tremors registered for a couple of seconds, these occurred rather more slowly, over a minute.)

The new earthquakes were traced almost exclusively to Greenland, where they were found to be specifically associated with large, fast-flowing outlet glaciers. There have been 200 of them in the last dozen years; in 2005 there were six times as many as in 1993.

Nettles nimbly explains the science as she heaves bags of equipment on to a helicopter, which will fly her to study Kangerlussuaq glacier. 'It's quite a dramatic increase, and that increase happened at the same time as we were seeing dramatic retreats in the location of the calving fronts of the glaciers, and an increase in their flow speed,' she says. 'The earthquakes are very closely associated with large-scale ice loss events.'

In other words, the huge chunks of ice breaking off from the glaciers and entering the oceans are large enough to generate a seismic signal that is sent through the earth. They are happening more regularly and, when they occur, it appears that the glacier speeds up even more.

The scientists rightly wrap their latest observations in caution. Their studies are still in their infancy. Some of the effects they are observing may be short term.

The Greenland ice sheet has survived natural warmer periods in history, the last about 120,000 years ago, although it was much smaller then than it is now. Those still sceptical of the scientific consensus over climate change should perhaps listen to the voices of those who could not be accused of having anything to gain from talking up climate change.

Inuit warnings

Arne Sorensen, a specialist ice navigator on *Arctic Sunrise*, began sailing the Arctic in the 1970s. Journeys around Greenland's coast that would take three weeks in the 1970s because of sea ice now take a day. He pays heed to the observations of the Inuit. 'If you talk to people who live close to nature and they tell you this is unusual and this is not something they have noticed before, then I really put emphasis on that,' he says. Paakkanna Ignatiussen, fifty-two, has been hunting seals since he was thirteen. His grandparents travelled less than a mile to hunt; he must go more than sixty miles because the sea ice disappears earlier – and with it the seals. 'It's hard to see the ice go back. In the old days when we got ice it was only ice. Today it is more like slush,' he says. 'In ten years there will be no traditional hunting. The weather is the reason.'

The stench of rotting seal flesh wafts from a bag in the porch of his house in Tasiilaq as Ignatiussen's wife, Åne, remarks that, 'the seasons are upside down'.

Local people are acutely aware of how the weather is changing animal behaviour. Browsing the guns for sale in the supermarket in Tasiilaq (you don't need a licence for a gun here), Axel Hansen says more hungry polar bears prowl around the town these days. Like the hunters, the bears can't find seals when there is so little sea ice. And the fjords are filled with so many icebergs that local people find it hard to hunt whales there.

Westerners may shrug at the decline of traditional hunting but, in a sense, we all live on the Greenland ice sheet now. Its fate is our fate. The scientists swarming over this ancient mass of ice, trying to understand how it will be transformed in a warming world, and how it will transform us, are wary of making political comments about how our leaders should plan for one metre of sea-level rise, and what drastic steps must be taken to cut carbon emissions. But some scientists are so astounded by the changes they are recording that they are moved to speak out.

What, I ask Hamilton, would he say to Barack Obama if he could spend ten minutes with the US president standing on Helheim glacier?

'Without knowing anything about what is going on, you just have to look at the glacier to know something huge is happening here,' says the glaciologist.

We can't as a scientific community keep up with the pace of changes, let alone explain why they are happening. If I was, God forbid, the leader of the free world, I would implement some changes to deal with the maximum risk that we might reasonably expect to encounter, rather than always planning for the minimum. We won't know the consequences of not doing that until it's way too late. Even as a politician on a four-year elected cycle, you can't morally leave someone with that problem.

2009

*

Although Helheim suddenly increased the rate at which it discharged ice into the ocean in the early 2000s, ice loss has since slowed and the glacier has advanced by about three of the more than six kilometres it retreated. Despite this, Greenland's glaciers continue to shift ice into the ocean, amidst projections of dramatic sea-level rise.

A 2020 scientific study of the Helheim, Kangerlussuaq

and Jakobshavn glaciers found their melting added 8.1 mm to sea-level rise since 1880 but could add up to 14.9 mm to sea level rise by 2100. Global sea levels rose by 17 cm during the twentieth century. Current scientific predictions for sea-level rise suggest between 70 cm and 200 cm by 2100 – enough to engulf Tuvalu.

Since I visited Sermilik fjord in 2009, Arctic sea ice has twice reached its lowest seasonal levels in forty years during the last decade – just 3.41 km^2 in the summer of 2012 and 3.74 km^2 in the summer of 2020. Scientists' models continue to show that sea ice is likely to disappear from the Arctic Ocean during summer before 2050.

The glaciologist Gordon Hamilton died in 2016 when the snowmobile he was riding in Antarctica plunged into a crevasse. He was fifty years old.

2021

PART VI

The Future of Nature

The introductionists:
a maverick rebellion on extinction

In a beautiful meadow filled with wildflowers and bird-song, a man of late middle age wearing a faded camouflage sun hat knelt beside a clump of clover and prepared to break the law. Martin White removed a carrier bag from his battered rucksack and began quickly opening the lids of dozens of matchbox-sized pots. As he shook each pot, a flake of brilliant blue fluttered free. Over the course of about five minutes, White released seventy-two mazarine blues, a small butterfly named after the striking colour used in seventeenth-century porcelain. For the first time in more than a century, this rare insect took to the skies of Britain.

One by one, the butterflies spread out on the pink clover. Some flashed silver-blue as they zigzagged across the meadow. White watched closely. A darker-coloured female curled its abdomen around a clover flower. 'She's dossing an egg off,' he murmured. The butterfly placed tiny white pinheads inside the flower. Satisfaction spread across White's face for a second. Then he scanned the dark woods beyond the meadow.

'I'd be worried if someone came out of there,' he said, pointing to the distant trees. 'But I'd pick up my bag,

357

amble off, and they probably wouldn't notice a thing.' It was against the law to release a species here, an area designated as a site of special scientific interest. What if White was caught and prosecuted? 'There would be an immense public outcry,' he told me in his blunt Nottinghamshire accent. 'I would be an instant martyr, and that's the last thing they want me to be.'

'They' are the government agencies, scientists and charities who for seventy years have decided how nature should be protected in Britain. These illustrious groups and experts have tried to save wild places and stop the loss of species. They've scored some notable successes – once-endangered species such as peregrine falcons have been revived and the Wildlife Trusts alone have created more nature reserves than there are branches of McDonald's – but, broadly speaking, they've failed. Britain has lost more of its nature than most other countries in the world. Almost every species or measurable wild habitat produces a graph plummeting downwards.

Over the last seventy years, 98 per cent of wildflower meadows in England and Wales have been destroyed; three-quarters of ponds and heaths have vanished; half the remaining fragments of ancient woods have been obliterated. The creatures inside this habitat have gone too: since 1970, more than half of Britain's farmland birds have disappeared, while a quarter of mammals are endangered and three-quarters of butterfly species have declined. Overall one in ten species are threatened with extinction; 500

species have already disappeared from England. Most alarmingly, this dramatic loss of biodiversity has accelerated in the last decade. During the same period, government funding for British wildlife and the environment has been cut by 30 per cent.

Can one individual do anything about an extinction crisis caused by the way we live, farm and build? White is doing something. For almost all of his sixty-one years, he has laboured mostly alone; for the last ten years, he has been breeding native butterflies from his modest terraced house in the East Midlands for release across the country. He is part of a small, scattered band of secret breeders - or 'introductionists' as they prefer – who have taken it on themselves to bring back wild species that have fallen victim to what one nature writer calls 'the great thinning' of non-human life.

White and his peers have quietly released captive-bred wild animals that were once commonplace in Britain: beavers, turtle doves, butterflies, even glow-worms. One introductionist I spoke to, Graham Wellstead, has released hundreds of polecats into the English countryside, helping this once-persecuted small carnivore spread across the south and east of the country once again. Another man's captive-breeding programme has revived the endangered sand lizard.

The introductionists are not fêted. To the conservation establishment, these men – and it is overwhelmingly men – are not allies, but pests, who do more harm than good.

Professional conservationists complain that unsanctioned reintroductions mess up their data. If conservation scientists can't accurately measure whether a wild population is increasing or falling, they can't understand what's causing a decline or take steps to stop it. Releasing a captive-bred water vole into the wild won't save that creature if the marshland where it lives has been drained; releasing a swift won't save the species if air pollution has removed the insects on which it fed.

Conservation organisations in the UK tend to focus not on saving individual species, but on saving habitats. Conservationists act slowly because they must bring people with them, while maverick releases are more likely to antagonise. Illegally releasing a beaver on to a Scottish river, say, which then floods farmers' fields, leads to the persecution of that species. No one wins. Professional conservationists disparage White's work. 'I'm just seen as an interloper, an attention-seeker. They called me a "schoolboy introductionist" until recently,' he said. 'Anything to undermine what I'm doing.'

White believes introductionists face such opprobrium because they challenge the power of the establishment. But, according to White, public opinion – suspicious of experts, hungry for change – is on their side. Besides, he said: 'I've been releasing butterflies since I was eight years old. I can't stop now.'

I first met White on a bright winter's day at Worksop railway station in Nottinghamshire. He was a tall but unremarkable-looking middle-aged man who seemed to have a knack for blending into his surroundings. He led me, on foot – he does not drive, and usually cycles everywhere – to his home, where he lives a spartan existence. He was virtually zero-carbon long before it was fashionable. His electricity comes from solar panels and his last holiday was to Blackpool, in 1974.

His narrow back yard was filled with dozens of large plant pots. Each one was covered by a neat dome of green wire, double-wrapped in netting. Inside were bonsaied blackthorn, clovers and violets; on them, or in the soil below, were hidden hundreds of butterfly eggs and hibernating caterpillars. He told me he had undertaken 2,500 successful butterfly reintroductions over the years, 'putting down' forty species of butterfly and three moth species, mostly in the Midlands, returning native insects to nature reserves, golf courses, even disused coal tips. Seeing White's meticulous notes – he recorded in blue ringbinders the progress of every release – his claims were believable.

'Technically,' said White, who punctuates his sentences with a big barking laugh, 'I started when I was three.' He retains a vivid picture of that moment: he was gazing at some Michaelmas daisies when a red admiral flew in. 'I was blown away. A jet-black butterfly with scarlet markings. I was hooked for life.' Like other boys growing up in the 1960s, he collected and killed butterflies, stowing them in drawers treated with an insecticide, paradichlorobenzene, the strong-smelling substance used in old mothballs, which also repels mites and beetles. Aged eight, he began to breed live ones. Beyond the house where he grew up was 2.5 hectares of glorious meadow. Every summer afternoon, after school, he would walk through it, alongside thousands and thousands of butterflies. 'That meadow was destroyed when I was eleven,' he said. 'That crucified me. It just broke my heart.'

As a teenager in the 1970s, White became a life member of Butterfly Conservation, a charity set up in the previous decade to protect British butterflies. He trained as a horticulturalist to learn about the plants on which caterpillars feed, and his first job was in a council parks department. In his twenties, however, he quit and began supporting himself by selling captive-bred butterflies to other enthusiasts. (These days, he sells them online.) 'I probably spent one day a week making a living, six days a week doing something else,' he said. That something else was releasing butterflies.

He also quit his life membership of Butterfly Conservation. One of the group's founding principles was 'to breed rare butterflies in captivity and where practicable introduce them into the wild'. But by the 1980s the charity was run by conservation scientists who sought to save species through habitat management, rather than 'throwing out' captive-bred butterflies. White felt that amateur introductionists were no longer welcome. Breeding and releasing into the wild was 'my mantra', said White. 'It's like listening to Buddha, and his words completely gel with what you think – and then Buddha says: "I didn't say that."'

Aged twenty-six, White did his first major reintroduction. He spotted on butterfly distribution maps that there were no marbled whites across a 140-kilometre swathe between the Midlands and the Yorkshire Wolds. 'I thought, I'm going to fill that gap,' he said. 'I got marbled whites into about a hundred sites. I'd plugged that gap by about 1991.'

Since then, he has released dozens of species. Some days, he will take a rucksack full of, say, captive-bred dingy skippers, get on a train, and head off to release them at six new locations, often derelict mining sites that are rich in wildflowers. He uses botanical distribution data to identify potential sites, and spends days inspecting their soils, food plants and 'companion' species, which some butterflies need.

White's claims about the return of the marbled white is supported by data from the UK Butterfly Monitoring Scheme, the world's longest-running dataset for butterfly distribution. It shows how the marbled white was absent from the Midlands in the 1980s, but is today found continuously in a northwards line through Nottinghamshire and South Yorkshire. The dingy skipper is also found on dozens of former mining sites around Worksop, where it was absent thirty years ago.

How much of this is due to White, and how much is

caused by climatic or habitat change, remains a matter of dispute. Although plenty of his reintroduced species reproduce and survive for a couple of summers, White concedes that many soon disappear again, for the same reasons they originally vanished – lack of wild habitat, say, or destructive human interference. Conventional conservationists occasionally give White grudging credit. It's widely accepted that he put the purple emperor back into Lincolnshire – but critics argue that the butterfly would have returned eventually. White acknowledges that climate change has 'hugely' helped warmth-loving butterflies expand their range.

In January White was in the midst of his most ambitious reintroduction yet: to return the mazarine blue to Britain. Unlike other reintroductions in which he helped a surviving British species recover its former range, the mazarine blue had completely vanished from the UK. White studied the reasons for its decline and set about identifying sites abundant with the things it needs to survive: black ants and zigzag clover. A friend caught four ageing butterflies for him from a site in France and smuggled them back to Britain. White kept them in his cages; they laid 680 eggs. Over two years, he released the offspring on to five meadows in the Midlands.

It was a big project, and White was working alone, apart from occasional conversations with a few fellow breeders. This attempt would probably fail, he said, but at least he would learn from his mistakes, and future tries might succeed. And it would cost almost nothing. Authorised reintroductions require surveys, forms, permissions and lots of money.

'Good luck to the people who want to go through the paperwork, but you'll get nothing done,' said White. 'We've reached crisis point. I come along and my first reintroduction of mazarine blues cost £6.28.' He checked himself. 'I don't know the exact amount, but it was less than a tenner.'

Given the climate and global extinction crises, and the dramatic loss of nature in Britain, is it time for the conservation establishment to welcome these maverick reintroductions as complementary to NGOs' slower, more scientific work? When I put this to Nigel Bourn, Butterfly Conservation's director of science and policy, I sensed him gamely trying to entertain this argument. But when I mentioned that two secret butterfly breeders had told me the purple emperor had moved back into eastern England in the last decade because of their reintroductions, including from breeding stock sourced in Germany, he was unimpressed.

'Introducing the purple emperor from 300 miles away – I'm sorry, that's just not right,' said Bourn. 'That's just a shallow argument. That's made me quite angry. If you're bringing other species from Germany, you're increasing the likelihood of pathogen spread.' As well as spreading disease, breeders change the genetics of a captive-bred species, which can adapt very quickly to life in a cage. ('Rubbish,' responded White.)

Bourn said that to suggest maverick work could complement conservation science was to underestimate its negative impact. The scientists' picture of the purple emperor's expansion, for instance, has been muddied by breeders. 'We'll never be totally sure if the purple emperor is responding to climate change, or changing woodland management practices, or whether people have been shoving them out the back of their cars.' The risk, argued Bourn, was that unofficial reintroductions 'corrupted' datasets, research priorities and, ultimately, the practical act of actually saving a species.

Society could not learn from rogue reintroductions, argued Bourn, since mavericks rarely publicised their work – often because it was illegal. But Bourn was overseeing an 'official' reintroduction himself: to return the chequered skipper to England, after it vanished from Rockingham Forest, Northamptonshire, in 1977. 'Reintroductions have a role to play. I'm slightly nervous of calling all reintroduction projects vanity projects, because that would include me,' he laughed.

Bourn insisted that his project was based on solid research, including four PhDs and good habitat management. British-born offspring of wild butterflies collected from Belgium (authorised by the Belgian authorities) and brought to Rockingham Forest via Eurostar (an operation costing around £10,000) were doing well so far.

Successful reintroductions usually require money and

time. Bourn's chequered skipper reintroduction is part of the Back from the Brink project, a £4.6 million Heritage Lottery-funded multi-charity programme to revive 200 species and their habitats. This will fund one further year of chequered skipper releases from Belgium, but Bourn said Butterfly Conservation retained a long-term commitment to the reintroduction effort, and to monitoring its success.

Rewilding – allowing nature to take care of itself by removing human influences from land, rivers or sea – has animated people in recent years. Its less radical sister, restoration, which means returning natural habitats to their former glory, is increasingly influential in conservation. But many conservationists still believe that scarce resources are ultimately best devoted to preserving what's left. 'This has to be the top priority,' argued Bourn. 'We know this country is one of the least wooded in Europe. We know this country's wildlife has been in severe decline for a long time. We know we need to do more about it, but the scale of what needs to be done is massive.'

Many of those who buy butterflies from White in order to conduct their own releases are well-meaning landowners and wildlife-loving farmers. But Bourn argues that what will be much more decisive for the future of nature in Britain are big structural changes to the way we produce food. 'We need to switch all the drivers that have destroyed our wildlife, such as the Common Agricultural Policy. If we get the new farm payments policy right post-Brexit, and get farmers well paid to restore the countryside, we'll fix it, and make the country much more able to cope with the horrors of climate change. That is how you conserve habitats and species in the UK.'

I met Britain's most notorious and successful introductionist in a Devon pub at the start of the year. That morning, Derek Gow had released a pair of beavers into a large enclosure on the National Trust's Holnicote estate, as part of an officially approved conservation scheme. Gow, who is widely known as Mr Beaver, had transported the animals from Scotland. The door of a wooden crate carrying the first beaver was lifted up in front of a tempting pool of water. Cameras were raised, but no beaver emerged. Six minutes passed. Still no beaver. Gow walked over to the crate and peered inside. 'The beaver is asleep,' he muttered, so he reached into the crate and gently pulled it out on to the bank. The beaver slipped into the water without complaint.

Later, Gow's assistant, Coral Edgcumbe, quietly ticked him off for not following protocol. He should not have grabbed the beaver. But Gow is someone who has dedicated his life to breaking the rules.

The beaver was hunted to extinction in Britain more than three centuries ago, but is today the rewilding movement's pin-up. Beavers are sometimes admiringly referred to as 'ecosystem engineers'. By damming streams, they reshape valley bottoms, creating new ponds and waterways that rapidly fill with birds, amphibians, dragonflies,

THE FUTURE OF NATURE

and other insects and fish. Research also shows how dams filter polluted water, and store huge quantities of floodwater. Beavers' dams can even prevent towns being flooded. But the water has to go somewhere – and the farmers whose fields are flooded as a result tend to detest these rodent engineers.

Most people agree Gow has almost single-handedly brought back the beaver. Quite how is a little mysterious. 'Somewhere in Derek's barn there's a big red button,' joked one scientist at the Exmoor beaver jamboree. 'It's like a Bond film,' laughed another – '"Release. The. Beavers."' Alongside 'unofficial' releases in Scotland and Devon (where the animals were first rumoured to be living wild in 2006 and first filmed in 2013) was an official trial that began in 2009, carefully placing beavers in a Scottish glen from which they couldn't spread. By 2016 the Scottish government recognised that more than 400 wild beavers, most released unofficially, were now so dispersed that they should once again be considered a native species. The government in England this year declared that Devon's unofficially released beavers, which have multiplied to a population of more than fifty on the River Otter, could stay there permanently.

'Derek did very consciously adopt the strategy of, what's the phrase, "creating facts on the ground", and it worked,' one conservationist told me. 'If something is there, it becomes a reality. I'm not saying it was him,' they added hurriedly of the unofficial releases. 'And it's not always brilliant if it's not well considered. You can lose the animals or the animals can cause problems.' Others have called Gow a 'one-man wrecking-ball' and a 'cowboy operating outside the law'. But these days, most conservation scientists give him grudging respect.

Gow, who runs a wildlife consultancy from a former sheep farm he is rewilding in Devon, is a charismatic talker who affects to despise both conservationists ('children and idiots whose idea of production is to do a lot of tedious reports that nobody ever reads, which cost a lot of money and sit on a shelf in a cupboard') and farmers ('They say: "Poor me, we're struggling on, despite the fact that somebody's given us £40,000 of taxpayers' money just to fuck about, own a pickup, shoot a few foxes and get pissed with my mates."')

He was inspired by Gerald Durrell's books as a boy, worked in farming for a few years, and then began to manage zoos. He started captive-breeding water voles, which are on the 'red list' of mammals in danger of extinction in Britain. Since 2000, working with conservation organisations and landowners, Gow has supplied 25,000 water voles for release into twenty-five wetlands across the country. In Queen Elizabeth Forest Park in Scotland, 1,000 water voles released in the mid-2000s have expanded to occupy more than fifty-seven square kilometres.

Gow admits to plenty of failures as well, and acknowledged that even this tiny mammal required major habitat restoration:

These animals are hanging on in a landscape that's shattered. There are very few environments suitable for them. Then you begin to look at beavers. You see them living in Poland in vast swamps full of orchids, the huge clusters of frogs, the damsel and dragonflies, the small fish jumping in profusion in the dams. You see how around this animal, 'the water saver', all life revolves. It became abundantly obvious that this animal could be the mechanism that provided living space for so many other things.

Gow's consultancy makes around £50,000 profit a year from work including wildlife photography courses and services for wildlife film-makers. His services are increasingly in demand from a new generation of rewilders, including wealthy landowners wanting to bring back beavers, as well as harvest mice, wildcats and white storks. Gow helped release the storks on the Knepp estate in West Sussex, where nesting pairs fledged chicks in the wild for the first time this summer. But even this has attracted opposition from some conservationists who argue that these large omnivorous birds should not have been released without a scientific assessment of their impact on rare amphibians.

Gow is scathing about such arguments. 'A conservation culture says: "We need to spend £100,000 looking at the genetics of a glow-worm before we can move it from Berkshire to Basingstoke, and now we've run out of money and we've achieved absolutely fuck all," and the farmers hate you for it – and they're right.' The government's own conservation agencies 'are so [financially] broken, or so science-based, they have very little practical experience of doing anything any more', he argued. Meanwhile, charities have lost government grants and EU funding, and cannot risk wasting money challenging the government to allow radical changes in the countryside.

According to Gow, the official beaver trial in Scotland was so hidebound by caution that without the unofficial releases it would never have led to them becoming officially recognised as a native wild animal again. Ultimately, however, as Gow reveals in an enjoyably rude book he's written about reintroducing the beaver, it was not maverick action by 'little people' that brought back the beaver, but political machinations. Gow has been financially supported by the multimillionaire board member of Defra, Ben Goldsmith, brother of environment minister Zac, for more than a decade. He obtained backing from wealthy landowners such as Knepp's Charlie Burrell and the philanthropist Lisbet Rausing, who owns swathes of the Highlands. Civil servants and politicians were lobbied at the highest level.

'Yes, without them we would've been screwed,' said Gow:

That's what's wrong. The reason some individuals are able to talk to government [about beavers] –

and we can probably still drop notes in to Boris
if we want to – is because people at the top of this
'meritocratic' chain want it to happen. I appreciate
that tremendously, and I am very grateful, but I do
not think that that is a fair or responsible way for
governments to act. It is actually abhorrently wrong.

I planned to meet White again in the summer, to follow the release of his 2020 crop of mazarine blues on to a
secret site in Lincolnshire. Could it work? As the world
became convulsed by the coronavirus pandemic, it seemed
impossible. When I phoned White as lockdown eased,
he uncharacteristically asked if I might drive him to his
release site, which he had always cycled to – seventy-four
kilometres in three hours – since he was a teenager.

White had survived the threat of coronavirus, but had
been diagnosed with advanced cancer of the throat and
oesophagus. He could hardly eat, had lost two stone and
had undergone a blood transfusion to strengthen him for
radiotherapy and, later, if he was fit enough, chemother-
apy. Doctors gave him a one-in-four chance. Normally,
he'd spend sixteen hours each day ensuring his plants and
caterpillars were in perfect condition. Now he was struggling to do two. 'I want to get these butterflies out before
treatment,' he said. 'This is what's keeping my sanity up,
keeping this project going.'

When I picked him up, White was wearing a jumper
the same hue as the male mazarine blue. His skin was

yellow. He had liberated most of his stock, giving rarities to breeder friends, putting out common species in promising sites. During the drive, he talked about the butterflies he had put down around a secret meadow in Lincolnshire. It was a wildlife-rich nature reserve, lovingly managed by the conservation charities that White scorned. Like so many parts of lowland Britain, it was encircled by huge stretches of intensively farmed land. Species that had vanished from the reserve needed help to ever find it again.

Many of White's reintroductions appeared doomed to fail. On this site alone, he had tried the high brown fritillary, Scotch argus, small heath, marbled white, grizzled skipper, wood white and chequered skipper. All had failed. So much diversity and complexity had already been stripped from ecosystems that it seemed beyond the ingenuity of humans to put anything back. But White had some notable successes, particularly with butterfly species that lived in trees – black and brown hairstreaks, and the purple emperor. 'Remember, none of my actions have ever resulted in the loss of any butterfly colony, rare or otherwise,' he said. According to White, clumsy 'habitat management' by mainstream conservationists has resulted in local extinctions of some colonies.

White and I walked somewhat furtively to the meadow. He looked relieved once the mazarine blues had flown free. Then he abruptly declared: 'I do believe the whole thing is going to be a failure.' That month, the species had failed to emerge on four of five sites where he had released them last year. He blamed the sunny, dry spring shrivelling up their clover food plant. 'I acknowledge all my failures. The conservation charities don't do that,' he said. 'I've discovered a hell of a lot about its habitat and zigzag clover. It's not a waste of time. Although it will be if I die of cancer and don't bloody write it up.'

As the afternoon sun dipped and softened, we sat on the verge of the lane beyond the meadow. White was in no hurry to leave. 'It's been bloody wonderful to get out. They'll be all over the meadow now. There'll be a hundred eggs at least.' Will he see mazarine blues here in a year's time? 'I don't think I'll be alive in a year's time.'

He was not shocked to get cancer. He believed his butterflies were to blame. 'I like a nice bit of irony, really black irony,' he said. 'I used paradichlorobenzene in my butterfly collection. It's the worst, the most carcinogenic of the lot. It's in my bedrooms, my store boxes, cabinets, everything. My mother used to complain about "that horrible stink coming from your room". I didn't want pests. I wanted an immaculate collection. A mate of mine had exactly the same cancer in the same place. A lot of breeders have died the same way.'

He was content:

My life hasn't been a waste. I would have loved to have had another thirty years, I could've done so much bloody more, I really could. But when I was a teenager I would've never imagined doing so much.

375

It sounds a bit big-headed, a bit crass, but you do realise how much you've put back. All other people seem to do is criticise you for doing something. They've done nothing. I like to think I'm leaving some sort of legacy, I must admit. I don't personally believe humanity is going to survive very long. Stephen Hawking's prediction is 500 years, and recovery from humans might take one million. I hope some of my butterflies might still be around.

2020

*

Martin White died on 12 October 2020. His story was published in the *Guardian* the following day, with Martin's blessing. His breeding butterfly stock was taken in by a good friend, Richard Priestley. In the region where Martin undertook most of his reintroductions, there has been an outpouring of appreciation for his work. Although many conservation scientists still disapprove of his methods, some scientists and amateur members of Butterfly Conservation are keen to follow up his attempts with the mazarine blue and see if they are successful in the long term.

2021

Big cats: Britain needs the lynx effect

Last Wednesday, at dusk, a good friend of mine went to close his curtains overlooking the Norfolk countryside. About a hundred metres away an animal stood, motionless, in a field. At first my friend, a farmer and wildlife-lover, assumed it was a deer, but then it moved. The creature bounded off with feline grace. It had an unusually long body and a distinct tail. My friend, a smart, sane man who has twenty-twenty vision and knows the difference between muntjac, Dobermann and panther, is convinced it was a big cat.

The idea that big cats roam the British countryside is often seen as a great urban myth to be filed alongside sightings of the Loch Ness monster. Most eyewitness accounts of big cats are a kind of collective delusion, argues George Monbiot, reawakening 'genetic memories' of ancestors facing sabre-toothed tigers; they answer today's unmet need for wildness.

I agree with Monbiot on all important issues, but on this more trivial matter his theory seems less plausible than the likelihood that hundreds of sensible individuals are not deluded but have seen real big cats.

This has been proved in Norfolk where in 1991 a game-keeper shot dead a 27-kilogram lynx a mile from where I grew up. For years, reliable locals spotted what we called 'the Beast of Booton', but the truth was only revealed when police records were published in 2006: a constable visited a gamekeeper to ask what was in his freezer. 'Oh, only some pigeons and a lynx,' the keeper replied. That lynx probably escaped from a wildlife park that has now closed. Other big cats are also escapees or illegally kept pets.

Many big-cat witnesses emphasise not what they've seen, but the alarmed responses of dogs or horses around them. These animals are not deluded. It is poignant that my friend may not see another big cat in his life. 'It was good but I want more,' he says. 'I want it to be within ten metres and growl at me.'

Big cats in our countryside stimulate our senses and spark our imaginations. They show how rewilding, and reintroducing the harmless-to-humans lynx, if done properly, would inspire us to spend more time in the wild. Our countryside can still offer such thrilling unpredictability.

2015

The magic nature farm: Knepp, in Sussex

Orange tip butterflies jink over grassland and a buzzard mews high on a thermal. Blackthorns burst with bridal white blossom and sallow leaves of peppermint green unfurl. The exhilaration in this corner of West Sussex is not, however, simply the thrilling explosion of spring. The land is bursting with an unusual abundance of life; rampant weeds and wild flowers, insects, birdsong, ancient trees and enormous hedgerows, billowing into fields of hawthorn. And some of the conventional words from three millennia of farming – 'hedgerow', 'field' and 'weed' – no longer seem to apply in a landscape which is utterly alien to anyone raised in an intensively farmed environment.

This is Knepp, a 1,400-hectare farm in densely populated lowland Britain, barely seventy kilometres from London. Once a conventional dairy and arable operation, at the turn of this century, Knepp's owners, Charlie Burrell and Isabella Tree, auctioned off their farm machinery, rewilded their land and, as much by accident as design, inched towards a new model of farming. Some view the result as an immoral eyesore, an abnegation of our responsibility to keep land productive and tidy. Others find it inspiring proof that people and other nature can coexist.

A pair of storks circle in the spring sky, great white egrets stalk the waterways and violet dor beetles – previously unseen in Sussex for fifty years – mine the cowpats on the front lawn of Burrell and Tree's historic, castellated home. The farm employs a full-time ecologist rather than farm labourers these days. Its advisory board of ecologists and other conservationists help analyse the rapid changes to their land and its animals. These changes are almost always uplifting. They used a drone for the first time to count grey heron nests this year and found twenty-four rather than the sixteen of last year.

This wild nature helps Burrell and Tree have a thriving glamping site and ecotourism business but they are still producing food from their free-roaming, 'rewilded' livestock. 'It's just like ranching really,' says Tree. She has just written a book, *Wilding*, which tells the story of the Knepp's transformation, and their own personal transformation too. She met Burrell through mutual school friends when she was eighteen; he attended agricultural college and then, aged twenty-three, inherited the Knepp estate in 1987. His family have farmed this land since it was a medieval deer park but what sounds like an archetypically privileged aristocratic tale is a little more complicated. Burrell inherited the estate from his grandparents, just after the twin blows of the hurricane that destroyed millions of trees in southern England and the Black Monday stock market crash. The farm is on the famously heavy clays of the Sussex Weald. It's no coincidence that Sussex folk have more than thirty dialect words for mud, from 'clodgy' to 'gubber': this poorly draining 'marginal' soil sets like concrete in summer and porridge in winter, and will never provide high yields of crops.

For seventeen years, Burrell did what the conventional farming world told him to do: intensify, and diversify. Tree quotes Burrell's aunt: 'We were all brought up to believe we would go to heaven if we made two blades of grass grow where one had grown before.' They invested in better machinery, unleashed the latest pesticides and launched their own brand ice-cream. They almost doubled their wheat yields. It didn't work. After fifteen years of farming, they made a cash surplus in only two. Both Burrell and Tree enjoyed wildlife. 'We'd go all over the world looking for nature, never thinking about what we were doing to it here, or how it could be here,' says Tree. In 1999 the ancient oaks on their land were inspected by an expert, Ted Green. He told the couple that their trees were in poor health because of their farming system's ploughing of roots and the destruction of mycorrhizae, a vast subterranean fungal network that is crucial to plant health. His visit, writes Tree, coming just when they realised their farm business was unequivocally failing, was an epiphany.

Nearly two decades on, Knepp is a completely different farm to its neighbours. In fact, after two decades, it is still unique: the only sizeable farm in lowland Britain to rewild itself. Its land is no longer a place of conventional food production. Arable fields have been left to run wild and the way animals and plants have bounced back has been constantly surprising, and rapid. Taking their lead from Dutch ecologist Frans Vera, Burrell and Tree have introduced free-roaming herbivores to mimic the grazing of extinct animals such as aurochs and tarpans. They 'farm' 350 head of English longhorn cattle (a hundred cows and their youngsters), Tamworth pigs, red and fallow deer and Exmoor ponies. Knepp challenges agricultural conventions but also tears up the orthodox conservation rulebook. Rather than set targets to protect specific rare species, their principle is to allow 'natural processes' to unfold. So there are no internal fences, and no predator control – to say, stop foxes predating ground-nesting lapwing (a declining bird in Britain) – and no 'scrub-bashing' so favoured by conventional conservationists. The uniqueness of Knepp poses three questions. Why did Burrell and Tree do it? Why has no one else in Britain done it yet? And can Knepp's success be replicated elsewhere?

Tree believes the answer to the first question is their unusual personal situation. They both acknowledge their good fortune: Burrell is not a tenant farmer but inherited the estate from his grandparents. Because Burrell was so young when he took over, when he realised conventional farming was failing he was still young and energetic enough to try something different. 'Naivety,' laughs Burrell. Unlike many young farmers, because Knepp skipped a generation, he was also not burdened by farmer parents criticising change: intergenerational dynamics are a huge influence on how farmers farm. Tree also believes that because Burrell spent his childhood in Africa and the Australian bush he was familiar with Serengeti-type landscapes, and a vision of free-roaming animals was not an anathema.

Many might assume Knepp has not been adopted by other British farms because it cannot be financially viable for anyone but the wealthiest of farmers. 'We're always going to get this criticism levelled at us – "It's alright for you, you live in a castle and you went to public school,"' says Tree. Tenant farmers or farmers with massive mortgages might not be able to start a Knepp (although Knepp was overdrawn when it changed its farming model) but this is not a self-indulgent hobby. Knepp's economics are striking. The farm today makes a £50,000 annual profit from one 2.5-hectare field – one-third of the average annual income its entire conventional farm of mixed crops, beef, sheep and 600 dairy cows used to make. 'That's bloody mad,' says Burrell. This magic field is worthless in agricultural terms but sits in a scenic valley surrounded by ancient trees and rewilding excitement, and now features yurts and an outdoor bath for glampers.

In their previous incarnation as an intensive farm, Knepp may have averaged £150,000 a year profit but lost money in all but two years because of endless capital investments in new machinery, such as dairy technology or new slurry lagoons or sewage systems to adhere to new legislation. A wilded farm has much fewer capital demands. Apart from glamping's £230,000 turnover (not profit) in

2016/17, annual farm incomes totalled £120,000 from selling seventy-five tonnes of live-weight high-grade organic meat, £500,000 from renting former farm buildings to local businesses (attracting 200 full-time jobs to the local economy) and £118,000 from renting seven former workers' cottages. As Burrell and Tree accept, such lucrative income streams are not available to every farmer; Knepp benefits from its proximity to Brighton and London. Finally, the farm currently receives £220,000 for having its land in the highest level of environmental stewardship scheme and £195,000 in 'basic payments', which every British farmer receives via EU funds. As all British farmers know, Brexit is certain to see the end of such generous subsidies.

It may not look like farming but Knepp's animal husbandry is subtle and complex. Conventional beef cattle reared on silage and grain are slaughtered at 24–26 months; Knepp's free-range cows are 28–30 months old. (If they are slaughtered over 30 months they are priced less because of old regulations from the BSE health scare.) So in farming terms, 'we're losing four months from a conventional system', explains Burrell, 'but we've not had to put any inputs into growing the animals – we're not making silage, growing wheat, housing them, getting rid of the dung, treating them with antibiotics. We have none of the costs associated with the production.'

The farm's sole conventional employee is its stockman, Pat Toe. The animals roam wild but cows still need to be periodically rounded up for TB tests and for slaughter

– not easy when they are hiding in Knepp's burgeoning sallow thickets. 'Just checking is a massive part of it,' says Toe. 'This kind of system doesn't take much labour but the labour is pretty intense sometimes.'

When he arrived ten years ago, he rounded up the cows on quad bikes. 'It's as near to chasing them as it could be and we just thought "no" – it's dangerous, and it's not good for the animals. There were seven of us and we still wouldn't get them all in.' So Toe watched long and rather tedious videos of American cow whisperer Bud Williams, who teaches ranchers how to round up cows simply by walking them. 'There's no running, no hitting with sticks,' says Toe. Instead, subtle movements help start the process, and each herd gathers its members together on its perambulation through unfenced former fields.

Much of Toe's job is observing animals, assessing their condition, and making sure Knepp's stock density is just right for the natural food available. While the farm wants to allow 'natural' environmental processes to unfold, if they let livestock populations grow too high, the animals will starve in the winter. The land will also suffer – grassy fields become muddy and 'poached' while trees are eaten and destroyed. At first, Burrell and Tree worried that there wouldn't be enough grass for the animals over winter because 'weeds' such as fleabane ran rampant in the early years of rewilding. But they discovered how nature is usually self-regulating and weeds, and species that devour them, boom and bust. Also, watching 'wild' cows has been a revelation. 'What's extraordinary when you allow animals free rein in the landscape is that you suddenly see their behaviours,' says Tree. 'They are endlessly surprising.' The biggest surprise has been to discover the pigs dive into waterways to collect swan mussels to eat. Tree is also amazed by the amount of sustenance that cows browse from trees and hedges, particularly in winter.

Each February a vet observes the cows' condition. In 2012 they had to reduce their cows in their northern section by 10 per cent because the herd had rapidly grown too large. If winters are hard, the vets help determine if animals require supplementary feeding. 'Natural' starvation isn't permitted; animals must be slaughtered well before that point. 'The key concern, as farmers, is to ensure [herd] numbers are always low enough so that, even in the harshest or wettest winter, the animals can come through it in good condition,' says Tree. Surprisingly, perhaps, even after the latest unusually wet and cold winter, their animals did not require any supplementary feed. Tree has seen what organic farmer Rosamund Young has observed in her book, *The Secret Life of Cows*: free-ranging animals will 'self-medicate' with certain plants if they are poorly, and find alternatives when there's no grass growing.

While Knepp's organic meat already has a premium price, Tree believes the basic 'organic' label is underselling it. 'Nobody knows that it's free-roaming, self-medicating, conservation-project rewilding meat. It's as ethical a meat as you can get. It's doing the least possible damage to the animal, it's positively good for the environment and it's positively good for us nutritionally because it's entirely pasture-fed,' she argues. Tree hopes they can create their own brand and sell more meat direct to consumers. Vegetarian campsite guests 'will actually eat our meat because all their objections are invalid when they see what we are doing,' says Tree. 'Our daughter will eat our meat but she won't eat dairy.'

Knepp is attracting the attention of both farmers and environmentalists, and Tree's new book must be unique in receiving glowing endorsements from both George Monbiot, the bête noir of sheep farmers, and James Rebanks, the sheep farmer and author who defends the cultural value of upland farming. Both have visited Knepp. And yet the farm attracts criticism from all sides too – farmers, traditional conservationists and rewilding purists, who dismiss Knepp as insignificant 'rewilding-lite' with its fenced enclosures and absence of apex predators such as wolves. Meanwhile, some traditional conservationists have suggested that Knepp is already 'overgrazed', albeit in a less extreme way than Oostvaardersplassen, the rewilded nature reserve in the Netherlands where herbivores roam free with minimal intervention.

How much livestock can Knepp's land carry? 'We've got no preconceived idea,' says Burrell. A conventional farm may put five, six or seven 'Grazing Livestock Units' (one modern dairy cow; a lowland ewe is 0.11 livestock units) on each hectare. 'Conservation grazing' according to Natural England, the government's conservation watchdog, should be no more than 1.4 livestock units per hectare. Knepp graze much less than conventional farms, and much less than conservationists too – just 0.3 livestock units per hectare. Burrell has long discussions with Knepp's advisory board about 'overgrazing' in certain areas of Knepp:

It's always used as a derogatory term, rather than 'highly grazed' or 'tightly grazed'. OK, overgrazed – for what? Dor beetles love tightly grazed 'lawns' but Essex Skippers [butterflies which require long grass] don't. If you are a botanist and want more flowers you'd say it was overgrazed. The carrying capacity of the land is often much higher than one might think because we're unused to seeing it.

Of the charge that Knepp is not 'proper' rewilding, Burrell and Tree never claim that they are. They can't bring back wild boar which, despite populations re-establishing themselves in the Forest of Dean and elsewhere, are classified as dangerous wild animals in law. They can't even put a stallion among their Exmoor ponies for fear of scaring the horses that are ridden on public byways through Knepp. 'We're not a big area, we're not a national park, we're not a wilderness, we haven't got apex predators,' says Tree, 'but we can still do something really interesting by introducing drivers of change [herbivores] and then letting go.' They would like to introduce more but Burrell even found an innocuous-sounding plan to reintroduce storks was thwarted when some members of Sussex Wildlife Trust opposed the scheme. Knepp has gone ahead and brought in storks anyway, and next hopes to bring back the beaver. Environment Secretary Michael Gove has approved schemes releasing beavers into fenced enclosures to alleviate flooding and benefit biodiversity but beavers are still controversial with many farmers. While conservationists endlessly debate such issues, Burrell and Tree, like all farmers, are ultimately doers. 'Of course you want to carry popular opinion with you but when you can see something in the flesh it's often more powerful than the analytical argument,' says Burrell. 'As soon as you see them [storks or beavers] you think, actually, it's fine.'

To return to the question of whether more British farmers will follow Knepp, landscape change and new species are 'scary', says Tree:

People come here the whole time and think, 'how amazing' but going back and doing it in your own backyard is a different thing. If a landowner is in a position like us, quite often they have parents who are still alive who think it's appalling. Partly it's fear of what the neighbours think. People really mind being criticised. Even just leaving dead wood on the ground, people say, 'It's so untidy.' If we've grown up having a happy childhood roaming barren hills, seeing it scrub

389

up is very difficult. It's challenging an aesthetic. Once it happens, you learn to love it but it's making that leap. So many farmers are on the cusp of doing this. It's just a little incentive – whether that's removing the subsidies, or being paid for some ecosystem services to make something a bit wilder.

Burrell and Tree firmly believe their model is applicable to other farms, and smaller farms too, but it will depend on whether society is willing to pay for 'ecosystem services' such as unpolluted water, flood protection and restored soils provided by truly sustainable farming. In Britain, it will also depend on what sort of farm payments post-Brexit Britain decides it can afford. Environment Secretary Michael Gove's mantra is 'public money for public goods', suggesting farmers will be rewarded for supporting ecosystem services. Some predict that marginal agricultural land will become 'environmental' land while fertile lowland areas will be ever more intensively farmed. But Burrell and Tree hope this vision doesn't come to pass in Britain. 'There has to be nature put back into landscapes which are fertile farming land – it can't just be the marginal land that gets turned back to nature,' says Burrell. As Tree puts it: 'To expect people living in good agricultural land to have no access to nature – everybody should have access to nature.'

Burrell understands that farmers are sometimes reluctant to embrace wildlife-friendly farming because they fear that regulators such as the government's wildlife watchdog, Natural England, will then step in to protect that wildlife. 'This has always been aimed at me by farmers – "If you turn your land into something good for nature, [the regulators] will screw you. They will stop you ever farming again,"' says Burrell. So his big idea is 'pop-up Knepps' with government regulation to support farmers devoting land to wildlife as Knepp as done for a limited period of twenty-five years. After this period, the restored soil can be turned back to agriculture if required, and the wildlife that has made the area its home can move to another pop-up rewilding project nearby. It's a super-scale, long-term rotational farming system for nature. Burrell and Tree won't turn their land back to conventional farming, and Burrell guesses his children won't either, but he's pragmatic enough to recognise that some farmers might need to, and it needn't be bad for nature if there's replacement land nearby. Perhaps our static conceptions of landscape, farming and nature reserves are outmoded?

Burrell is also interested in GPS fencing – using GPS collars on livestock to create virtual fencing, which graziers in America, France and Norway are already trialling. These could exclude livestock from certain areas for certain periods, mimicking the behaviour of apex predators. Burrell and Tree know wolves won't be returned to southern Britain any time soon. 'We need to rebuild ecosystems so that future generations will be able to choose whether they want to bring back wolves and bears,' says Tree:

The rewilding word is useful shorthand for the layperson – you can say 'rewilding' and people have an idea but it means so many things to so many different people. But unlike that little suffix, 're', we're not trying to go back. The world is so changed we can't possibly ever go back to the past, if we could even understand what that was. We want to get some dynamism back into the landscape, because that's where you get all the knock-on effects like soil restoration and water purification. What does seem to be true is that herbivores can kickstart dynamism into the system again, and lift the glider into the sky. Whether it's cows or beavers, something exciting happens when you get free-roaming herbivores in the landscape again.

2018

*

Storks and beavers have been successfully reintroduced to Knepp, which has become hugely influential in the British rewilding movement. Dozens of landowners are now following the estate's lead. The popularity of Isabella Tree's book, *Wilding*, has almost made Knepp a victim of its own success, however, with some wild areas of the estate under pressure from the number of visitors desperate for close communion with its wildlife.

2021

Dam it!
Can beavers save Britain from flooding?

At a secret location in the rolling pasture of west Devon lies a marshy patch of farmland protected by £35,000-worth of solar-powered electric fencing. This isn't to keep people out but to restrain the tree-chomping, river-damming residents of these three hectares. Outside the fence is a typical small valley, with a trickle of a stream, willow thickets and pasture grazed by cattle. Inside the enclosure, the tiny stream has been blocked by thirteen dams, creating pools and half-metre-wide canals. These have been built by Britain's newest wild mammal, the beaver, which uses its waterways like we do – to transport goods. And as the beavers have coppiced trees, the willow thicket has been replaced with sunny glades of wild flowers – marsh thistles, watermint, meadowsweet – which dance with dragonflies and butterflies.

'The beavers have transformed this little trickle of a stream into a remarkable, primeval wetland,' says Mark Elliott, lead beaver project officer of Devon Wildlife Trust, which released two beavers here in 2011. 'This is what the landscape would have looked like before we started farming, and it's only six years old.'

The return of beavers to Britain half a millennium after we hunted them to extinction is both thrilling and controversial. The Eurasian beaver has been reintroduced into virtually every European country in recent decades, including densely populated nations such as the Netherlands, where conservationists laugh at Britain's agonies over the animal. While Britain remains a member of the EU, it is obliged to reintroduce extinct species 'where feasible'. In Scotland, the government last year declared the animal a native, protected species after an official trial and unofficial releases – the first ever formal reintroduction of a once-native British mammal. In England, several Bavarian beavers unofficially let loose on to the River Otter in east Devon are now part of an official trial licensed by Natural England, the government's conservation watchdog. In 2020, the government will decide whether to allow them back for good.

In Europe, beavers have stimulated ecotourism, but they may also benefit human communities in other ways. Scientific studies show that their dams remove pollutants from water – they are particularly effective at filtering out harmful phosphates – and reduce floodwater peaks. Enthusiasts proclaim these large herbivores could become 21st-century water engineers, protecting towns from flooding. But some farmers hate beavers because their dams can also flood productive land. In one Scottish valley, where beaver numbers are estimated to have risen to several hundred, beavers have been shot before the formal legal protection is in place. Beavers can live in Britain, but can the British live with beavers?

The experimental site in Devon is proof of how beavers create a wildlife paradise, re-engineering small valleys with amphibian- and insect-friendly ponds. Exeter University scientists counted ten clumps of frogspawn here in 2011; this year there are 681. There were eight species of water beetle in 2011; twenty-six in 2015. Herons, grass snakes, kingfishers, willow tits and rare barbastelle bats have all returned. In Scotland, ecologists recently found that beavers increased the number of plant species by nearly 50 per cent because they create such a rich variety of habitats.

But it's the beavers' water works that have really struck those studying the site in west Devon. Its small beaver ponds and soil saturated by damming hold nearly one million litres of water. Scientific instruments measure water flows and quality above and below the site. Exeter University researchers have collated data in a remarkable graph showing flood events. During heavy rain, the volume of water flow increases rapidly above the site, creating a dramatic spike in the graph. But when the floodwater is measured again below the site, there is a gentle curve. In other words, the beavers dramatically reduce the peak flow of floodwater on this stream.

The experimental site is on farmland owned by retired beef and sheep farmer John Morgan. He sees the beavers' impact on flooding in the real world. Before the enclosure, country lanes below this land used to flood in heavy rain; since the beavers came in, the roads haven't flooded. 'It proves that [using beavers as a form of flood defence] works,' says Morgan. Should beavers be reintroduced? 'I think it's a good idea. They do a lot of work that these different water companies have to do. If a dam gets washed out, the beavers put it back overnight. They do a twelve-hour shift every day of the year. They don't take holidays.'

Over in east Devon, holidaymakers from China and New Zealand are among those coming to watch the twenty-one beavers on the River Otter. Summer evenings are the best time to see their kits and families gather on the bank after 6.30 p.m. I walk across fields over the broad valley with Elliott.

The bucolic countryside looks unperturbed by beavers. When Natural England announced plans to remove this 'non-native' animal, which was mysteriously found breeding on the river in 2013, locals objected and Devon Wildlife Trust offered to fund an official £500,000 trial. The trust has raised money via crowdfunding and selling novelty 'beaver chips' – bits of wood gnawed by the beavers – but Elliott admits the charity is still 'desperately in need' of funding. At least the beavers are thriving: from just one pair, there are now twenty-one individuals, with almost a dozen kits this summer. 'Clearly, they are expanding to fill the available space,' says Elliott.

On the Otter there are more storylines than a soap opera. A nosy dog recently got a nip from a beaver for straying too close to its lodge. The other night a badger slipped into the water and was hustled out by a beaver. Locals named one adult Bob, but were surprised when it returned with a pink ear-tag. So it's now Mrs Bob, its mate Mr Bob; their kits Miss Bob, Master Bob, Bobby Junior and Roberta.

'It's the little ones that have really enthralled me,' says local Gaynor Cooper, who comes out most nights. 'They are tranquil and seem very gentle.' These slow-moving herbivores don't eat fish and are much more easily spotted than otters. Five minutes after the first picnic blanket is laid down, there's a plop of flat tail against water and Mrs Bob glides into view.

I can't find any dissenting voices on the riverbank 'but beavers do create issues, there's no two ways about it', says Elliott. 'They are not marauding across farms causing damage but they do engineer water and they could change the way we drain land.' His most crucial task is to work with local farmers. 'We're not seeing any persecution [of beavers] on the river at all.'

In Scotland, farmers complain they have lost valuable farmland to flooding caused by beaver dams and have spent thousands clearing ditches blocked by the animals. They are negotiating with the Scottish government to cull if beavers threaten agricultural land.

Elliott says that, in Devon, 'the farmers say to us: "We don't mind the beaver, but if they return we need to be able to deal with problems quickly."' This doesn't necessarily mean killing them. In two instances so far on the

Otter, dams have flooded small areas of grazing pasture. Under the trial's terms, Devon Wildlife Trust pays to solve the problem. In one case, it installed a 'beaver deceiver'. This pipe goes through the dam, lowering the water level and stopping flooding. The pipe is concealed and covered with mesh, so busy beavers can't block it. Important trees are protected with a sandy-textured anti-beaver paint – the animals hate chewing it. The trust hopes that such technologies will allow beavers back into human-dominated countryside, but also knows that farmers' acceptance may depend upon government payments if land is given over to beaver-created flood defence.

For centuries in Britain, we have sought to remove water from land to farm it, and channel rainwater out to sea. We have built houses on so many floodplains downstream that we need to slow the flow, and hold more water on land upriver to stop towns flooding. Beavers installed in every headwater – at the top of small streams – look like ideal, cost-effective flood engineers, providing landowners are compensated. But, as Elliott explains, it isn't so simple. Beavers are territorial and like deep water. Small streams require intensive beaver-labour to create dams and deep-enough water. Beavers won't naturally inhabit these locations unless all the better territory downstream is occupied by other beavers.

'If you're trying to protect people from flooding downstream, we've got to have this type of dam system in the headwaters. But if you put beavers in, all they will do is move downstream,' says Elliott. 'You've either got to hold them with fencing or have beavers back in the landscape, so they are forced into these sub-optimal habitats.'

In Cornwall, holding beavers in a pen upstream is exactly what one local farmer has started doing this year, in a bold attempt to protect the village of Ladock from flooding. There's a proposal for a similar scheme in the Forest of Dean, Gloucestershire. But fenced-in beavers won't be affordable in the long term. Will the beaver be permitted back into the wider landscape? Elliott believes there are plenty of suitable rivers – from the Severn to the Thames – but fears that they could cause more problems than benefits for intensively farmed lowlands such as the East Anglian Fens or the Somerset Levels.

On the banks of the Otter, David White comes most nights to photograph his new neighbours. 'It's a shame the government won't put any money behind the beavers,' he says. 'The beaver can influence ecosystems but it is a big animal and it will need space. And I don't know how good humans are at giving it space.'

2017

*

More scientific evidence has been gathered that reveals the beaver's beneficial impacts on pollution, flood control and wider biodiversity. In 2020 the government announced that the wild beavers on the River Otter could remain there indefinitely. Dozens of projects to release beavers into fenced enclosures in England and Wales have been authorised. While the beaver is still not freely released into the English and Welsh countryside, wild populations are living secretly on some river systems. Culls of beavers permitted by the Scottish government are being challenged in court. Opinion polls have found the beaver is by far the most popular animal to be reintroduced. This rodent is becoming a cherished part of the new British countryside.

2021

How the sea eagle was brought back to life

We are lurching along the loch when the twenty-five seagulls hanging above our boat suddenly scatter. 'It's coming,' says David Sexton quietly. A dark shape materialises low over the water, gaining on us fast.

With wings like planks and a meat-cleaver for a beak, the white-tailed eagle fixes its eyeballs (twice as large as ours) on the boat. Taking great scoops of air with each flap, it stretches yellow talons to pluck a fish from the water.

Britain's biggest bird of prey passes three milestones this spring. It is forty years since a revolutionary re-introduction programme began to return the white-tailed eagle, also known as the sea eagle, to the Scottish Highlands. Thirty years since the first chicks fledged and this year, the number of nesting pairs will exceed a hundred for the first time. But for all the celebrations, some people still detest our biggest carnivorous creature.

The most easily spotted animal pairing on the island of Mull is Mr and Mrs Goretex. Everywhere you go, holidaymakers train their binoculars on the twisting coastline, searching for sea eagles, golden eagles and otters. For David Sexton of the RSPB, the man responsible for managing the complex relationship between people and eagles here, spring is a stressful time. The birds are hatching their chicks, which are vulnerable to late snow, and he begins to get some difficult phone calls. 'It's usually, "Your eagles are attacking my lambs,"' he sighs. Just that morning, a farmer found an eagle plucking at a dead lamb in a field.

'I sympathise completely,' says Sexton. 'Farmers are out from 5 a.m. until last light and when they see a sea eagle sat on a lamb, they aren't going to ask whether it's actually killed it. We're not used to having a big predator around. It's our version of the wolf, in a way.'

Sexton takes me to Mull's modest golf course. In the woods beyond is a white-tailed eagle nest the size of a treehouse. 'The eagle with the sunlit eye,' as it is called in Gaelic, once flew everywhere from the Isle of Wight to Shetland. With its 2.5-metre wingspan and massive nests, it is conspicuous and, unlike the notoriously wary golden eagle, an inquisitive animal. A totemic symbol for Neolithic people who buried their dead with white-tailed eagles on Orkney, it was all too easily trapped, poisoned and shot to extinction, the last bird killed in 1918.

Over a decade from 1975, eighty-two young eagles were brought from Norway and released on the island of Rùm. Typically, the eagles did things their way and flew over to Mull, where they began nesting. In 1984 Sexton came to the island to undertake covert nest surveillance. It was so secretive he even had a cover story – he was studying rare red-throated divers. At that point, the reintroduction was in crisis: none had bred successfully in nine years. During his first year, the only breeding pair's nest failed. 'It was a big disappointment. You're not exactly incubating the eggs yourself but it feels like that,' he says. The next year, the same pair tried again: one chick survived to take its maiden flight. 'It was a life-changing moment, really,' says Sexton.

We shelter from a torrential spring shower under some trees, a respectful distance from the eagles' nest. When I peer through Sexton's telescope, I'm not sure what is nest and what is bird. Then I realise: the female is half the nest, an enormous mound of mottled brown feathers. Sexton is relieved: 'We know she's OK and she's sitting on her eggs.'

Augmented by further reintroductions on Wester Ross and Scotland's east coast, a healthy population of British-born eagles, and a few Norwegian old-timers, now in their thirties, grace the Highlands. The reintroduction has proved a model for others around the globe, such as the Californian condor project, and also provides inspiration for the burgeoning rewilding movement and its ambitious moves to bring back beavers, lynx and even wolves.

But the story of the sea eagles shows that returning large animals to live among people who have no memory of residing alongside big predators is contentious. Mull covers a bigger area than Birmingham and its population is just 2,800. It appears wild and empty and yet human interests – and bird-disturbing bustle – are everywhere:

not just sheep farming but forestry, hydro schemes, and the holidaymakers.

'The eagles have done a grand job bringing in visitors,' says David Clowes, who runs a guest house. But postcards of puffins and golden eagles far outnumber images of the reintroduced bird in shops. When I canvass opinion, everyone acknowledges the tourism dividend but several say there are now too many, or worry about the white-tailed eagles' impact on other inhabitants – hares, golden eagles and farmers.

'Older people are more resistant,' thinks John Clare, a seasonal eagle ranger employed by a partnership between Forestry Commission Scotland, Police Scotland, Scottish Natural Heritage, the Mull and Iona Community Trust and the RSPB (which shows the institutional backing for this bird). 'I'm great friends with an islander who has lived here all his life. He loves golden eagles but sees white-tailed eagles as interlopers.'

Golden eagles are smaller but more aggressive preda-tors than white-tailed eagles, which often steal prey from other predators – crows, gannets and even otters. Sexton studies leftovers found in white-tailed eagles' nests: these include everything from hedgehogs to herons, and the occasional lamb. Mull rumours say cat collars are found in nests ('a complete fabrication', says Sexton – though the eagles do snatch feral cats, which does all wildlife a favour). Critics also claim the eagles wipe out eider ducks (mink is the culprit, corrects Sexton) and Irish hares (another misconception, says Sexton: hare numbers have fallen partly because of disease). 'Sea eagles get blamed for absolutely everything,' he says.

The fiercest opposition comes from farmers, even though some have holiday cottages and benefit from tourism. Lachlan MacLean farms 1,800 ewes with his brother. 'The eagles are here to stay but I was better off before they were here,' he says. On the morning we spoke, two lambs had gone missing. One disappeared from a field where he has a 'particular problem' with the eagles. 'I'm 99 per cent certain it was a sea eagle. It has a huge impact on your income. Last year I was able to identify nineteen lamb carcasses on the ground. That was the ones I found.'

Sexton has never witnessed a white-tailed eagle actually seize a lamb. The birds do swoop in after hooded crows or great black-backed gulls have attacked a lamb and pecked out its eyes but scientific studies in Scotland and Norway have found they rarely take live lambs. Sexton has watched the eagles ignore lambs in favour of apparently more difficult catches. 'They seem focused on wild prey – I've seen them overfly a whole field of lambs and go for a greylag goose or snatch a rabbit caught by a buzzard.'

Has MacLean ever seen a white-tailed eagle take a lamb? 'I've not actually seen it but I've found a number of lambs with talon marks in them,' he says. And he knows several people who have witnessed a white-tailed eagle 'lift' a lamb. Scottish Natural Heritage last year acknowledged that white-tailed eagles do take lambs, and this year is offering financial assistance – up to £5,000 per farmer each year – to help farmers protect flocks from predation. But for MacLean, such sums do not compensate for the stress, and lost bloodlines when lambs are killed. '"Eagle Island" has been a huge attraction but now even some of the wildlife folk think there are too many,' he says. 'There has to be some form of control on that but if they want to keep folk farming in this part of the world there also has to be proper compensation. We don't just want to be here providing a food supply for the eagles.'

I take an eagle-spotting trip on a boat named *Lady Jayne*. Its skipper, Martin Keivers, used to cut grass; now he makes a living from taking tourists to see the eagles. His boat bucks along the windy loch and, in the dark woodland beyond our vision, an eagle's eye is caught by the gathering gulls. The enormous bird bears down on us and, at the last moment, Keivers throws a small dead fish into the water. A dozen holidaymakers' camera shutters click furiously to catch the eagle's swoop. 'It's like clay-pigeon shooting while trampolining,' says Keivers of the camera skills required. 'We've had people in tears as the birds come down.' Are the birds an accepted part of the landscape now? 'Yes.' Keivers pauses. 'Although people don't want to see them sat on every lamp post.'

2015

*

The white-tailed eagle continues to expand over the Highlands of Scotland. There were around 130 breeding pairs in 2020. Young Scottish birds have been successfully relocated to the Isle of Wight in England, with a further five-year reintroduction project in Norfolk proposed by farmers – once the sworn enemy of the eagle.

2021

Play God with small things

The possibility of lynx or wolves being brought back to our land thrills and terrifies in equal measure. But one creature has already been successfully returned to the wild that many people may find scarier: one of Britain's largest arachnids, the palm-sized, fish-devouring fen raft spider. This handsome and completely harmless-to-humans spider, which can walk across the water thanks to its eight-centimetre leg span and enjoys a varied diet of pond skaters, water beetles and newt tadpoles, was threatened with extinction five years ago.

Reduced to just three locations, it is now thriving on four new sites on the Norfolk and Suffolk Broads after a pioneering project in which ecologist Helen Smith hero-ically hand-reared 6,000 baby spiders and released these three-month-old spiderlings on nature reserves in the Yare and Waveney valleys.

Environmental groups including the RSPB, Suffolk Wildlife Trust, the Broads Authority and Natural England have restored habitat so the spiders can prosper. On my local RSPB reserve, Strumpshaw Fen, more than 480 of the spider's beautiful, crystal-like 'nursery' webs have been counted this autumn, compared with 184 last year.

Critics argue that 'playing God' with individual species

is expensive but this restoration (a form of rewilding) is the best hope for the conservation movement. The great inhibitor to saving our environment is that horrible feeling that we can't make a difference. Bringing back species – red kites, sea eagles, otters, great bustards, beavers and large blue butterflies are a few recent success stories – fires imaginations and inspires activism. It's not superficial work either – for any reintroduction to succeed, a wider environment must be put right: so the restoration of the short-haired bumblebee in Kent, for instance, requires the repair of thousands of acres of marshland, which benefits hundreds of other species too.

I've not yet seen a fen raft spider but I can't wait to pay homage when my impressive new neighbour emerges from hibernation in the spring, a living symbol of how a passion for small things might just save our planet.

2015

Newt kids on the block:
the teens rewilding Britain with reptiles

The new enterprise taking shape on a strip of derelict land beside a garden centre in Staffordshire would be extraordinary at any time. But the large pond, greenhouses, cabins and enclosures that will comprise this particular start-up are miraculous given that it is driven by two seventeen-year-olds, both studying for their A levels in the middle of a pandemic.

Childhood friends Harvey Tweats and Tom Whitehurst are on a mission – to rewild Britain by restoring reptile and amphibian species that have been extinct for centuries in this country. Their company, Celtic Reptile & Amphibian, will soon open what the pair believe will be the country's largest outdoor breeding facility for reptiles and amphibians. They hope it will be the first step in restoring lost species so that British ponds, lakes and wetlands again resound to the croak of pool frogs and other once-common lizards and frogs. In the long term, Tweats and Whitehurst hope that the European pond turtle and the Aesculapian snake, already unofficially released in a couple of UK sites, may be embraced as native species after being absent for thousands of years.

This may appear wildly ambitious but they are knowledgeable, passionate environmentalists with the financial

THE FUTURE OF NATURE

backing of leading rewilders, such as Ben Goldsmith, who has supported efforts to reintroduce the beaver, and Charlie Burrell of the Knepp estate.

It's incredible, I enthuse, when Tweats and Whitehurst show me around their back-garden facilities via video. 'It's not incredible,' replies Tweats, laughing drily. 'It's really hard work.'

That work includes building their new facility, which they are aiming to open for the spring breeding season. Their current operation is in their parents' back gardens. In the sunniest corner of Tweats' small garden is a greenhouse and a patio surrounded by open-topped plastic storage boxes. Inside each box grow plants that match the native habitat of the animals they are breeding.

Tweats dips his hand into a small pond and gently picks out a moor frog. The dun-coloured amphibian crouches on his fingers, glistening in the sunlight. 'This species is extinct in Britain but we want to bring it back,' he says. 'It's a male and it's hibernating at the bottom of the pond, in a state of torpor.'

In another enclosure, Tweats carefully pulls out a European pond turtle, a gorgeous small reptile that lives across mainland Europe. The turtles colonised Britain after the Ice Age, but are thought to have disappeared from the country after a period of climatic cooling. 'Who doesn't love a turtle?' says Tweats, beaming. 'The fact that they can sleep under ice and were once native to Britain . . . brilliant.'

They may be experts in breeding European species, but the pair are also nurturing less exotic species such as common toads, which have declined by 68 per cent in Britain since the 1980s. 'Conservationists focus so much on the endangered species that we don't actually have a clue how to breed common stuff,' says Tweats. 'You can learn so much from captive breeding. You can almost telepathically know how that animal is, whether it is sick or injured or in a breeding condition.'

Tweats' interest in frogs and lizards began when he was small. 'It's almost innate, as if it's in your DNA to love nature,' he says. 'My grandad was, and still is, a massive nature nut. He's taught me all about the countryside, ecology.' Tweats collected frogspawn and watched tadpoles become frogs. He reared butterfly and moth caterpillars, but his first captive breeding 'on quite a large scale' was stick insects. 'The babies would get out and climb up the walls,' he says. He was nine when he got a tortoise. Later, he kept pythons.

Every summer Tweats and his family holidayed near an area of lowland heathland in Devon, the Pebblebed Heaths. One year he and his grandad attended an evening looking for nightjars and the wildlife warden, Ed Lagdon, impressed with Tweats' enthusiasm, invited his family on a tour of the heath. They kept in touch and, when a population of beavers was discovered on the nearby River Otter, Lagdon invited Tweats to do work experience on a trial to study the beavers' impact in the valley.

By now a teenager, Tweats had been inspired by George Monbiot's book *Feral*. Working on the beaver project, 'I had that lightbulb moment,' he says. 'These beavers are creating incredible wetlands for amphibians and reptiles and yet they aren't there because they went extinct so long ago.'

Tweats saw how beavers are ecosystem engineers. By building dams, they create new wetlands for amphibians and reptiles but also dragonflies and other insects, and the birds and mammals that eat them. He now believes that many of Britain's 'missing' amphibians went extinct in medieval times – because the beaver was hunted to extinction.

Tweats and Whitehead began breeding amphibians in earnest when they were revising for their GCSEs. Was Whitehurst dragged along by Tweats' enthusiasm? 'You could say that,' says Whitehurst, laughing:

When Harvey started keeping European green lizards, that made me go: 'Hang on, this is something I want to be involved in.' They were so stunning. When you realise these vibrant green lizards are a European species and you can actually keep them outdoors, that inspired me.

We suddenly thought: 'If Harvey got some green lizards and I got some eyed lizards, why don't we start a Facebook page and see what connections we can make?'

413

So they merged garden-breeding operations and posted pictures online. 'It started to gain momentum and we eventually transformed it into a company,' says Whitehurst.

One day, on the beaver trial, Tweats met Derek Gow, an environmentalist known as Mr Beaver, and the talk turned to amphibians. 'I said: "I breed them." And boom! There you go,' Tweats says. He realised that he could scale up his hobby and contribute to big rewilding projects. Gow now sits on their advisory board and introduced Tweats and Whitehurst to financial backers. This allowed them to rent a half-acre patch of ground ten minutes' walk from their homes for their new breeding facility.

The friends are also in their final year of school, and are having to study from home. 'It's just been an absolute nightmare,' admits Tweats. 'We'll be fine,' says Whitehurst. 'We've got a lot of work to get on with so it kind of works in our favour.'

What do their peers think? Loving wildlife was once the badge of a teenage nerd. 'I do think that's changing,' says Tweats. 'Environmentalism is becoming almost sexy. I hate to use the term fashionable, because this isn't just a Gucci handbag, this is something we really need to take seriously as stewards of the earth. But it has become a bit more of a trend.'

So pupils never call him 'newt boy'? 'I am a people person and I'm very confident in social situations,' says Tweats. 'I will make a joke about it and we'll have a laugh, but overall it's been incredibly positive.'

In fact, friends – bribed with bacon butties and beer – have dug the pond for their breeding centre. Do they have time for girlfriends or partners? 'No, we don't,' says Whitehurst. 'We'd much rather crack on with this before we start looking for something serious.'

There is still a lot of work to do – they will soon build enclosures with rat-proof mesh and a quarantine area. 'Biosecurity is vital because of pathogens such as the chytrid fungus [a big cause of global amphibian declines],' says Tweats.

Tweats and Whitehurst hope to become self-sustaining with revenue from breeding animals for sale to hobbyists and also making money from social media and providing animals for filming. They are already earning sponsorship from their YouTube channel and one of their European pond turtles has appeared on *Countryfile* on BBC One.

Ultimately, however, they want to breed thousands of amphibians and reptiles to support conservation programmes and bring back species to Britain's new beaver-created wetlands. And they are dismayed by the modest attempts made so far, such as returning the pool frog to a couple of pools in Norfolk.

'If that's the imagination we're going to have, considering we're in the sixth mass extinction, we may as well admit defeat,' says Tweats. 'If we want to get this species back, it needs to be in every single pond in the UK. End of.'

While wolves or lynx capture the imagination, the significance of smaller creatures is underestimated, he says, citing a US study that found the weight of juvenile amphibians on ten hectares of healthy marshland to be equivalent to a black rhino – and 1,400 kilograms of amphibians in a marsh is a lot of food.

'Although we think of amphibians as small, collectively they assemble into a massive superorganism that feeds so many species,' says Tweats. 'People ask why do we want to bring back the pool frog or the moor frog or the agile frog? It's simply food. All these different species inhabit slightly different niches in the ecosystem and open up the availability of food to many other species. If we want to bring back white storks at Knepp, then we've got to think about returning food to the landscape, as well as the inspiration and beauty that comes from these mini-dragons.'

Tweats says they have had so much 'wonderful' support over the past year. 'The interest in these species has just been insane. They used to be completely vilified – toads were once seen as the spawn of witches. It's come full circle and these animals are a symbol of hope and restoration.'

I ask Tweats and Whitehurst to name their favourite reptile or amphibian. They look pained at the prospect of choosing one. Tweats' favourites include the sand lizard and European pond turtle; Whitehurst loves eyed lizards ('the largest mainland lizard in Europe'), common lizards ('they give live birth, incubating the eggs inside them') and tree frogs.

'What about *Gallotia goliath*?' says Tweats. 'It was a giant species of lizard that lived on the Canary Islands and it went extinct when the Conquistadors arrived. There are still remains, so there's the potential to do a *Jurassic Park*-style resurrection on them.'

'We'll be at the forefront of that,' says Whitehurst with a gleam in his eye. 'When we're famous and we've got enough cash,' adds Tweats, laughing. Will the next Jurassic Park be found in Leek? I wouldn't bet against it.

2021

Acknowledgements

I'd like to thank Fred Baty, Francisco Vilhena, Laura Hassan and Djinn von Noorden for their dedicated work on this anthology, and Robert Hahn and Karolina Sutton, my agent at Curtis Brown, for helping it happen.

I don't mean to sound grandiose but this seems like a good place to thank some of the inspiring journalists I've worked with over the years. I have learned a lot, forgotten too much, and I continue to learn every day from colleagues who genuinely number too many to mention. My first boss on the paper, Ed Pilkington, taught me a lot about how to tell a story and he also made me laugh. Other editors have devised some of the greatest commissions any journalist could wish for or given me the freedom to pursue my own ideas: thank you Kath Viner, Ian Katz, Emily Wilson, Clare Margetson, Clare Longrigg, David Wolf, Jonathan Shainin, Katherine Butler, Hugh Muir, Sam Wollaston, Jamie Wilson, Ian Cobain, Tim Lusher, Merope Mills, Malik Meer, Liese Spencer, Charlotte Northedge, Alex Needham, Melissa Denes, Steve Chamberlain, Harriet Green, Kira Cochrane, Homa Khaleeli, Phil Daoust, Liz McCabe, Andy Pietrasik and Jane Dunford.

In recent years, I've been lucky enough to be based on the environment desk where toil some of the very nicest

419

editors, reporters and human beings: thank you Alan
Evans, Natalie Hanman, Bibi van der Zee, Damian Car-
rington, Jon Watts, Sandra Laville, Matt Taylor and Fiona
Harvey.

Editors are mostly unseen alongside the administrators
– thank you Suzie Worroll – lawyers, librarians and particularly the subeditors who've saved many an embarrassing
slip. Also unseen in this anthology are the photographers
with whom I travelled on some of the most interesting and
challenging stories. They always help me see more. Special
thanks to Graeme Robertson, Martin Godwin, Graham
Turner, David Levene and Chris Thomond.

Journalists are a much maligned species but at their
best they are stimulating, amusing, infuriating, enlighten-
ing and passionate. I've been motivated and schooled by
many *Guardian* legends over the years who have spoken
the truth to power, from George Monbiot to John Vidal,
Gary Younge, Mike White and Polly Toynbee.

It has also been a joy to become close friends with some
brilliant colleagues during very different periods of my
life. Deep thanks to John Crace, Simon Hattenstone, Paul
MacInnes, Hannah Pool, Emine Saner, Adam Holling-
worth, Lee Glendinning, Nic Fleming, Robert Orr, Richard Alleyne and Steve Bird.